BIRDS OF THE WEST INDIES

BIRDS
OF THE
WEST INDIES

Herbert Raffaele, James Wiley,
Orlando Garrido,
Allan Keith, and Janis Raffaele

Principal Illustrators:
Tracy Pedersen and Kristin Williams

Supporting Illustrators:
Cynthie Fisher, Don Radovich, and Bart Rulon

Princeton University Press
Princeton and Oxford

DEDICATION

To the people of the Caribbean Islands and the conservation of the unique avifauna which is their heritage.

ACKNOWLEDGMENTS

The authors, artists, and publishers would like to express their gratitude to the following organizations for providing sponsorship and support in the production of this book: World Wildlife Fund U.S., National Fish and Wildlife Foundation, U.S. Fish and Wildlife Service, and U.S. Forest Service.

ARTIST CREDITS

Tracy Pedersen: 1–3, 6 (Franklin's Gull), 8 (Black Noddy), 10–14, 15 (Wood Sandpiper), 16 (Curlew Sandpiper), 19 (Common Greenshank), 22, 23 (except grebes), 24 (Orinoco Goose), 25–7, 35, 39–41, 44–58, 60 (thrushes), 61–2, 65–6, 69 (Townsend's Warbler), 83–4, 86 (Tawny-shouldered Blackbird, Yellow-shouldered Blackbird), 91–2, 94 (Swamp Sparrow, Northern Wheatear).
Kristin Williams: 4, 5, 6 (exc. Franklin's Gull), 7, 8 (exc. Black Noddy), 9, 23 (only grebes), 24 (exc. Orinoco Goose), 31–4, 36–8, 42–3, 59, 60 (solitaires), 63–4, 80–2, 85, 86 (exc. Tawny-shouldered Blackbird, Yellow-shouldered Blackbird), 87–90, 93, 94 (exc. Swamp Sparrow, Northern Wheatear).
Don Radovich: 67–8, 69 (exc. Townsend's Warbler), 70–9.
Cynthie Fisher: 15 (exc. Wood Sandpiper), 16 (exc. Curlew Sandpiper), 17–8, 19 (exc. Common Greenshank), 20–1.
Bart Rulon: 28–30.

Plates and illustrations copyright © 2003, 1998 by Herbert Raffaele, James Wiley, Orlando Garrido, Allan Keith, Janis Raffaele, Tracy Pedersen, Kristin Williams, Roman Company, Christopher Cox, Cynthie Fisher, Don Radovich, Bart Rulon

Library of Congress Cataloging-in-Publication Data
Birds of the West Indies/Herbert Raffaele ... [et al.] ; principal illustrators, Tracy Pedersen and Kristin Williams.
    p. cm.—(Princeton field guides)
Includes bibliographical references (p.).
ISBN 0-691-11319-X (pbk. : alk. paper)
    1. Birds—West Indies—Identification. I. Raffaele, Herbert A. II. Series.

QL688.A1B47 2003
598'.09729—dc21   2003041865

This book has been composed in Galliard (main text) and MetaPlus (headings and labeling)

Printed on acid-free paper.

www.pupress.princeton.edu

Edited and designed by D & N Publishing, Hungerford, Wiltshire, UK

Printed in Italy by EuroGrafica

10 9 8 7 6 5 4 3 2 1

CONTENTS

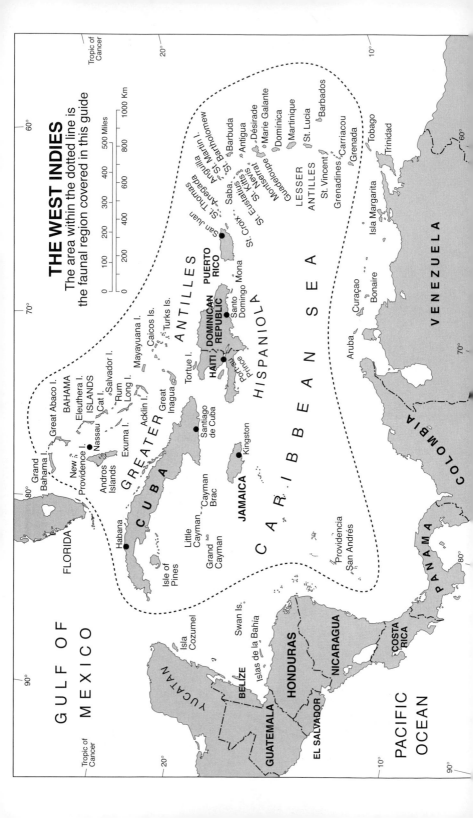

THE WEST INDIES

The area within the dotted line is
the faunal region covered in this guide

INTRODUCTION

GOAL

The primary goal of this guide is to promote an interest in birds among the local people of the Caribbean islands. It is only when people appreciate and respect their birdlife that they ever come to protect it. The book also aims to facilitate the study of West Indian birds by both novice and professional alike.

GEOGRAPHIC COVERAGE

The West Indies are taken to include all islands of the Bahamas, Greater Antilles, Virgin Islands, Cayman Islands, Lesser Antilles, San Andrés and Providencia.

Omitted are Trinidad and Tobago and other islands off the north coast of South America. Though Trinidad and Tobago appear contiguous to the Lesser Antilles, their origins, and consequently their birdlife, are entirely different.

SPECIES COVERAGE

The text presents accounts of 564 bird species known to occur in the West Indies. Species included in the book are those for which there exist a minimum of either two specimens or photographs from the region, or six separate sight records by reliable observers.

Several species considered by some to be extinct are included in the book. We have chosen to do this firstly because there is always a chance that a bird thought to be extinct might be rediscovered after many years of going undetected. The Puerto Rican Nightjar is one example. Collected in 1888, the species went undetected for 73 years until being rediscovered in 1961. One can only hope that this will also be the case for the Jamaican Petrel, which occupies remote precipices and is entirely nocturnal during its brief stint on land. Secondly, it is important to remember what we have lost, or are about to lose. Our hope is that this book will encourage a greater appreciation of what we still have, an awareness of its fragility, and a wider recognition that extinction is irreversible.

Numerous other bird species have become extinct in the West Indies during historic time. At least 15 species of parrot alone fall into this category. These birds are not included in this book.

TAXONOMY

Much more work remains to be carried out before the taxonomy of West Indian birds is adequately understood. Recent studies have revised the tanager *Spindalis* from what was formerly considered to be one very variable species into four distinct ones. Contemporaneous research suggests that the two indigenous *Contopus* flycatchers should be split into six species, and that the Palm Crow be divided into Hispaniolan and Cuban species. Additional work is under way on several other bird groups. In general, for the purpose of this guide, the authors followed the taxonomy and use of common names proposed in the American Ornithologists' Union (AOU) Checklist of North American Birds (1998). There are a few exceptions. We divided the Lesser Antillean Pewee into three species: the Lesser Antillean, St Lucia, and Puerto Rican Pewee. We based our decision upon revisions in progress which, we feel, justify the split and have strong potential to be adopted by the AOU's classification and nomenclature committee. A few English common names were also changed to better represent certain species. An example is the substitution of the name Rose-throated Parrot for the long-standing, but inaccurate, Cuban Parrot. This change was made to eliminate the implication that this parrot is unique to Cuba when, in fact, it is a flagship species of the Bahamas and Cayman Islands. Efforts to conserve these parrots are not enhanced by such a misnomer.

USING THE GUIDE

SPECIES ACCOUNTS

These have been kept brief in order to fit opposite the bird illustrations. To a large extent they follow the sequence used by the AOU. However, in some cases, particularly among marine and aquatic birds, species have been grouped according to similarity of appearance to help facilitate comparison.

DESCRIPTIVE PARTS OF A BIRD

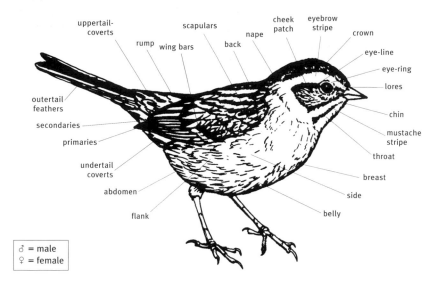

uppertail-coverts
rump
wing bars
scapulars
back
nape
cheek patch
eyebrow stripe
crown
eye-line
eye-ring
lores
chin
mustache stripe
throat
outertail feathers
secondaries
primaries
undertail coverts
abdomen
flank
breast
side
belly

♂ = male
♀ = female

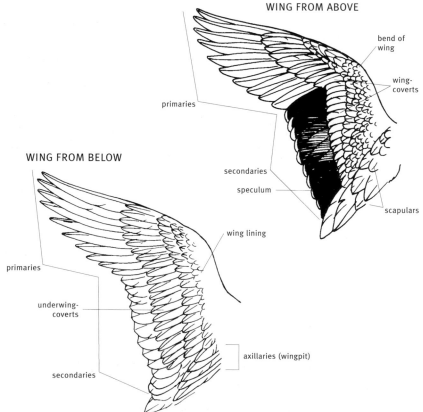

WING FROM ABOVE

bend of wing
wing-coverts
primaries
secondaries
speculum
scapulars

WING FROM BELOW

wing lining
primaries
underwing-coverts
axillaries (wingpit)
secondaries

IDENTIFICATION

Size is a basic tool in bird identification. Where length varies, because of the presence or absence of tail plumes for example, several measurements are provided.

Only salient field marks are presented. These are key features to look for when identifying the bird. No attempt is made to describe the species comprehensively since this is better discerned in the plates. Most field marks pertain to plumage, but they do sometimes include peculiar habits such as tail-bobbing.

Plumages which vary by age, sex, or season are differentiated. So are variations when a species differs substantially among islands. For species that occur in the West Indies for only a part of the year, the plumage most likely to be seen is presented first, with the least likely plumage presented last. For example, of the various gull species that occur in the West Indies but do not breed, immature birds occur much more regularly than adults. Consequently, the sub-adult plumages are described before those of the adults. For species that do not breed in the West Indies and which rarely occur, the breeding plumage may not be illustrated in every case.

Flight: Described when it is a specific asset to identification.

Voice: The calls, songs, and notes as known in the West Indies are described when important for identification.

Status and range: The extent to which the bird depends upon the West Indies during its life-cycle is presented. Some species reside on a single island during their entire lives. Others may pass through the islands only during certain migratory periods.

The following terms are used to represent the overall status of each species:

Endemic: A species which is confined to a specific island or small group of islands and is found nowhere else in the world.

Resident: A species which spends its entire life-cycle on a particular island or group of islands.

Breeding resident: A species which breeds on a particular island or group of islands and then migrates elsewhere during the non-breeding season.

Non-breeding resident: A species which breeds elsewhere, but occurs on a particular island or group of islands during the non-breeding season. Sometimes referred to as a 'visitor' or 'visitant'. Other bird guides often refer to such birds as 'winter visitor'. This term has been deliberately avoided in this work since 'winter' is not a term used on all islands, so it would represent a bird's status from a North American perspective.

Migrant: A species which migrates between islands or to areas outside the West Indies on a seasonal basis. Sometimes referred to as a 'transient'.

Wanderer: A species which moves between islands at irregular intervals.

The terms used to describe the likelihood of observing a given species are defined below:

Common: 5 or more individuals likely to be seen daily.

Fairly common: 1–4 individuals likely to be seen daily.

Uncommon: Not likely to be seen on every trip, but can be expected at least twice per year.

Rare: Fewer than 2 records per year; at least one occurrence every 5 years.

Very rare: Occurs once every 5 to 10 years.

Vagrant: Occurs less frequently than once every 10 years.

These categories are based upon a skilled observer seeking the bird in the right place at the right time. In some cases, this means visiting a very specific habitat such as coastal marshes during the migration season. For birds which roost or breed communally (e.g. herons and terns), the status given represents the likelihood of encountering the species under more general field conditions and does not include flocks flying to or from a roost.

The terms have several ramifications. Some species are substantially more detectable than others. For example, every Snowy Egret in a small swamp can be located easily. However, a single Yellow-breasted Crake in that same swamp would be harder to detect. This would be the case even if crakes were substantially more abundant than egrets. To address this, we have tried to indicate species that are particularly difficult to detect. This is either stated in the text, or implied in the description of the bird's habitat, which might be 'at sea'.

This issue is particularly important with regard to endangered species. The critically endangered Yellow-shouldered Blackbird might be seen during every trip to its roosting or feeding areas in Puerto Rico, thus classifying it as 'locally common'. This is not to say that the total population size of the species is large. We have tried to indicate, at least for threatened and endangered species, cases where a species is classified as locally common, whereas in fact its population is small.

Misconceptions can be created by these terms when they are applied to small islands. A small island with a small pond may sustain only one pair of Pied-billed Grebes or a single Great Blue Heron. Yet these birds might be observed on every trip to the island and are thus classified as 'common'. Similarly, if that particular pond is only full seasonally, grebes may be present whenever it has water but will be absent when it is dry. We leave it to the common sense of the observer to determine how circumstances such as these apply to any particular species or island.

Habitat: The specific environment in which the bird is likely to be found is presented.

MAPS

The map displays the range of the species within the West Indies. Maps are included only in cases where they can be helpful in portraying a species' distribution at a glance. Maps are omitted for species that occur throughout the West Indies or inhabit only one or two islands. Green indicates that a species is a permanent resident on an island, though the birds may move periodically among islands, for example the White-cheeked Pintail. Maroon indicates that the species occurs on the island for only a portion of the year and migrates elsewhere to breed. Species that breed in the West Indies but migrate elsewhere during the non-breeding season are represented by orange.

PLATES

The color plates depict every species for which there is an account in the text. The plumage of some birds differs noticeably from island to island, for example the ubiquitous Bananaquit. In such cases, various island forms are illustrated. Variations in plumage between male and female, adult and immature, breeding and non-breeding birds are also depicted if important for identification purposes. For species that do not breed in the West Indies, the breeding plumage may not be illustrated.

CONSERVATION

THE PROBLEM

The growth of human populations and extensive changes in land use practices have resulted in major impacts on the earth's biological resources, especially its birdlife. Directly as a result of these human impacts, several hundred species and subspecies of birds have become extinct worldwide over recent centuries. Of particular conservation concern to the West Indies is the fact that approximately nine out of every ten of these extinct species were island forms.

Island species are particularly vulnerable for two reasons. First, most species occupy very limited ranges, leaving few areas to serve as safe havens where small populations might manage to survive. Second, island species have generally evolved in the absence of terrestrial predators such as cats, dogs, pigs, mongooses, and humans. Consequently, they often lack appropriate mechanisms with which to defend themselves and their young.

Endangerment and extinction can be part of the natural evolutionary process. However, this is only considered to be the case when naturally occurring events, such as hurricanes, are the cause of the decline. Bulldozing the last remaining stand of trees sheltering a species, or releasing exotic animals that prey on the young of ground-nesting birds, are hardly natural events. Not surprisingly, given the extensive development of the Caribbean over the past few centuries, virtually every bird species presently considered endangered or threatened in the West Indies has become so as the result of human-induced causes.

PRINCIPAL CAUSES OF ENDANGERMENT AND EXTINCTION

Habitat destruction and disturbance: Every natural habitat known to the West Indies has been significantly altered by humans. Some of these alterations are obvious, such as the cutting of lowland forest and its replacement with cattle pastures or housing developments. Others are less so, for example, the channelization of wetlands as a means of mosquito control. Some might argue that our most remote mountain forests are unaltered, but this too can be challenged. Puerto Rico's uncut Luquillo rainforest is infested with feral cats and rats which prey on native birds including the young of the endangered Puerto Rican Parrot. St Christopher's Mount Misery has suffered the affliction of the African green monkey (*Cercopethicus aethiops*) for centuries. In fact, it is often these insidious, inconspicuous changes we cause to our environment which are the most threatening because their impacts often go so long undetected.

Given the extent of development in the West Indies, it is not surprising that habitat destruction and disturbance are by far the primary causes of endangerment to West Indian birds. Unless a serious attempt is made to manage these development trends wisely, through integrated planning efforts focused on each ecosystem as a whole, the list of endangered and threatened species in the West Indies will continue to grow.

Heavy deforestation in the West Indies began soon after European colonization. Lowland forests were the first to disappear, followed by those of the foothills and lower mountain slopes. Timber extraction for house construction, fuelwood, and furniture, along with clearing for agriculture and cattle production, quickly took a heavy toll on the native vegetation. Flat islands were denuded most rapidly; those with precipitous mountains or otherwise remote localities more slowly. Nevertheless, by the late 1800s most forests of the West Indies had either been felled by ax or saw, or cleared by ox or fire. The 20th century has brought the bulldozer and chainsaw as new threats to native forests along with the expansion of roads into previously inaccessible areas. Fortuitously, this has been counteracted on some islands by natural forest regeneration resulting from the use of gas and electricity as a replacement for charcoal, and by the abandonment of marginal agricultural lands resulting in a shifting of rural populations to cities.

The forests of some West Indian islands are in better shape now than they were a century ago, but others are decidedly worse off. Considering the ever-increasing threat of the chainsaw, population growth, and expansive development, increased care must be taken to ensure that habitat destruction does not continue to be the single greatest threat to West Indian birdlife.

Hunting: Historically, hunting is a traditional pastime on most islands of the West Indies. It was widely practiced without adequate attention to the biology of the game species hunted, or to controls regarding the numbers of birds taken. This has resulted in dramatic declines of formerly common species, particularly among pigeons, doves, and waterfowl. This is one area in which conservation measures can benefit all involved including hunters, bird aficionados, and the birds themselves.

Introduced predators: Prior to colonization of the West Indies, either by Amerindians or Europeans, the avifauna evolved on most islands in the absence of mammalian predators. Colonization dramatically altered that situation with the introduction of black and brown rats, cats, dogs, pigs, and mongooses, among others. These non-indigenous creatures have doubtless had dramatic effects on many local bird species, particularly ground-nesters. Various seabirds, ducks, rails, doves, owls, goatsuckers, and songbirds that nest on or near the ground have suffered significantly as a result of such predation. Doubtless tree-nesters have also suffered, but to a lesser extent. It is difficult to know precisely the extent to which these introduced predators have affected local species, but it appears likely that they played major roles in the serious decline of several rail and goatsucker species.

Other causes: Various other factors have a negative impact upon the avifauna of the West Indies. Capturing wild birds for house pets or for the international bird trade has reduced native parrot numbers particularly. The collecting of eggs for food has been detrimental to flamingos and a number of colonial nesting seabirds. The shooting of birds considered to be pests has affected parrots and several other species. The Shiny Cowbird, a parasite on the nests of other birds and a recently arrived species from South America, is wreaking havoc with several native orioles and other species. Introduced bird species, primarily parrots and finches, compete with native relatives for food or nest sites. Such exotics also pose a serious threat of unknowingly introducing diseases which can decimate native bird species unadapted to foreign diseases. Chemical pollutants, ranging from agricultural pesticides and herbicides to industrial and chemical wastes, have notorious negative impacts on birds. Though reports of such impacts are rare in the West Indies, this does not mean damage has not occurred. The near-absence of insect-eating birds on New Providence in the Bahamas may well be the result of intensive spraying for mosquito control. While none of these factors individually has been proven to be a major factor in the decline of the West Indian avifauna, each is, or has the potential to be, important in species' declines. They all warrant the attention of decision-makers and managers of natural resources.

ISLAND CONSERVATION NEEDS

Discussions with preeminent conservationists from throughout the Caribbean reveal a number of conservation priorities requiring particular attention.

Probably the salient need facing most islands is for public outreach at all levels—to schools, to the general public, and to decision-makers. This remains true despite the fact that several Lesser Antillean islands have undertaken some of the most comprehensive bird conservation outreach campaigns conducted anywhere in the world. Most of these campaigns have been impressively successful, as demonstrated by the remarkable recovery of the St Lucia Parrot. These advances only go to show the importance of expanding such outreach programs if local conservation objectives are to have any hope of being achieved.

Another high priority need is for more effective implementation of existing legislation. Most, if not all, the islands have conservation laws to protect birds. Developing a conservation ethic and the institutional capacity to implement these statutes would contribute significantly to conservation on the islands. Some islands need to update their local laws and regulations.

The setting aside of protected areas—conserving habitat—is decidedly important. This is because habitat destruction is clearly the most important factor threatening the birdlife of the region. However, it is not the most essential conservation measure. It seems that Caribbean islanders believe that what is in the hearts and minds of the people is more important than what is set aside by decree, fiat or legal mandate. They lead most other nations in advancing this concept.

ENDANGERED SPECIES LIST

The table below lists birds considered to be extinct, extirpated, endangered or threatened in the West Indies. Listed birds represent either: (1) endemic species; (2) endemic subspecies (races); or (3) any species or subspecies which is threatened or endangered throughout all, or the greater portion of, its range.

Where local populations are endangered or threatened, but the status of the species is stable throughout the remainder of its range, whether within or outside the West Indies, such mention is made only in the text. Examples include the Pine Warbler on Haiti. The table also identifies what are believed to be the primary causes of the species' endangerment. These causes include both past and present impacts.

This list is derived from the published literature, from discussions with resident West Indian bird experts, and from personal observation by the authors.

EXTINCT AND EXTIRPATED

DEFINITION—Species and subspecies believed to no longer exist and which are represented by museum specimens.

Species	Subspecies
Jamaican Petrel	Uniform Crake (Jamaica race)
Passenger Pigeon	Hispaniolan Parakeet (Puerto Rico race)
Cuban Macaw	Puerto Rican Parrot (Culebra Island race)
Brace's Hummingbird	Burrowing Owl (St Kitts, Nevis and Antigua race)
Grand Cayman Thrush	Burrowing Owl (Marie Galante race)
	House Wren (Martinique race)
	Cuban Solitaire (Isle of Youth race)
	Puerto Rican Bullfinch (St Kitts race)
	Jamaican Oriole (Grand Cayman race)

CRITICALLY ENDANGERED

DEFINITION—Species and subspecies that have declined dramatically to such low population levels that their continued survival is in serious jeopardy. Active steps must be taken to ensure their survival. In some cases extinctions may have already occurred.

	CAUSES				
Species	Habitat loss	Hunting	Harvest or trade	Introduced predators	Other
Black-capped Petrel			X	X	
Hook-billed Kite (Grenada race)	X	X			
Cuban Kite	X	X			
Spotted Rail	X			?	
Eskimo Curlew		X			
Grenada Dove	X	?		X	
Puerto Rican Parrot	X	X	X	X	X[1]
St Vincent Parrot	X	X	X		
Imperial Parrot	X	X	X		
Puerto Rican Screech-Owl (Virgin Islands race)	X				X1
Stygian Owl (Hispaniola race)	X	X			
Jamaican Poorwill	X			X	
Ivory-billed Woodpecker	X	X			
Euler's Flycatcher (Grenada race)	Unknown				
Golden Swallow (Jamaica race)	Unknown				
House Wren (Guadeloupe race)	X	X		X	
White-breasted Thrasher	X			X	
Bachman's Warbler	?				
Semper's Warbler	?			X	
Yellow-shouldered Blackbird	X				X[2]

1 Competition with introduced species and egg predation by the Pearly-eyed Thrasher.
2 Population decline as a result of brood parasitism by the Shiny Cowbird.

ENDANGERED

DEFINITION—Species and subspecies that have declined significantly to such low population levels that unless this trend is halted in the immediate future, the survival of the species will be in jeopardy.

Species	Habitat loss	Hunting	Harvest or trade	Introduced predators	Other
West Indian Whistling-Duck	X	X	X	X	
Zapata Rail	X			?	
Gundlach's Hawk	X	X			
Sharp-shinned Hawk (Puerto Rico race)	X			X	X[1]
Ridgway's Hawk	X				
Piping Plover	X				
Plain Pigeon	X	X		X	
Gray-headed Quail-Dove (Dominican Republic race)	X	X		X	
Blue-headed Quail-Dove	X	X		X	
Red-necked Parrot	X	X	X		
St Lucia Parrot	X	X	X		
Cuban Parakeet	X	X	X		
Bay-breasted Cuckoo	X	X			
Puerto Rican Nightjar	X			X	
Rufous Nightjar	X			X	
Fernandina's Flicker	X				
Giant Kingbird	X				
Golden Swallow (Hispaniola race)	X				
Brown-headed Nuthatch	X				
Cuban Palm Crow	Unknown				
La Selle Thrush	X				
Kirtland's Warbler	X				X[3]
White-winged Warbler	X				
Gray-crowned Palm-Tanager	X				
Western Chat-Tanager	X				
Martinique Oriole					X[2]
Montserrat Oriole	X				X[2,4]
White-winged Crossbill	X				

1 Egg and young chick predation by Pearly-eyed Thrasher.
2 Population decline as a result of brood parasitism by Shiny Cowbird.
3 Population decline as a result of brood parasitism by Brown-headed Cowbird.
4 Volcanic eruption.

THREATENED

DEFINITION—Species and subspecies that have experienced moderate declines or face imminent threats thus warranting specific conservation measures.

Species	Habitat loss	Hunting	Harvest or trade	Introduced predators	Other
			CAUSES		
White-cheeked Pintail	X	X		X	
Sharp-shinned Hawk (Hispaniola race)	X			X	
Broad-winged Hawk (Puerto Rico race)	X				
Black Rail	X			X	
Caribbean Coot	X	X		X	
Limpkin (Hispaniola race)	X	X		?	
Sandhill Crane	X	X		X	
Snowy Plover	X			X	
Double-striped Thick-knee	X	X			
Roseate Tern	X		X	X	
White-crowned Pigeon	X	X	X	X	
Ring-tailed Pigeon	X	X			
Gray-headed Quail-Dove (Cuba race)	X	X		X	
Hispaniolan Parakeet	X	X			
Rose-throated Parrot	X		X		
Yellow-billed Parrot	X		X		
Black-billed Parrot	X		X		
Hispaniolan Parrot	X	X	X		
Stygian Owl (Cuba race)	X	X			
Least Poorwill	X			X	
White-tailed Nightjar (Martinique race)	X			X	
Bee Hummingbird	X				
Hispaniolan Trogon	X				
West Indian Woodpecker (Grand Bahama race)	X				
White-necked Crow	X	X			
Forest Thrush	X	X			X[3]
House Wren (St Vincent and St Lucia races)	X	X		X	X[1]
Zapata Wren	X			?	
Cuban Solitaire	X				
Elfin-Woods Warbler	X				
Green-tailed Warbler (Isla Beata race)	Unknown				
Whistling Warbler	X				
Eastern Chat-Tanager	X				
Greater Antillean Oriole (Bahamas race)	Unknown				
Jamaican Blackbird	X				
Tawny-shouldered Blackbird (Hispaniola race)	X				X[1]
St Lucia Oriole	X				X[1,4]
Zapata Sparrow					X[2]

1 Population decline as a result of brood parasitism by Shiny Cowbird.

2 Small, local populations put all three races at risk to overnight losses resulting from such natural sources as hurricanes or from human-related causes such as habitat destruction.

3 Competition with Bare-eyed Robin and parasitism by Shiny Cowbird.

4 Population decline as a result of pesticide spraying.

GREATER SHEARWATER *Puffinus gravis* 48cm (19in). One of two large shearwaters in West Indies; noticeable white bands on hindneck and rump contrast with black cap and dark grayish-brown upperparts. **STATUS AND RANGE:** Uncommon non-breeding resident among Bahamas and off Puerto Rico primarily May through July, but can occur any month. Likely rare through rest of West Indies during these months. **HABITAT:** At sea.

CORY'S SHEARWATER *Calonectris diomedea* 46–53cm (18–21in). Large shearwater, appears featureless at distance. Pale yellowish bill, white uppertail-coverts variable in extent; coloration of cheek and neck blend with underparts. **FLIGHT:** Leisurely on broad, loosely held wings, noticeably angled at wrist. **STATUS AND RANGE:** Uncommon migrant among Bahamas primarily May and June, but until September. Rare in rest of West Indies; likely transits off all islands. **HABITAT:** At sea.

BLACK-CAPPED PETREL *Pterodroma hasitata* 35–40cm (14–16in). Upperparts blackish except for white rump, hindneck and forehead. Extent of white variable. **FLIGHT:** Black front-edge of underwing. Wrist more bent than shearwater's and flight more erratic. **STATUS AND RANGE:** Rare and very local breeding resident in West Indies. Critically endangered. **HABITAT:** At sea.

JAMAICAN PETREL *Pterodroma caribbaea* 35–46cm (14–18in). Dark gray overall, except white rump and uppertail-coverts; legs and feet pinkish-white. **STATUS AND RANGE:** Endemic to Jamaica, but believed extinct. May persist in John Crow Mountains. **HABITAT:** At sea.

SOOTY SHEARWATER *Puffinus griseus* 40–46cm (16–18in). Medium-sized, blackish overall with whitish underwings. Wings long and narrow. **FLIGHT:** Swift and direct, with rapid flapping ascents and long glides usually close to the water. **STATUS AND RANGE:** Apparently rare migrant in West Indies primarily late May through July, but some through November. Might be expected any month. **HABITAT:** At sea.

MANX SHEARWATER *Puffinus puffinus* 30–38cm (12–15in). Medium-sized; short tail. Blackish above and white below, including wing linings and undertail-coverts. **FLIGHT:** Four or five distinctive snappy wingbeats and a rocking glide in light winds or flat seas. **STATUS AND RANGE:** Rare migrant in West Indies primarily November through March. **HABITAT:** At sea.

AUDUBON'S SHEARWATER *Puffinus lherminieri* 30cm (12in). Relatively small, long-tailed shearwater, blackish-brown above and white below, but with dark undertail-coverts. **STATUS AND RANGE:** The only shearwater regularly encountered in West Indies. In the Bahamas, a common breeding resident primarily March through July; uncommon in other months. Elsewhere in West Indies a generally uncommon and local breeding resident, rare outside breeding season. **HABITAT:** At sea.

BAND-RUMPED STORM-PETREL *Oceanodroma castro* 19–21cm (7.5–8in). Medium-sized; black head and upperparts. Conspicuous narrow white rump band contrasts with blackish tail and underparts; square tail. **FLIGHT:** Buoyant and direct, though sometimes erratic and shearwater-like with deep wingbeats. Feet do not extend beyond tail. **STATUS AND RANGE:** Very rare off Bahamas, Cuba, and Antigua. Expected primarily May through August. Status in West Indies poorly known. **HABITAT:** At sea.

LEACH'S STORM-PETREL *Oceanodroma leucorhoa* 20cm (8in). A small, brownish-black seabird with white rump. Has slightly forked tail, pale brown wing band, and white rump patch appearing divided at close range. **FLIGHT:** Feet do not extend beyond tail. **STATUS AND RANGE:** Rare non-breeding resident throughout West Indies primarily November through June, but sometimes in other months. **HABITAT:** At sea.

WILSON'S STORM-PETREL *Oceanites oceanicus* 18–19cm (7–7.5in). Small, dark brownish-black seabird with white rump. Blacker, wings shorter, broader and more rounded with less angled wrists than Leach's Storm-Petrel, also tail more square. **FLIGHT:** Feet, with yellow toe-webbing, extend beyond tail. Regularly follows boats, swooping over wake and touching sea with feet. **STATUS AND RANGE:** Rare non-breeding resident in much of West Indies primarily May and June. Most frequent among Bahamas where uncommon. **HABITAT:** At sea.

GREATER SHEARWATER

CORY'S SHEARWATER

JAMAICAN
PETREL

SOOTY SHEARWATER

BLACK-
CAPPED
PETREL

atypical
coloration

◄MANX SHEARWATER

◄BAND-RUMPED
STORM-PETREL

LEACH'S
STORM-
PETREL

WILSON'S
STORM-
PETREL

AUDUBON'S SHEARWATER

Jamaican Petrel not to scale

WHITE-TAILED TROPICBIRD *Phaethon lepturus* 81cm (31in) (with plumes), 37–40cm (15–16in) (without plumes). **ADULT:** White overall; long tail feathers; heavy black stripes on upperwing and outer primaries. Bill yellow or orange. **IMMATURE:** Barred back; short central tail feathers. Bill yellowish, ringed with black. **VOICE:** Raspy *crick-et*. **STATUS AND RANGE:** Widespread; very locally common breeding resident in West Indies primarily March through June (through October in Bahamas). The typical tropicbird of Bahamas, Greater Antilles, and Cayman Islands; scarcer in Lesser Antilles. **HABITAT:** At sea.

RED-BILLED TROPICBIRD *Phaethon aethereus* 91–107cm (36–42in) (with plumes), 46–51cm (18–20in) (without plumes). **ADULT:** White overall; black barred back; long tail plumes; red bill. **IMMATURE:** Similar to White-tailed, but back less boldly barred, darker black band across hindneck. **VOICE:** Long, harsh, raspy *keé-arrr*. **STATUS AND RANGE:** Common in Virgin Islands; uncommon and very local resident throughout Lesser Antilles and on Culebra off Puerto Rico. **HABITAT:** At sea.

AMERICAN WHITE PELICAN *Pelecanus erythrorhynchos* 125–165cm (49–64in). Huge size, massive bill, white coloration. Black primaries and outer secondaries. **BREEDING ADULT:** Bill orange-yellow, knob on upper mandible; hindcrown and hindneck tan. **NON-BREEDING ADULT:** Bill orange-yellow; hindcrown and hindneck gray. **IMMATURE:** Bill gray. **STATUS AND RANGE:** Very rare non-breeding resident in Cuba and Puerto Rico. Vagrant elsewhere in West Indies. May occur in any month. **HABITAT:** Freshwater lakes and coastal bays.

BROWN PELICAN *Pelecanus occidentalis* 107–137cm (42–54in). Large size, massive bill, dark coloration. **BREEDING ADULT:** Reddish-brown hindneck and back of head, though infrequently the hindneck remains white. **NON-BREEDING ADULT:** White hindneck and back of head. **IMMATURE:** Overall grayish-brown; paler below. **STATUS AND RANGE:** Common resident in southern Bahamas, Greater Antilles, and locally in northern Lesser Antilles east to Montserrat. Uncommon to rare through rest of West Indies. **HABITAT:** Bays, lagoons, other calm coastal waters.

Illustrations not to scale

WHITE-TAILED
TROPICBIRD

adult

RED-BILLED
TROPICBIRD

adult

imm

AMERICAN WHITE
PELICAN

non-br
adult

br

BROWN PELICAN

imm

RED-FOOTED BOOBY *Sula sula* 66–76cm (26–30in). **ADULT:** BROWN PHASE Brown, with white hindparts and tail. WHITE PHASE All white, with black primaries and secondaries. **IMMATURE:** Sooty brown; paler below, sometimes slightly darker breast band. **VOICE:** Guttural *ga-ga-ga-ga*, of variable length—trails off. Also distinctive squawk. **STATUS AND RANGE:** Widespread, but very local resident in West Indies. Abundant near remote roosting and nesting islands. Not often seen from shore. **HABITAT:** At sea.

BROWN BOOBY *Sula leucogaster* 71–76cm (28–30in). **ADULT:** Entirely brown head sharply demarcated from white belly and abdomen. **IMMATURE:** Light brown belly and abdomen. **VOICE:** Hoarse *kak*. **STATUS AND RANGE:** Fairly common resident offshore throughout West Indies; locally abundant near breeding grounds. Very rare or absent only from northern Bahamas. **HABITAT:** Bays, coastal areas, and at sea.

MASKED BOOBY *Sula dactylatra* 81–91cm (32–36in). **ADULT:** Primarily white; black tail, primaries, and secondaries. **SUBADULT:** Similar to adult, but upperparts brown on head and rump; brown flecks on wing-coverts. **IMMATURE:** Head and upperparts brown with white hindneck. Underparts white except throat, undertail and flight feathers. **STATUS AND RANGE:** Very rare and local resident in West Indies. Threatened. **HABITAT:** At sea.

MAGNIFICENT FRIGATEBIRD *Fregata magnificens* 94–104cm (37–41in). Long, forked tail; long, slender, pointed wings sharply bent at wrist; floats motionless in air. **ADULT MALE:** Black. During courtship, inflatable throat pouch bright red. **ADULT FEMALE:** Blackish, white breast. **IMMATURE:** Blackish; head and breast white. **STATUS AND RANGE:** Common but somewhat local resident throughout West Indies. **HABITAT:** Bays, inshore waters and offshore cays.

NORTHERN GANNET *Morus bassanus* 100cm (40in). **IMMATURE:** Dark gray above, flecked white on wings and mantle. Paler below. **ADULT:** White with tan crown and black wingtips. Immatures are most likely in West Indies. **STATUS AND RANGE:** Rare in Bahamas September through May. **HABITAT:** At sea.

Illustrations not to scale

adult, brown phase

BROWN BOOBY

adult

RED-FOOTED BOOBY

adult, white phase

MASKED BOOBY

adult

adult ♂

MAGNIFICENT FRIGATEBIRD

adult ♀

adult ♂

imm

adult

NORTHERN GANNET

imm

● **GREAT BLACK-BACKED GULL** *Larus marinus* 69–79cm (27–31in). **STATUS AND RANGE:** Uncommon in northern Bahamas October through March; rare in Puerto Rico; vagrant elsewhere in West Indies. Numbers are increasing. **HABITAT:** Beaches and calm bays. (*See also* Plate 5.)

● **LESSER BLACK-BACKED GULL** *Larus fuscus* 53–63cm (21–25in). **STATUS AND RANGE:** Fairly common locally in northern Bahamas. Very rare elsewhere in West Indies November through April. Numbers increasing. **HABITAT:** Beaches, calm bays, and dumps. (*See also* Plate 5.)

● **RING-BILLED GULL** *Larus delawarensis* 46–51cm (18–20in). **STATUS AND RANGE:** Fairly common but local non-breeding resident in northern Bahamas and Puerto Rico; uncommon in southern Bahamas, Cuba, Hispaniola, Cayman Islands, and Barbados; rare in Jamaica, Virgin Islands, and Lesser Antilles south to St Vincent. Occurs in all months, but primarily December through March. Numbers increasing. **HABITAT:** Coastal harbors, lagoons, and open ground from parking lots to grassy fields. Often urban areas. (*See also* Plate 5.)

● **HERRING GULL** *Larus argentatus* 56–66cm (22–26in). **STATUS AND RANGE:** Generally uncommon and local non-breeding resident in Bahamas, Cuba, Hispaniola, and Cayman Islands September through May and rare June through August. Rare in Jamaica, Puerto Rico, and Virgin Islands; very rare in Lesser Antilles October through March. Numbers increasing. **HABITAT:** Coastal areas, harbors, and lagoons. (*See also* Plate 5.)

● **BLACK-LEGGED KITTIWAKE** *Rissa tridactyla* 43cm (17in). **STATUS AND RANGE:** Very rare in Bahamas December through March; vagrant elsewhere. **HABITAT:** Far offshore. (*See also* Plate 6.)

● **BLACK-HEADED GULL** *Larus ridibundus* 39–43cm (15–17in). **STATUS AND RANGE:** Rare and local non-breeding resident in Bahamas, Puerto Rico, Virgin Islands (St Thomas and St Croix), Guadeloupe, and Barbados. Vagrant elsewhere in West Indies. Occurs November through June. Numbers increasing. **HABITAT:** Coastal harbors. (*See also* Plate 6.)

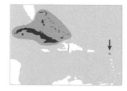

● **BONAPARTE'S GULL** *Larus philadelphia* 30.5–36cm (12–14in). **STATUS AND RANGE:** Uncommon non-breeding resident in Cuba and locally in Bahamas August through April. Rare on Barbuda. Vagrant elsewhere. **HABITAT:** Coastal harbors, lagoons, and at sea. (*See also* Plate 6.)

● **BLACK SKIMMER** *Rynchops niger* 40–51cm (16–20in). Unmistakable scissor-like black and orange bill with lower mandible longer than the upper. Often nocturnal. Plows water surface with bill. **STATUS AND RANGE:** Very rare migrant October through April in Bahamas, Cuba, Hispaniola, Puerto Rico, and Virgin Islands. Vagrant elsewhere in West Indies. **HABITAT:** Calm coastal bays and lagoons.

● **LAUGHING GULL** *Larus atricilla* 38–43cm (15–17in). **STATUS AND RANGE:** Widespread resident in West Indies, breeds locally. Generally common April through September; irregular and rare through most of West Indies remainder of year. **HABITAT:** Calm bays, coastal waters, and islets. (*See also* Plate 6.)

2nd-year

2nd-year

LESSER
BLACK-BACKED
GULL

non-br
adult

GREAT
BLACK-BACKED
GULL

non-br adult

non-br adult

RING-BILLED GULL

non-br adult

HERRING GULL

BLACK-LEGGED
KITTIWAKE

BONAPARTE'S
GULL

BLACK-HEADED
GULL

non-br adult

non-br adult

non-br adult

adult

non-br
adult

immature

BLACK SKIMMER

LAUGHING GULL

GREAT BLACK-BACKED GULL *Larus marinus* 69–79cm (27–31in). Very large, with massive bill. **FIRST YEAR:** Mottled grayish-brown; head white with pale flecks on rear and hindneck; bill black; tail has broad, black band. **SECOND YEAR:** Bill pinkish with large black band near tip, rump white, mantle with black blotches. **NON-BREEDING ADULT:** Black mantle, pink legs, pale flecks on head, bill yellow with red spot near tip. **BREEDING ADULT:** Head white. (*See also* Plate 4.)

LESSER BLACK-BACKED GULL *Larus fuscus* 53–63cm (21–25in). Large, with large bill. **FIRST YEAR:** Mottled grayish; head brownish in contrast. **SECOND YEAR:** Bill pinkish with large black band near tip. Broad, black tail band; white rump; brownish-gray wings with no white spots at tip. **NON-BREEDING ADULT:** Dark grayish-black mantle, pale yellow legs, yellow bill with red spot near tip. **BREEDING ADULT:** Head and neck white. (Great Black-backed Gull larger; bill more massive. Adult Herring Gull has paler mantle and pink legs; first and second year birds have less pronounced white rump patch.) (*See also* Plate 4.)

HERRING GULL *Larus argentatus* 56–66cm (22–26in). Large, with large bill. **FIRST YEAR:** Back and wings heavily streaked grayish-brown, bill pinkish at base, tipped black; tail lacks clear band; legs pink. **SECOND YEAR:** Variable gray on back and wings; outer primaries black; bill pinkish with pale gray band beyond nostril. **THIRD YEAR:** Tail white with broad black band; bill yellowish with dark band. **NON-BREEDING ADULT:** Heavy yellow bill with red spot near tip of lower mandible; head and underparts white; legs pink. **BREEDING ADULT:** Head and underparts white. (*See also* Plate 4.)

RING-BILLED GULL *Larus delawarensis* 46–51cm (18–20in). Fairly large, with medium-sized bill. **FIRST YEAR:** Mottled grayish-brown wings; gray back. Broad black tail band; bill pinkish, tipped black. **SECOND YEAR:** Upperparts and mantle mostly gray; black primaries with white spot at tip. **NON-BREEDING ADULT:** Bill yellowish with black band; legs yellowish-green. **BREEDING ADULT:** White head and underparts. Smaller than Herring Gull, more delicate head and bill, yellowish-green or grayish-green legs. (Herring Gull lacks bill ring and has pink legs.) (*See also* Plate 4.)

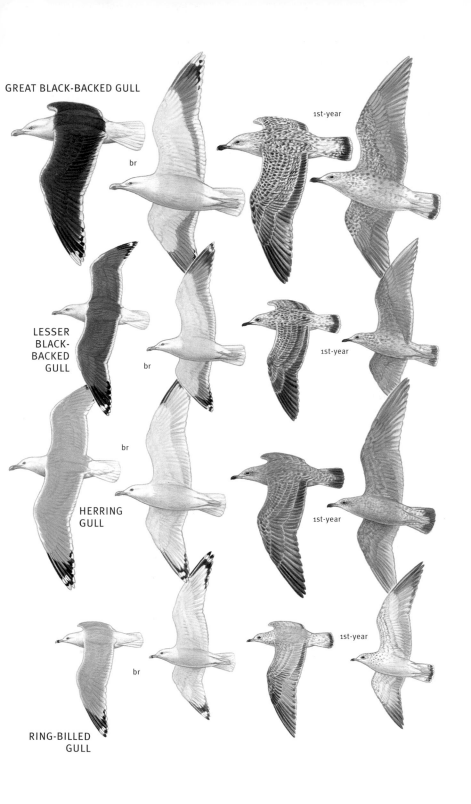

GREAT BLACK-BACKED GULL

1st-year

br

LESSER
BLACK-
BACKED
GULL

br

1st-year

HERRING
GULL

br

1st-year

br

1st-year

RING-BILLED
GULL

● **LAUGHING GULL** *Larus atricilla* 38–43cm (15–17in). **BREEDING ADULT:** Black head; dark gray mantle; black wingtips; reddish bill. **NON-BREEDING ADULT:** Similar, but diffuse gray mark on rear of white head; bill black. **IMMATURE:** Mottled gray-brown; belly whitish. **FIRST YEAR:** White rump; gray sides and back; broad black tail band. **SECOND YEAR:** Partial hood; spotting on tail; mantle slaty. **VOICE:** Squawky, variable *caw* and *caw-aw*. Also laugh-like *ka-ka-ka-ka-ka-ka-ka-kaa-kaa-kaaa-kaaa*. (*See also* Plate 4.)

● **BLACK-LEGGED KITTIWAKE** *Rissa tridactyla* 43cm (17in). **FIRST YEAR:** White head; black ear-spot, bill, and terminal tail band. **NON-BREEDING ADULT:** Yellow bill; white head, black mark behind eye; gray mantle; black wingtips with no white. **BREEDING ADULT:** Head entirely white. First year distinguished from Bonaparte's Gull by black half collar on hind-neck and white trailing edge of secondaries. **FLIGHT:** Wings and mantle marked with contrasting 'W'. (*See also* Plate 4.)

● **BLACK-HEADED GULL** *Larus ridibundus* 39–43cm (15–17in). **FIRST YEAR:** Black ear-spot; two-toned bill; narrow, black tail band; gray undersides to primaries. **NON-BREEDING ADULT:** Bill reddish, black tipped; mantle pale gray; outer primaries white, tipped black. **BREEDING ADULT:** Head black; bill red. (Bonaparte's Gull lacks pale gray undersides to primaries.) (*See also* Plate 4.)

● **BONAPARTE'S GULL** *Larus philadelphia* 30.5–36cm (12–14in). **FIRST YEAR:** Black ear-spot; thin black bill; narrow black tail band; whitish undersides to primaries. **NON-BREEDING ADULT:** Mantle pale gray, tail and outer primaries white; legs red. **BREEDING ADULT:** Head black. (Black-headed Gull has gray undersides to primaries.) (*See also* Plate 4.)

● **FRANKLIN'S GULL** *Larus pipixcan* 37cm (14.5in). **FIRST YEAR:** Narrow black tail band; white breast and underparts; gray back; partial blackish hood, and white forehead. **NON-BREEDING ADULT:** Similar, but only partial black hood; whitish forehead. **BREEDING ADULT:** Black head; slaty mantle and wingtips with black bar bordered with white on both sides. First year and non-breeding adults have more distinctive partial black hood and white forehead. **STATUS AND RANGE:** Vagrant in West Indies. **HABITAT:** Bays and estuaries.

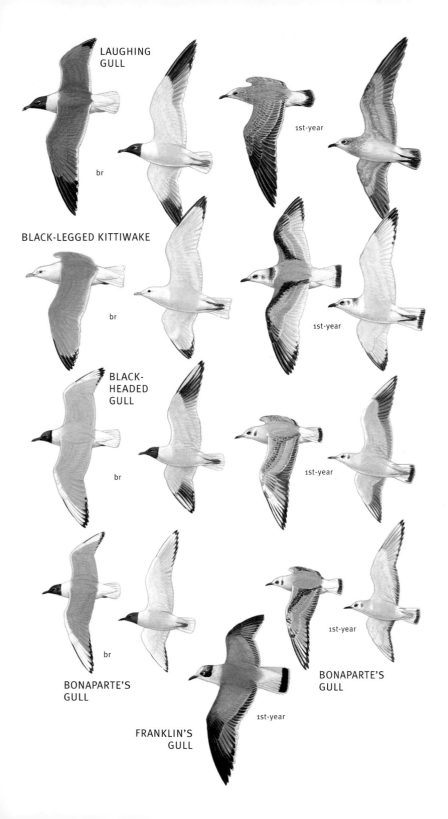

LAUGHING
GULL

br

1st-year

BLACK-LEGGED KITTIWAKE

br

1st-year

BLACK-
HEADED
GULL

br

1st-year

BONAPARTE'S
GULL

br

1st-year

BONAPARTE'S
GULL

1st-year

FRANKLIN'S
GULL

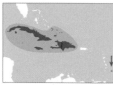

● **CASPIAN TERN** *Sterna caspia* 48–58cm (19–23in). Large tern with long, stout, red bill; black crest; dark gray underside to primaries. **NON-BREEDING ADULT:** Crest flecked white. **BREEDING ADULT:** Crest black. **IMMATURE:** Bill orange-red. (Royal Tern smaller, bill orange-yellow, underside of primaries pale; forehead white in non-breeding plumage.) **STATUS AND RANGE:** Common very locally and may breed in Cuba. Rare non-breeding resident locally in Bahamas, Jamaica, Hispaniola, and Barbados. Very rare in Puerto Rico and Cayman Islands. Occurs any month. **HABITAT:** Coastal lagoons.

● **ROYAL TERN** *Sterna maxima* 46–53cm (18–21in). Large tern with orange-yellow bill and black crest. **BREEDING ADULT:** Crown entirely black. **NON-BREEDING ADULT AND IMMATURE:** Forehead white. **VOICE:** Harsh, high-pitched *kri-i-ik.* **STATUS AND RANGE:** Common, but local resident in Bahamas, Greater Antilles, Virgin and Cayman Islands; generally fairly common in Lesser Antilles. Breeds very locally. **HABITAT:** Coastal lagoons.

● **LEAST TERN** *Sterna antillarum* 21.5–24cm (8.5–9.5in). Smallest West Indies tern. **BREEDING ADULT:** Black crown; V-shaped white forecrown; pale yellow bill with black tip. **STATUS AND RANGE:** Generally common, but local breeding resident in Bahamas, Greater Antilles, Cayman Islands, St Martin, Antigua, and Barbuda primarily May through August. Migrants occur September to March through all West Indies where uncommon to very rare. **HABITAT:** Coastal lagoons.

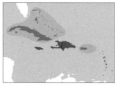

● **SANDWICH TERN** *Sterna sandvicensis* 41–46cm (16–18in). Relatively large. **BREEDING ADULT:** Appears white; shaggy black crest; slender black bill tipped yellow. Sometimes bill patched or entirely dull yellow. **NON-BREEDING ADULT:** Crown white, flecked black. **STATUS AND RANGE:** Common resident in Bahamas and Cuba; uncommon in Puerto Rico, Virgin Islands, and possibly on Sombrero Island (Anguilla). Non-breeding birds range to other islands where common on Jamaica, St Bartholomew, and Antigua primarily October through March; uncommon on Hispaniola, St Martin, Guadeloupe, Martinique, and Barbados; rare elsewhere. **HABITAT:** Coastal lagoons.

● **GULL-BILLED TERN** *Sterna nilotica* 33–38cm (13–15in). Chunky, gull-like. Heavy black bill; broad wings; shallow fork to tail. **BREEDING ADULT:** Black crown and hindneck. **NON-BREEDING ADULT:** Crown whitish with pale gray flecks; gray spot behind eye. **VOICE:** Raspy 2–3 syllables. **STATUS AND RANGE:** Uncommon breeding resident in Bahamas April through August. Uncommon and local in Hispaniola, Puerto Rico, larger Virgin Islands, Cayman Islands, and Sombrero Island (Anguilla) during same months. Disperses among other islands September through March. **HABITAT:** Ponds, lagoons, fields.

● **ARCTIC TERN** *Sterna paradisaea* 35–43cm (14–17in). **NON-BREEDING ADULT:** Blackish line along trailing edge of primaries; short black bill; short red legs. **BREEDING ADULT:** Bill entirely blood-red; underparts gray; cheek patch white. **IMMATURE:** Incomplete black cap and indistinct shoulder bar; tail shorter than adult's. **FLIGHT:** 'Neckless' appearance. **STATUS AND RANGE:** Rare non-breeding migrant in Puerto Rico June through October. **HABITAT:** Generally far out at sea.

● **FORSTER'S TERN** *Sterna forsteri* 35–42cm (14–16.5in). **NON-BREEDING ADULT:** Silvery-white primaries; large black spot enclosing eye; forked tail extends beyond folded wings. **BREEDING ADULT:** Bill orange with black tip. **STATUS AND RANGE:** Rare non-breeding resident in Bahamas, Cuba, Hispaniola, and Cayman Islands November through April. Very rare in Puerto Rico and Virgin Islands. **HABITAT:** Coastal lagoons.

● **COMMON TERN** *Sterna hirundo* 33–40cm (13–16in). **BREEDING ADULT:** Black cap; red bill with black tip; partly black outer primaries; tail does not extend beyond tips of folded wings. **NON-BREEDING ADULT:** Bill blackish; shoulder with dark bar; forehead white past eye. **VOICE:** Strong *kee-arr-r.* **STATUS AND RANGE:** Uncommon to rare migrant through most of West Indies. Occurs primarily May through October. **HABITAT:** Coastal lagoons.

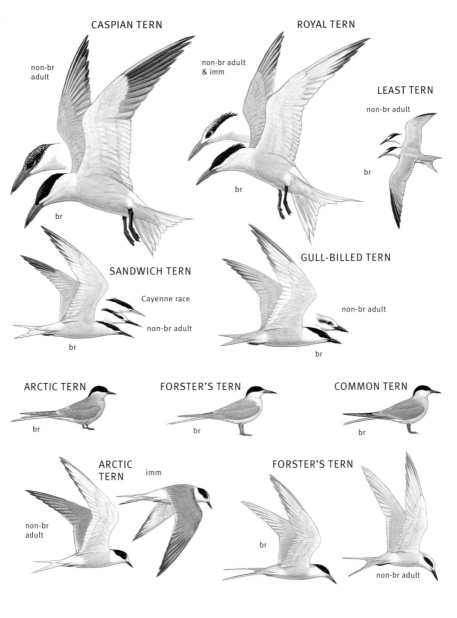

CASPIAN TERN

non-br adult

br

ROYAL TERN

non-br adult & imm

br

LEAST TERN

non-br adult

br

SANDWICH TERN

Cayenne race

non-br adult

br

GULL-BILLED TERN

non-br adult

br

ARCTIC TERN

br

FORSTER'S TERN

br

COMMON TERN

br

ARCTIC TERN

imm

non-br adult

FORSTER'S TERN

br

non-br adult

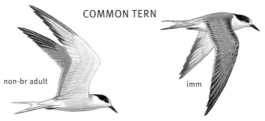

COMMON TERN

non-br adult

imm

ROSEATE TERN *Sterna dougallii* 35–41cm (14–16in). Very long, deeply forked tail; pale gray mantle and primaries; tail extends well beyond wingtips; underside of primary feather tips with little or no blackish. **BREEDING ADULT:** Bill black with some red (much more than North American birds); cap black. **NON-BREEDING ADULT:** Bill blackish; indistinct dark marking on shoulder; forehead white past eye. **IMMATURE:** Dark forehead and crown; bill blackish; back mottled; shoulder with indistinct marks. (Adult Common Tern's mantle darker gray and primary wing feathers have noticeable blackish on underside. Immature Common Tern has distinct black shoulder mark.) **VOICE:** Raspy *krek* and soft 2-syllable *tu-ick*. **STATUS AND RANGE:** Widespread, but generally uncommon to rare and very local breeding resident in West Indies primarily April through September. Common only in Virgin Islands. **HABITAT:** Coastal bays and lagoons.

SOOTY TERN *Sterna fuscata* 38–43cm (15–17in). **ADULT:** Blackish above and white below; tail deeply forked; white outertail feathers; white of forehead extends only to eye. (Bridled Tern has white line from forehead to behind eye, and white hindneck.) **IMMATURE:** Dark brown with whitish spots on mantle and wings; tail less deeply forked. **VOICE:** Distinctive, plaintive *wide-a-wake* or *wacky-wack*. **STATUS AND RANGE:** Generally a common breeding resident throughout, May through August. Rare in other months. **HABITAT:** Far offshore.

BRIDLED TERN *Sterna anaethetus* 38cm (15in). **ADULT:** Grayish-brown above and white below; white hindneck, and white line above and behind eye. (Sooty Tern is blacker above, lacks white hindneck, and white on forehead does not extend behind eye.) **IMMATURE:** Upperparts flecked pale gray. **VOICE:** Puppy-like *yep* or whining *yerk*. Also continuous *ah-ah-ah....* **STATUS AND RANGE:** Generally fairly common, but local breeding resident throughout West Indies April through August. Infrequent in other months. **HABITAT:** Far offshore.

WHISKERED TERN *Chlidonias hybridus* 25cm (10in). Small, with slightly notched tail. **NON-BREEDING ADULT:** Primarily pale gray above with ample black in primaries. Rear of crown black extends to eye; legs red. **BREEDING ADULT:** Black crown and dark gray underparts highlight white cheek. (Non-breeding Black Tern is darker above and has dark patch on side of neck. Non-breeding White-winged Tern's whitish rump contrasts with darker back.) **STATUS AND RANGE:** Vagrant in Barbados. **HABITAT:** Inland freshwater bodies, also calm coastal waters.

WHITE-WINGED TERN *Chlidonias leucopterus* 24cm (9.5in). Small, with slightly notched tail. **NON-BREEDING ADULT:** Black ear-spot and rear of crown; white rump; lacks dark neck mark. **BREEDING ADULT:** Black except for white tail and rear of body. Wings pale gray with black underwing linings; legs red. (Non-breeding Black Tern has gray rump, dark mark on side of neck, dark legs, and darker wings especially upper forewing.) **STATUS AND RANGE:** Vagrant. **HABITAT:** Inland freshwater bodies.

BLACK TERN *Chlidonias niger* 23–26cm (9–10in). **NON-BREEDING ADULT:** Gray above; forecrown, hindneck, and underparts white except dark patches on sides of breast. Dark patch behind eye. **BREEDING ADULT:** Head, breast, and belly black. **IMMATURE:** Upperparts washed brownish, sides washed grayish. **FLIGHT:** Buoyant and slightly erratic. Often hovers. **STATUS AND RANGE:** Fairly common migrant in Jamaica and Puerto Rico. Uncommon in Cayman Islands, Antigua, and Barbados. Rare in Cuba, Hispaniola, and most of Bahamas. Very rare or absent elsewhere in West Indies. Occurs April through November. **HABITAT:** Fresh and brackish ponds and rice fields. Well out at sea during migration.

BROWN NODDY *Anous stolidus* 38–40cm (15–16in). **ADULT:** Entirely dark brown except silvery-white forecrown fading to brown on hindneck. **VOICE:** Harsh *karrk*. **STATUS AND RANGE:** Locally common and widespread resident throughout Bahamas, Greater Antilles, Virgin Islands, and Lesser Antilles. Vagrant in Cayman Islands. Away from breeding islets, usually seen only at sea. **HABITAT:** Far offshore.

BLACK NODDY *Anous minutus* 34cm (13.5in). Entirely blackish-brown with white crown. Very similar to Brown Noddy, but with longer, thinner bill; white of crown extends farther down hindneck; neck noticeably more slender; underwings darker. Best distinguished by voice. **VOICE:** Sharp, dry nasal cackles, chatters, and squeaky notes. Also plaintive, piping whistle *wheeeaeee*, with rising inflection. **STATUS AND RANGE:** Vagrant in West Indies. **HABITAT:** Well offshore and around rocky islets.

ROSEATE TERN

imm

non-br adult

br

SOOTY TERN

adult

imm

BRIDLED TERN

adult

WHITE-WINGED TERN

non-br

WHISKERED TERN

non-br

BLACK TERN

non-br adult

br

BROWN NODDY

imm

adult

BLACK NODDY

GREAT SKUA *Stercorarius skua* 51–66cm (20–26in). Large, bulky, powerful, gull-like. Extremely similar to South Polar Skua. Dark brown; reddish-brown highlights; golden or reddish-brown streaks on head and neck. Underparts paler. Indistinct dark cap. **FLIGHT:** White wing patch. **STATUS AND RANGE:** Likely occurs through West Indies primarily November through May. **HABITAT:** Well out at sea.

SOUTH POLAR SKUA *Stercorarius maccormicki* 53cm (21in). Extremely similar to Great Skua but slightly smaller. Three color phases. Dark phase—As above, but darker underparts and lacks reddish tones. Intermediate phase—Light brown head, neck and underparts, light hindneck, may have dark cap. Light phase—Pale gray underparts, head and neck. **FLIGHT:** White wing patch. **STATUS AND RANGE:** Likely occurs through West Indies primarily November through May. **HABITAT:** Well out at sea.

PARASITIC JAEGER *Stercorarius parasiticus* 46–67cm (18–26.5in). Small jaeger. **ADULT:** Light phase—Dark brownish-gray above, whitish below; grayish-brown cap; narrow, dark upper breast band. Dark phase—Dark brown overall. **SUBADULT:** Finely barred below; often reddish cast to plumage. Pointed tips to central tail feathers. **FLIGHT:** Strong and direct, showing white patch on primaries. **STATUS AND RANGE:** Uncommon migrant and rare non-breeding resident in West Indies August through May. **HABITAT:** Well out at sea.

POMARINE JAEGER *Stercorarius pomarinus* 65–78cm (25.5–31in). Heavy-bodied; the largest jaeger. Two color phases with intermediate variation. **ADULT:** Central tail feathers can be long, but are usually twisted to give a spoon-like appearance. Light phase—Blackish cap and broad, dark band across breast. Dark phase—Less frequent; entirely dark ranging from brown to black. **SUBADULT AND IMMATURE:** Usually heavily barred below, especially sides under the wings. Central tail feathers may not extend beyond rest of tail. Parasitic Jaeger smaller; more buoyant flight; lacks heavy barring on sides. **FLIGHT:** White patch on primaries. **STATUS AND RANGE:** Uncommon non-breeding resident October through May in West Indies, especially off Hispaniola, west of Lesser Antilles, and in Bahamas. **HABITAT:** Well out at sea.

LONG-TAILED JAEGER *Stercorarius longicaudus* 50–58cm (19.5–23in), including 15–25cm (6–10in) tail. The smallest jaeger. **ADULT:** Long central tail feathers; grayish-brown cap; no breast band; back and secondaries grayish contrasting with darker primaries. **SUBADULT:** Dark phase—Uniform grayish-brown; darker cap; tail feathers not extended. Light phase—Finely barred below; fine white barring on back. Some have pale head and hindneck. Tail feathers not extended. **FLIGHT:** Graceful, tern-like; small white wing patch. **STATUS AND RANGE:** Very rare migrant through West Indies primarily August through October and March through May. **HABITAT:** Well out at sea.

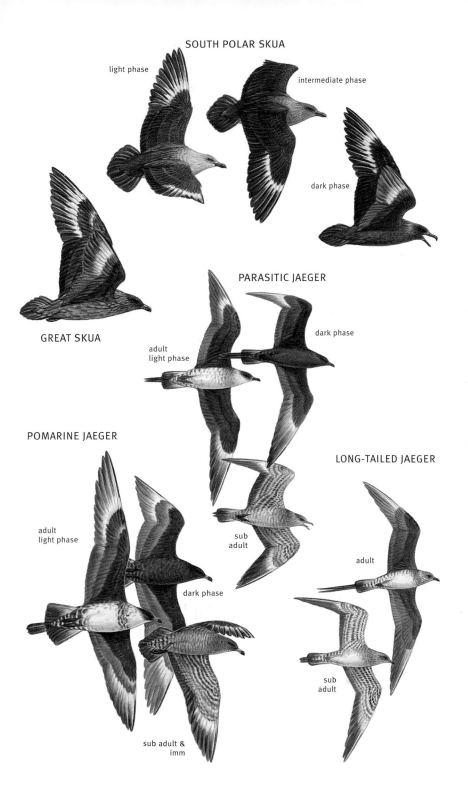

SOUTH POLAR SKUA

light phase

intermediate phase

dark phase

GREAT SKUA

PARASITIC JAEGER

adult
light phase

dark phase

POMARINE JAEGER

adult
light phase

dark phase

sub
adult

LONG-TAILED JAEGER

adult

sub adult &
imm

sub
adult

⬤ **LITTLE BLUE HERON** *Egretta caerulea* 56–71cm (22–28in). Medium size; bill grayish, tipped black. **ADULT:** Dark gray. **IMMATURE:** Initially white; later mottled with dark feathers. **STATUS AND RANGE:** Common resident throughout West Indies. **HABITAT:** Calm, shallow freshwater and saltwater areas; swift-flowing rivers and streams.

⬤ **TRICOLORED HERON** *Egretta tricolor* 61–71cm (24–28in). **ADULT:** Gray with white belly and undertail-coverts. **IMMATURE:** Browner. **STATUS AND RANGE:** Common resident in Bahamas, Greater Antilles, Virgin and Cayman Islands, and San Andrés. Generally rare in Lesser Antilles. **HABITAT:** Mangrove swamps and saltwater lagoons, infrequently freshwater wetlands.

⬤ **LITTLE EGRET** *Egretta garzetta* 55–65cm (22–25.5in). **BREEDING ADULT:** White phase— White; usually 2 long head plumes; bill and legs black, feet yellow; lores reddish. Dark phase— Gray; sometimes white chin and throat. **NON-BREEDING:** Gray-green lores. **STATUS AND RANGE:** Uncommon breeding resident in Barbados. Rare wanderer or non-breeding resident in St Lucia. Vagrant elsewhere. Numbers increasing. **HABITAT:** Coastal ponds and lagoons.

⬤ **SNOWY EGRET** *Egretta thula* 51–71cm (20–28in). **ADULT:** Legs black; feet and lores yellow; bill thin and black. **IMMATURE:** Legs dark in front and greenish-yellow in back. **STATUS AND RANGE:** Common resident in Bahamas, Greater Antilles, Virgin and Cayman Islands, Antigua, Guadeloupe, and Barbados. Generally uncommon non-breeding resident or transient elsewhere in Lesser Antilles, though breeds on St Martin. Uncommon on San Andrés. **HABITAT:** Freshwater swamps, but also river banks and saltwater lagoons.

⬤ **REDDISH EGRET** *Egretta rufescens* 69–81cm (27–32in). **ADULT:** Black-tipped bill, pinkish at base; ruffled neck feathers; dances in water. Dark phase—Grayish; head and neck reddish-brown. White phase—White. **IMMATURE:** Bill entirely dark; neck feathers unruffled. **STATUS AND RANGE:** Locally common resident in Bahamas and Cuba; uncommon in Cayman Islands and Hispaniola; uncommon and very local in Jamaica; and very rare wanderer to Puerto Rico. **HABITAT:** Shallow, protected coastal waters, also swamp edges.

⬤ **GREAT BLUE HERON** *Ardea herodias* 107–132cm (42–52in). Very large. Dark phase— Primarily gray; large, straight bill; black eyebrow stripe. White phase—White; yellow bill and legs. **STATUS AND RANGE:** Common non-breeding resident in Bahamas, Greater Antilles, Virgin and Cayman Islands primarily October through April. Uncommon in Lesser Antilles. Decidedly uncommon in other months, during which some breed. White phase extremely rare in West Indies. **HABITAT:** Ponds and lagoons.

⬤ **GRAY HERON** *Ardea cinerea* 90–98cm (35–38in). Very large; gray; white thighs in all plumages. (Great Blue Heron darker, particularly on hindneck and abdomen; thighs reddish-brown.) **STATUS AND RANGE:** Vagrant on Montserrat, Martinique, and Barbados. Numbers increasing. **HABITAT:** Ponds and lagoons.

⬤ **GREAT EGRET** *Ardea alba* 89–107cm (35–42in). Very large, with yellow bill and black legs. **STATUS AND RANGE:** Common resident in Bahamas, Greater Antilles, Antigua, and Guadeloupe; uncommon in Virgin Islands. Common non-breeding resident in Cayman Islands, St Bartholomew, and Barbados; uncommon elsewhere in Lesser Antilles September through April. Uncommon on San Andrés and Providencia. **HABITAT:** Large freshwater and saltwater swamps, grassy marshes, river banks, and shallows behind reefs.

⬤ **WESTERN REEF-HERON** *Egretta gularis* 55–65cm (22–25.5in). Stout bill. Two color phases and intermediates. **BREEDING ADULT:** White phase—White; 2 long head plumes, legs dark olive-green, feet yellow, lores greenish-yellow or green, bill yellowish-brown, with paler lower mandible. Dark phase—Dark gray; white chin and throat, lower breast and belly tinged brown, black legs, bill brownish-black; feet yellowish-green. **IMMATURE:** White; variably brown; bill dull brown. **STATUS AND RANGE:** Very rare on Puerto Rico (Culebra), St Lucia, and Barbados. Numbers increasing. **HABITAT:** Ponds and lagoons.

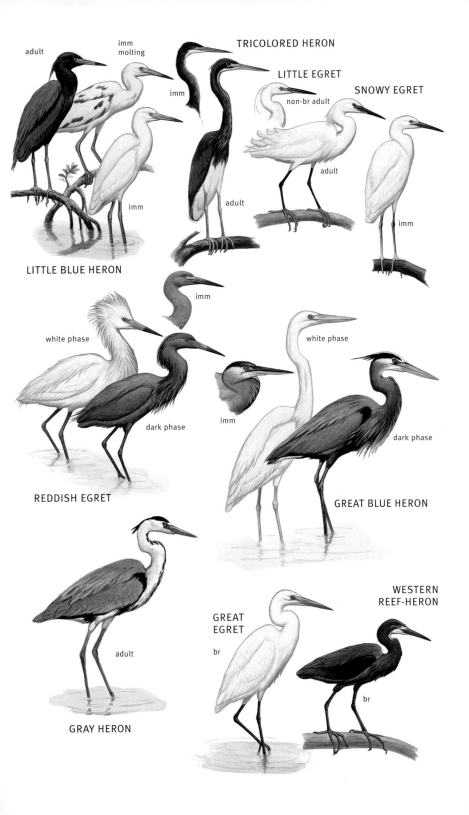

adult

imm molting

TRICOLORED HERON

imm

LITTLE EGRET

non-br adult

SNOWY EGRET

adult

imm

imm

adult

LITTLE BLUE HERON

imm

white phase

white phase

imm

dark phase

dark phase

REDDISH EGRET

GREAT BLUE HERON

adult

WESTERN
REEF-HERON

GREAT
EGRET

br

br

GRAY HERON

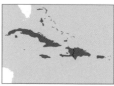

● **AMERICAN BITTERN** *Botaurus lentiginosus* 58–61cm (23–24in). Black neck mark, points bill upward. **FLIGHT:** Blackish wingtips. (Immature Night-heron darker and lacks black on neck and wingtips.) **VOICE:** Peculiar pumping sound, *oong-ka-chunk!* **STATUS AND RANGE:** Non-breeding resident in West Indies primarily October through March. Uncommon and local on larger islands of Bahamas and in Cuba; very rare in Cayman Islands, Jamaica, Hispaniola, and Puerto Rico. Vagrant elsewhere in West Indies. **HABITAT:** Dense vegetation of freshwater swamps.

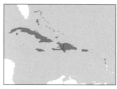

● **LEAST BITTERN** *Ixobrychus exilis* 28–35cm (11–14in). Small, reddish-yellow, with cream-colored patch on upperwing. **VOICE:** *Koo-koo-koo-koo*, almost a *coo*, first syllable often higher, call accelerates slightly. Also loud, harsh *kack*, sometimes in series. **STATUS AND RANGE:** Common resident in Cuba and Jamaica; fairly common in Cayman Islands (Grand Cayman) and Puerto Rico; uncommon in Hispaniola and Guadeloupe; uncommon to rare in Bahamas and Dominica; very rare in Virgin Islands. **HABITAT:** Dense vegetation of freshwater swamps, often with cattails; also mangroves.

● **YELLOW-CROWNED NIGHT-HERON** *Nyctanassa violacea* 56–71cm (22–28in). Nocturnal. Medium-sized, chunky appearance. **ADULT:** Gray underparts, black-and-white head markings. **IMMATURE:** Grayish-brown with white flecks. **VOICE:** Distinctive *quark*. **STATUS AND RANGE:** Common resident in Bahamas, Greater Antilles, Virgin and Cayman Islands, and northern Lesser Antilles; generally uncommon south of Barbuda; fairly common on San Andrés and Providencia. **HABITAT:** Mangrove swamps, but also freshwater areas, mud flats, and dry thickets.

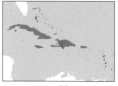

● **BLACK-CROWNED NIGHT-HERON** *Nycticorax nycticorax* 58–71cm (23–28in). Nocturnal, medium-sized, with chunky appearance. **ADULT:** Black crown and back; white face, underparts and head plumes. **IMMATURE:** Brown with white flecks. **FLIGHT:** Only feet extend beyond tail. Browner; larger white flecks on wings and upperparts, thinner bill and shorter legs than immature Yellow-crowned Night-heron. **VOICE:** Distinctive *quark*. **STATUS AND RANGE:** Uncommon and local resident in Bahamas, Greater Antilles, Virgin and Cayman Islands. Uncommon to rare non-breeding resident in Lesser Antilles October through April. **HABITAT:** Freshwater swamps; also brackish lagoons and salt ponds.

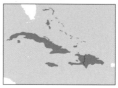

● **LIMPKIN** *Aramus guarauna* 69cm (27in). Large, long-legged, long-necked wading bird, brown with white streaks. Long, slightly down-curved bill. **VOICE:** Loud, piercing *carrao*. **STATUS AND RANGE:** Common resident on some northern Bahamas, Cuba, and locally in Jamaica; uncommon in Hispaniola; rare among other islands of Bahamas. **HABITAT:** Grassy freshwater wetlands, wooded floodplains, upland wet forests.

● **GREEN HERON** *Butorides virescens* 40–48cm (16–19in). Small, with short neck, dark coloration and greenish-yellow to orangish legs. **BREEDING ADULT:** Legs bright orange. **IMMATURE:** Heavily streaked below. **VOICE:** Distinctive, piercing *skyow* when flushed; softer series of *kek*, *kak* or *que* notes when undisturbed. **STATUS AND RANGE:** Common resident throughout West Indies. **HABITAT:** All water bodies.

● **CATTLE EGRET** *Bubulcus ibis* 48–64cm (19–25in). Small, with short, thick, yellowish bill; upland habitat. **BREEDING:** Reddish legs and eyes; reddish bill. Tan wash on crown, breast, and upper back. **NON-BREEDING:** Black legs and yellow bill. Tan wash reduced. **STATUS AND RANGE:** Common resident throughout West Indies. **HABITAT:** Pastures and fields. Roosts in mangroves or dense woods.

AMERICAN
BITTERN

LEAST BITTERN

imm

adult

YELLOW-CROWNED
NIGHT-HERON

imm

adult

imm

adult

BLACK-
CROWNED
NIGHT-HERON

imm

adult

imm

adult

BLACK-CROWNED
NIGHT-HERON

LIMPKIN

GREEN HERON

adult

imm

br

CATTLE EGRET

non-br adult

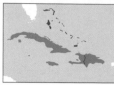

WHITE IBIS *Eudocimus albus* 56–71cm (22–28in). **ADULT:** White; long, down-curved reddish bill. **IMMATURE:** Brown; belly and rump white. **FLIGHT:** Outstretched neck, wingtips black. **STATUS AND RANGE:** Common resident in Cuba and Hispaniola; uncommon and local in Jamaica; rare non-breeding resident in Bahamas; rare wanderer in Cayman Islands. **HABITAT:** Freshwater swamps, rice fields, and saltwater lagoons.

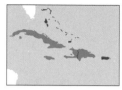

GLOSSY IBIS *Plegadis falcinellus* 56–64cm (22–25in). **ADULT:** Very dark, with long, down-curved bill. **IMMATURE:** Lighter. **STATUS AND RANGE:** Fairly common resident in Hispaniola; uncommon and local in Cuba and Jamaica. Uncommon in Bahamas where may breed; very local and irregular visitor to Puerto Rico and Cayman Islands; rare or vagrant elsewhere. **HABITAT:** Mud flats, marshy savannas and rice fields.

ROSEATE SPOONBILL *Platalea ajaja* 66–81cm (26–32in). **ADULT:** Pink, with spatula-like bill. **IMMATURE:** White, some pink. **STATUS AND RANGE:** Locally common resident in Cuba and Hispaniola. In Bahamas, common resident on Great Inagua, uncommon on Andros and rare on Caicos. Vagrant elsewhere. **HABITAT:** Shallow, saltwater lagoons and edges of mud flats.

SCARLET IBIS *Eudocimus ruber* 58.5cm (23in). **ADULT:** Unmistakable scarlet plumage; black wingtips. **NON-BREEDING:** Bill pinkish. **BREEDING:** Bill blackish. **IMMATURE:** White below; brownish above; pale back and rump tinged pink-buff. **STATUS AND RANGE:** Very rare wanderer to Grenada primarily January through June. Vagrant elsewhere. **HABITAT:** Coastal swamps, lagoons, and mangroves.

WOOD STORK *Mycteria americana* 100cm (40in). Large, with long legs. White coloration, black on wings, head dark. Bill large, down-curved at tip. **ADULT:** Head bald and blackish, bill black. **IMMATURE:** Head feathered and brownish, bill yellowish. **FLIGHT:** Black trailing edge of wing; feet trail beyond tail. **STATUS AND RANGE:** Rare resident in Cuba; very rare on Hispaniola, probably extirpated. Vagrant elsewhere. **HABITAT:** Swamps, mangroves, and coastal mud flats. Also rice fields, ponds, and inland water bodies.

GREATER FLAMINGO *Phoenicopterus ruber* 107–122cm (42–48in). Typically found in flocks. **ADULT:** Orangish-pink coloration; long legs and neck; strangely curved bill. **IMMATURE:** Much paler. **FLIGHT:** Head and neck outstretched and drooping; flight feathers black. **VOICE:** Goose-like honks. **STATUS AND RANGE:** Abundant resident on Great Inagua in Bahamas. Common but very local resident in Cuba and Hispaniola. Rare and very local in Jamaica and Puerto Rico. Numbers increasing. Reintroduced in Virgin Islands. **HABITAT:** Shallow lagoons and coastal estuaries.

SANDHILL CRANE *Grus canadensis* 100cm (40in). Very large, with long legs and long neck. **ADULT:** Gray; bare red crown. **IMMATURE:** Head and neck brownish; body gray mottled with brown. **VOICE:** High-pitched trumpet like call. **STATUS AND RANGE:** Rare and local resident in Cuba. Threatened. **HABITAT:** Marshes with emergent vegetation, swamp borders, edges of pine barrens, and natural savannas.

WHITE IBIS

adult

imm

adult

GLOSSY IBIS

adult

imm

ROSEATE SPOON-
BILL

imm

adult

adult

SCARLET IBIS

br

imm

WOOD STORK

imm

adult

GREATER
FLAMINGO

adult

imm

SANDHILL CRANE

adult

SEMIPALMATED PLOVER *Charadrius semipalmatus* 18.5cm (7.25in). Brown upper-parts; dark breast band; stubby bill; orange legs. Sometimes breast band shows only as bars on either side of breast. (Piping Plover much paler.) **NON-BREEDING:** Bill dark and may lack orange at base. **BREEDING:** Base of bill orange. **VOICE:** Plaintive *weet*. **STATUS AND RANGE:** Common non-breeding resident through most of West Indies August through May. Most frequent September and October. **HABITAT:** Tidal flats.

PIPING PLOVER *Charadrius melodus* 18cm (7in). Pale gray upperparts; short stubby bill; orange legs. **NON-BREEDING:** Bill black; breast band may be partial or absent. **FLIGHT:** White upper-tail-coverts and black spot near tip of tail. **BREEDING:** Base of bill orange; breast band may be partial or complete. **VOICE:** Thin, whistled *peep* and *pee-lo*. **STATUS AND RANGE:** Fairly common non-breeding resident in northern Bahamas; rare elsewhere in Bahamas, Greater Antilles, and Virgin Islands (St Croix) primarily late August through March. Vagrant elsewhere. Endangered. **HABITAT:** Dredged spoils and sandy water edges.

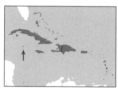

WILSON'S PLOVER *Charadrius wilsonia* 18–20cm (7–8in). Broad breast band; long, thick, black bill. **ADULT MALE:** Breast band black. **ADULT FEMALE AND IMMATURE:** Breast band brown. **VOICE:** Emphatic, raspy whistles, or quick *ki-ki-ki*. **STATUS AND RANGE:** Common resident in Bahamas, Greater Antilles, Virgin Islands, and some northern Lesser Antilles. Uncommon in Cayman Islands and Grenadines. Rare or vagrant elsewhere. **HABITAT:** Salt pond borders.

SNOWY PLOVER *Charadrius alexandrinus* 14–15cm (5.5–5.75in). Tiny, pale, slender, with black bill, dark neck marks, and blackish or dark legs. **BREEDING:** Black ear patch. **IMMATURE:** Lacks black markings. **VOICE:** Weak whistle, like calling someone's attention. **STATUS AND RANGE:** Common resident in southern Bahamas, Hispaniola, and Anguilla. Uncommon resident in Puerto Rico, Virgin Islands (Anegada), St Martin, and St Bartholomew. Very rare breeding resident on Cuba. Vagrant elsewhere. Threatened. **HABITAT:** Beaches and lagoon borders with extensive salt flats.

COLLARED PLOVER *Charadrius collaris* 15cm (5.75in). **ADULT MALE:** Reddish-brown hindcrown and hindneck; white forehead, throat and underparts; black band across breast. **ADULT FEMALE:** Thinner breast band; less reddish-brown. **IMMATURE:** Breast band limited to sides of neck; no black on crown; only hint of reddish-brown. **FLIGHT:** No wing stripe. **VOICE:** Sharp, metallic *peet* or *peep-peep* and *chitit*. **STATUS AND RANGE:** Uncommon to rare breeding resident in Grenada and perhaps in Grenadines (Mustique). Rare wanderer to Barbados. Vagrant elsewhere. **HABITAT:** Salt flats, coasts, and river banks.

KILLDEER *Charadrius vociferus* 25cm (9.75in). 2 black bands on breast. **FLIGHT:** Reddish-brown rump. **VOICE:** Plaintive, high-pitched *kee* and *dee-de*. **STATUS AND RANGE:** Common resident in Bahamas and Greater Antilles, less so in Virgin Islands. Migrants augment local numbers primarily September through March. Uncommon non-breeding resident in Cayman Islands, northern Lesser Antilles, Barbados, and San Andrés. Rare to very rare elsewhere in Lesser Antilles. **HABITAT:** Wet fields, short grass, mudholes, and freshwater pond edges.

SEMIPALMATED
PLOVER

br

non-br

PIPING PLOVER

br

non-br

WILSON'S PLOVER

♀

♂

SNOWY PLOVER

imm

br

COLLARED PLOVER

imm

adult ♂

KILLDEER

adult

NORTHERN LAPWING *Vanellus vanellus* 30cm (12in). Crest; broad black breast band. **IMMATURE:** Crest and color pattern less conspicuous. **STATUS AND RANGE:** Vagrant to West Indies. **HABITAT:** Grasslands and tidal flats.

BLACK-BELLIED PLOVER *Pluvialis squatarola* 26–34cm (10–13.5in). Large, stocky, with short bill. **NON-BREEDING:** Light mottled-gray; indistinct contrast between gray crown and whitish eyebrow stripe. **BREEDING:** Black underparts. **FLIGHT ABOVE:** White uppertail-coverts, white tail with dark bars and distinct white wing stripe. **FLIGHT BELOW:** Black wing-pits. **VOICE:** Plaintive *klee* or *klee-a-lee*. **STATUS AND RANGE:** Generally common non-breeding resident in West Indies August through May; also occurs June and July. **HABITAT:** Tidal mud flats and other coastal water edges.

AMERICAN GOLDEN-PLOVER *Pluvialis dominica* 26cm (10in). Fairly large and stocky, with short bill. **NON-BREEDING:** Mottled gray; contrast between dark crown and whitish eyebrow stripe. **BREEDING:** Black underparts; broad white patch edging breast; golden cast on mottled upperparts. **FLIGHT ABOVE:** Dark tail and uppertail-coverts; lacks white wing stripe. **FLIGHT BELOW:** Lacks black wingpits. **VOICE:** Loud whistle and soft, warbled *chee-dle-wur*, sometimes as loud whistle. **STATUS AND RANGE:** Rare southbound migrant throughout West Indies August through November and very rare northbound March and April. **HABITAT:** Fields and golf courses; also tidal flats

PACIFIC GOLDEN-PLOVER *Pluvialis fulva* 24cm (9.5in). Fairly large; slender; long-legged. More slender and longer-legged than American Golden-plover. **NON-BREEDING:** Golden cast (yellower than American Golden-plover) on back, face and eyebrow stripe; breast also yellower. **BREEDING:** Black below; mottled black and yellowish-brown above. **STATUS AND RANGE:** Vagrant on Barbados. **HABITAT:** Fields and golf courses; also tidal flats.

NORTHERN LAPWING

adult

non-br

non-br

non-br

BLACK-
BELLIED
PLOVER

br

AMERICAN
GOLDEN-PLOVER

non-br

br

non-br

non-br

PACIFIC GOLDEN-
PLOVER

non-br

br

SOLITARY SANDPIPER *Tringa solitaria* 19–23cm (7.5–9in). White eye-ring, dark upperparts, black barring of outertail feathers; dark greenish legs; black mark down center of rump with white on either side. Bobs tail. **VOICE:** Series of hard whistles. **STATUS AND RANGE:** Non-breeding resident throughout West Indies. Uncommon southbound migrant September and October; less frequent November through May. **HABITAT:** Freshwater edges. (*See also* Plate 21.)

WOOD SANDPIPER *Tringa glareola* 20cm (8in). Medium-sized, slender, with entirely white rump. Pale yellow or greenish-yellow legs; white eyebrow stripe. (Solitary Sandpiper lacks conspicuous eyebrow stripe, has more noticeable white eye-ring and darker wing linings.) **FLIGHT:** Pale gray underwings. **STATUS AND RANGE:** Rare on Barbados and Guadeloupe. **HABITAT:** Primarily freshwater edges.

WILSON'S SNIPE *Gallinago delicata* 27–29cm (10.5–11.5in). Long bill, striped head and back, reddish-brown tail. **VOICE:** Guttural squawk when flushed. **STATUS AND RANGE:** Fairly common non-breeding resident in Bahamas, Cuba, and Hispaniola; uncommon in Jamaica, Puerto Rico, Virgin and Cayman Islands, and Barbados, and rare through Lesser Antilles except Barbados. Occurs primarily October through April. **HABITAT:** Grassy freshwater edges and grassy or muddy savannas. (*See also* Plate 21.)

STILT SANDPIPER *Calidris himantopus* 20–22cm (8–8.5in). Dull greenish legs; whitish eyebrow stripe. Long bill, thick at base, slightly drooped at tip (Dowitchers have longer, straighter bills). **NON-BREEDING:** Grayish above, whitish below; pale eyebrow stripe. **BREEDING:** Reddish-brown ear-patch and heavily barred underparts. **VOICE:** Very soft, unmusical and unabrasive *cue*. **STATUS AND RANGE:** Generally uncommon in West Indies, though common locally in Cuba, Hispaniola, Puerto Rico, and Virgin Islands primarily late August through early November. Occurs in all months. **HABITAT:** Mud flats and shallow lagoons. (*See also* Plate 21.)

SHORT-BILLED DOWITCHER *Limnodromus griseus* 26–30cm (10–12in). Very long, straight bill. Feeds with vertical bill thrusts. **NON-BREEDING:** Gray above, whitish below, pale gray breast, white eyebrow stripe. **BREEDING:** Variable. Pale reddish-brown head and breast blending to white on belly. Breast finely barred, flanks heavily barred. **VOICE:** In flight, soft, rapid whistle *tu-tu-tu*, harsher when alarmed. **STATUS AND RANGE:** Fairly common, but local non-breeding resident in Bahamas, Greater Antilles, Cayman Islands, and Barbados August through April, and rarely May through July. Uncommon in Virgin Islands and uncommon to rare in Lesser Antilles. **HABITAT:** Tidal mud flats. (*See also* Plate 21.)

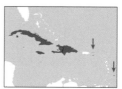

LONG-BILLED DOWITCHER *Limnodromus scolopaceus* 28–32cm (11–12.5in). Very long, straight bill. Feeds with vertical bill thrusts. Best distinguished from Short-billed Dowitcher by voice. **NON-BREEDING:** Gray above, paler below and with white eyebrow stripe. **BREEDING:** Reddish breast, belly, and abdomen. Breast finely barred, flanks moderately barred. **FLIGHT:** White patch extends well up back. **VOICE:** Thin, high-pitched *keek*, singly or in series. **STATUS AND RANGE:** Status uncertain as both dowitchers were until recently considered a single species. Apparently a very rare migrant. **HABITAT:** Primarily shallow fresh and brackish water, also tidal mud flats.

WOOD SANDPIPER

SOLITARY SANDPIPER

br

non-br

STILT SANDPIPER

WILSON'S SNIPE

br

non-br

SHORT-BILLED
DOWITCHER

br

non-br

LONG-BILLED
DOWITCHER

● **DUNLIN** *Calidris alpina* 20–23cm (8–9in). Heavy bill, distinctively drooping at tip; short-necked; hunched appearance. **NON-BREEDING:** Gray wash on breast, head, and upperparts. **BREEDING:** Black belly and reddish back. **VOICE:** Distinctive harsh, nasal *tzeep*. **STATUS AND RANGE:** Rare non-breeding resident in Bahamas; very rare in Cuba, Jamaica, Puerto Rico, and Virgin Islands; vagrant elsewhere. Occurs late August through April. **HABITAT:** Borders of still water, particularly mud flats. (*See also* Plate 21.)

● **CURLEW SANDPIPER** *Calidris ferruginea* 18–23cm (7–9in). Bill slightly down-curved throughout its length. **FLIGHT:** White rump. **NON-BREEDING ADULT:** Upperparts brownish-gray; underparts white. **BREEDING MALE:** Reddish-brown. **BREEDING FEMALE:** Duller. **VOICE:** A soft *chirrup*. **STATUS AND RANGE:** Primarily vagrant in West Indies. Occurs September through October and April through June. **HABITAT:** Mud flats, marshes, and beaches.

● **SEMIPALMATED SANDPIPER** *Calidris pusilla* 14–16.5cm (5.5–6.5in). Small, with black legs. Medium-length black bill slightly longer and more drooped at tip in female than in male. Flocks. The principal small sandpiper to know well. **NON-BREEDING:** Grayish-brown above; whitish below. **BREEDING:** Finely barred upper breast; reddish-brown tints on upperparts. **VOICE:** Soft chatter; also fairly deep, hoarse *cherk*. **STATUS AND RANGE:** Generally common non-breeding resident through most of West Indies August through October. **HABITAT:** Mud flats; still water edges from puddles to salt ponds. (*See also* Plate 21.)

● **WESTERN SANDPIPER** *Calidris mauri* 15–18cm (5.75–7in). Bill relatively long, heavy at base, narrower and drooping at tip. Bill characters overlap with very similar Semipalmated Sandpiper. Best distinguished by voice and in breeding plumage. **NON-BREEDING:** Grayish-brown above; whitish below. **BREEDING:** Reddish-brown crown, ear-patch, and scapulars. **VOICE:** *Kreep*, coarser and more querulous than Semipalmated Sandpiper. **STATUS AND RANGE:** Non-breeding resident throughout West Indies primarily September through March. Fairly common through much of the region. **HABITAT:** Primarily mud flats.

● **LEAST SANDPIPER** *Calidris minutilla* 12.5–16.5cm (5–6.5in). Tiny; brown with streaked breast. Yellowish-green legs distinguish it from all other small sandpipers.Thin bill has slightly drooping tip. **NON-BREEDING:** Brown above and on breast; white belly and abdomen. **BREEDING:** Plumage more mottled with reddish-brown tints. **VOICE:** Thin, soft whistle *wi-wi-wit*. Also whinny-like trill dropping in pitch and volume *tr-tr-tr-tr....* **STATUS AND RANGE:** Through most of West Indies a common migrant August through October and April through May; uncommon to rare non-breeding resident November through March. **HABITAT:** Mud flats and still water borders. (*See also* Plate 21.)

● **WHITE-RUMPED SANDPIPER** *Calidris fuscicollis* 18–20cm (7–8in). White rump. Easily overlooked. **NON-BREEDING:** Brownish-gray above and on upper breast, appearing hooded. **BREEDING:** Browner; reddish-brown tints on crown, upper back and ear-patch. **VOICE:** Mouse-like squeak, *peet* or *jeet*. Also thin, high-pitched trill. **STATUS AND RANGE:** Generally uncommon to rare migrant southbound through West Indies August through October; rarer northward migrant March and April. **HABITAT:** Rice fields, mud flats and borders of still water. (*See also* Plate 21.)

● **BAIRD'S SANDPIPER** *Calidris bairdii* 18–19cm (7–7.5in). Larger than Semipalmated and Western, and wings extend beyond tail. Best separated from White-rumped Sandpiper in flight; white rump of Baird's is divided by a dark central stripe. Baird's picks for food rather than probes. Occurs singly or in small groups. **NON-BREEDING:** Brownish-gray above and on breast. **BREEDING:** Browner, with faint reddish-brown tints. **STATUS AND RANGE:** Very rare migrant in West Indies. Status poorly known. Occurs primarily September and October. **HABITAT:** Edges of inland wetlands. Often some distance from water.

● **PECTORAL SANDPIPER** *Calidris melanotos* 20–24cm (8–9.5in). Yellowish-green bill and legs; sharp demarcation between heavily streaked breast and white belly. **NON-BREEDING:** Gray-brown upperparts, head and breast. **BREEDING MALE:** More mottled; breast heavily streaked with black. **VOICE:** Low, harsh *krip*. **STATUS AND RANGE:** Generally an uncommon southbound migrant August through early November through West Indies. Rare during northward migration March and April. **HABITAT:** Wet meadows, grassy areas after rains. (*See also* Plate 21.)

DUNLIN

non-br

br

CURLEW SANDPIPER

non-br

SEMIPALMATED
SANDPIPER

non-br

br

WESTERN
SANDPIPER

non-br

br

LEAST SANDPIPER

non-br

br

WHITE-RUMPED
SANDPIPER

non-br

br ♂

BAIRD'S SANDPIPER

non-br

br

non-br

br

PECTORAL
SANDPIPER

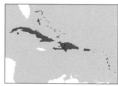

● **HUDSONIAN GODWIT** *Limosa haematica* 33–40cm (13–16in). Long, slightly upturned bill, pinkish at base; black tail with white base. **NON-BREEDING:** Gray overall, paler below; white eyebrow stripe. **BREEDING:** Dark reddish-brown below, heavily barred. Female paler. **FLIGHT ABOVE:** White wing stripe and base of tail. **FLIGHT BELOW:** Blackish wing linings and white wing stripe. **STATUS AND RANGE:** Very rare through most of West Indies primarily September and October. **HABITAT:** Grassy freshwater pond edges and mud flats.

● **MARBLED GODWIT** *Limosa fedoa* 40–51cm (16–20in). Large, with no white on rump. Long, slightly upturned bill. **NON-BREEDING:** Buff-colored underparts. **BREEDING:** Reddish-brown underparts barred black. **FLIGHT ABOVE:** Cinnamon-colored; blackish primary wing-coverts. **FLIGHT BELOW:** Cinnamon-colored wing linings with paler flight feathers. **STATUS AND RANGE:** Very rare migrant or vagrant in West Indies primarily late August through early April. **HABITAT:** Mud flats and marshes.

● **SANDERLING** *Calidris alba* 18–22cm (7–8.5in). Occurs in flocks, which typically advance and retreat with waves on the tideline. **NON-BREEDING:** The lightest-colored sandpiper; white underparts and light gray upperparts. Black mark on bend of wing. **BREEDING:** Reddish-brown head and breast. **VOICE:** Distinctive *whit*. **STATUS AND RANGE:** Generally fairly common non-breeding resident throughout West Indies September through April, and rare May through August. **HABITAT:** Sandy beaches. (*See also* Plate 21.)

● **SPOTTED SANDPIPER** *Actitis macularia* 18–20cm (7–8in). Has a distinctive teetering walk. **NON-BREEDING:** White underparts; dark mark on side of neck; orangish base of bill. **BREEDING:** Dark spots on underparts; orange bill with black tip. **VOICE:** Whistled *we-weet*. **STATUS AND RANGE:** Generally common non-breeding resident throughout West Indies August through May, less common other months. **HABITAT:** Water edges of mangroves, coastlines, and streams. (*See also* Plate 21.)

● **RED KNOT** *Calidris canutus* 25–28cm (9.75–11in). Medium-sized; chunky build, usually greenish legs, and relatively short bill. **NON-BREEDING:** Gray above; white below. **BREEDING:** Orangish-red face and underparts. **STATUS AND RANGE:** Generally rare through West Indies September and October, less frequent March and April. **HABITAT:** Sandy tidal flats. (*See also* Plate 21.)

HUDSONIAN GODWIT

br

non-br

non-br

SANDERLING

br

non-br

MARBLED GODWIT

br

non-br

br

RED KNOT

br

non-br

SPOTTED SANDPIPER

non-br

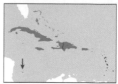

WILLET *Catoptrophorus semipalmatus* 38–40cm (15–16in). Large, light gray, with gray legs and thick bill. **BREEDING:** Fine black stripes on head, neck and breast. **NON-BREEDING:** More uniformly gray. **FLIGHT:** Black-and-white wing pattern. **VOICE:** Sharp *chip-chip-chip*; also sharp whistles. **STATUS AND RANGE:** Resident in Bahamas, Greater Antilles, and Cayman Islands where most common August through November. Uncommon to rare elsewhere. **HABITAT:** Tidal flats; also borders of saltwater and freshwater bodies.

UPLAND SANDPIPER *Bartramia longicauda* 28–32cm (11–12.5in). Orangish-yellow legs; thin, relatively short bill; small head; long slender neck; long tail. Occurs in grasslands, rather than water edges. **FLIGHT:** Dark primaries; long tail; stiff, shallow wingbeats. **STATUS AND RANGE:** Rare migrant in Bahamas, Cuba, Puerto Rico, and some Lesser Antilles primarily August through early October. Very rare or vagrant elsewhere in West Indies. **HABITAT:** Grasslands, pastures and savannas.

RUFF *Philomachus pugnax* Male: 30cm (12in); Female: 23–28cm (9–11in). **NON-BREEDING:** Fairly chunky; erect posture; whitish around base of bill; buffish breast, sometimes scaled; relatively short and slightly drooped bill. Legs often pale, varying from dull yellow to orange, green or brown. Feeds sluggishly. **BREEDING MALE:** Extremely variable but all have elaborate breast and head feathers. **BREEDING FEMALE:** Variable. Similar to non-breeding, but darker. **FLIGHT:** Long, oval white patches at base of tail. **STATUS AND RANGE:** Rare but regular migrant on Barbados; vagrant elsewhere in West Indies. Occurs primarily September and October. **HABITAT:** Mud flats and borders of ponds and lagoons.

ESKIMO CURLEW *Numenius borealis* 30–35cm (12–14in). Small curlew. Noticeably smaller than very similar Whimbrel and with shorter, straighter bill. **FLIGHT:** Cinnamon-colored wing linings; dark, unbarred primaries. **STATUS AND RANGE:** Vagrant in West Indies. Critically endangered if not extinct. **HABITAT:** Grasslands, plowed fields, sometimes mud flats.

WHIMBREL *Numenius phaeopus* 38–46cm (15–18in). Relatively large, with striped crown and long, down-curved bill. **FLIGHT:** Underwings barred, without cinnamon color. **VOICE:** Harsh, rapid whistle, *whip-whip-whip-whip*. **STATUS AND RANGE:** Generally uncommon to rare, but regular migrant throughout West Indies, primarily September. **HABITAT:** Ponds, swamps and marshes.

LONG-BILLED CURLEW *Numenius americanus* 51–66cm (20–26in). Large, with extremely long, down-curved bill. Mottled cinnamon-brown above, paler below, legs bluish. **FLIGHT:** Cinnamon wing linings. **STATUS AND RANGE:** Vagrant in West Indies. **HABITAT:** Mud flats, lagoons, wetlands, sand bars and shorelines.

WILLET

br

non-br

UPLAND
SANDPIPER

non-br

br ♂

br ♀

non-br

RUFF (FEMALE: REEVE)

ESKIMO
CURLEW

LONG-BILLED
CURLEW

WHIMBREL

COMMON GREENSHANK *Tringa nebularia* 32cm (12.5in). Large, with slightly upturned bill, thicker at base. **NON-BREEDING:** Greenish or yellowish legs. **BREEDING:** Breast heavily flecked with black. **FLIGHT:** White 'V' extends from uppertail-coverts onto back. (Greater Yellowlegs lacks this white 'V'.) **STATUS AND RANGE:** Vagrant in West Indies. **HABITAT:** Mud flats.

GREATER YELLOWLEGS *Tringa melanoleuca* 33–38cm (13–15in). Large, with orangish-yellow legs. Long, straight bill often appears slightly upturned and two-toned. (That of Lesser Yellowlegs is relatively shorter, thinner and darker at base.) Forms flocks. **FLIGHT:** Dark above; white uppertail-coverts. **VOICE:** Loud, raspy, 3- or 4-note whistle, *cu-cu-cu*, or *klee-klee-cu*. **STATUS AND RANGE:** Non-breeding resident throughout West Indies. Most common during southbound migration August through October. **HABITAT:** Mud flats and shallows of freshwater and saltwater bodies.

LESSER YELLOWLEGS *Tringa flavipes* 25–28cm (9.75–11in). Medium-sized, with orangish-yellow legs and thin, straight bill. Forms flocks. **VOICE:** 1- or 2-note *cu-cu*, softer and more nasal than Greater Yellowlegs. **STATUS AND RANGE:** Non-breeding resident throughout West Indies. Most common during migration August through October and March through May. **HABITAT:** Mud flats and shallows of both freshwater and saltwater bodies. (*See also* Plate 21.)

SPOTTED REDSHANK *Tringa erythropus* 30cm (12in). Red legs and base of lower mandible. **FLIGHT:** Large white patch on lower back. **NON-BREEDING ADULT AND IMMATURE:** Gray above, paler below; blackish lores, paler in immature; white eyebrow stripe. **BREEDING ADULT:** Black, heavily spotted white. **STATUS AND RANGE:** Vagrant in West Indies. **HABITAT:** Shorelines, tide pools, marshes.

WILSON'S PHALAROPE *Phalaropus tricolor* 23cm (9in). Thin straight bill. Phalaropes spin in water to stir up food. **NON-BREEDING:** White breast; thin dark gray mark through eye. **BREEDING MALE:** Reddish-tan wash on neck. **BREEDING FEMALE:** Dark reddish-brown band from shoulder blending to black behind eye. **STATUS AND RANGE:** Rare migrant and less frequently non-breeding resident August through May in Hispaniola and Barbados; very rare in Jamaica, Puerto Rico, Virgin and Cayman Islands. Vagrant elsewhere. **HABITAT:** Shallow ponds and lagoons. (*See also* Plate 21.)

RED-NECKED PHALAROPE *Phalaropus lobatus* 18cm (7in). **NON-BREEDING ADULT:** Black cap; white forehead; broad black bar through eye and ear-coverts; very thin, straight black bill. (Non-breeding Wilson's Phalarope has thin gray eye-stripe and longer bill.) **BREEDING FEMALE:** Black cap, dark back streaked white or pale buff, pale reddish-brown neck, golden wing-coverts. **BREEDING MALE:** Duller than female. (Wilson's Phalarope lacks white stripes on back.) **STATUS AND RANGE:** Very rare migrant in Bahamas, Cuba, and Hispaniola October through January. Vagrant other seasons and other islands. **HABITAT:** Usually out at sea; sometimes ponds and lagoons. (*See also* Plate 21.)

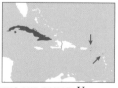

RED PHALAROPE *Phalaropus fulicarius* 21cm (8in). **NON-BREEDING ADULT:** Unstreaked pale gray above, underparts white. Bill stout and black except for yellow spot at base of lower mandible; hindcrown blackish; broad black bar through eye to ear-coverts. **BREEDING FEMALE:** Entirely dark reddish-brown below with a conspicuous white facial patch. **BREEDING MALE:** Dull orangish-brown below with less distinct whitish facial patch. **STATUS AND RANGE:** Very rare migrant in West Indies October through January. **HABITAT:** Usually out at sea; sometimes ponds and lagoons. (*See also* Plate 21.)

COMMON GREENSHANK

non-br

br

LESSER
YELLOWLEGS

GREATER
YELLOWLEGS

non-br adult
and imm

SPOTTED
REDSHANK

WILSON'S
PHALAROPE

br ♀

non-br

non-br
adult

br ♀

RED
PHALAROPE

non-br
adult

RED-NECKED
PHALAROPE

br ♀

● **RUDDY TURNSTONE** *Arenaria interpres* 21–23cm (8–9in). **NON-BREEDING:** Dark breast markings; orange legs. **BREEDING:** Unusual black-and-white facial markings; reddish-orange back. **FLIGHT:** Distinctive white pattern on upperwings, back and tail. **VOICE:** Loud, nasal *cuck-cuck-cuck*, increasing in volume. **STATUS AND RANGE:** Common non-breeding resident throughout West Indies in most months. **HABITAT:** Mud flats, pond edges, sandy and rocky coasts.

● **BUFF-BREASTED SANDPIPER** *Tryngites subruficollis* 19–22cm (7.5–8.5in). **ADULT:** Upperparts have scaled look. Large dark eye framed by pale eye-ring on clean buffish face; thin black bill. Underparts buff with spots on sides; yellow legs and feet; short tail not extending beyond folded wings at rest. (Upland Sandpiper larger, with longer neck, legs, and bill; streaked below.) **FLIGHT:** White wing linings. **STATUS AND RANGE:** Very rare in Lesser Antilles September through early November; rarer in April. Vagrant elsewhere. **HABITAT:** Fields, pastures, short grass.

● **DOUBLE-STRIPED THICK-KNEE** *Burhinus bistriatus* 38–43cm (15–17in). Large, plover-like, with large yellow eye, whitish eyebrow stripe, striped breast. Nocturnal; terrestrial. **FLIGHT:** Conspicuous white wing patches. **VOICE:** Loud, rattling *ca-ca-ca-ca-....* rising in volume then fading away. **STATUS AND RANGE:** Uncommon and local resident in Hispaniola. Threatened. **HABITAT:** Semi-arid open country, savannas, plantations, and rice fields.

● **AMERICAN OYSTERCATCHER** *Haematopus palliatus* 43–54cm (17–21in). Large, with black hood and long, heavy bill. **ADULT:** Orange-red bill; pinkish legs. **IMMATURE:** Dull pinkish bill, dark at tip. Gray legs. **FLIGHT:** Broad white wing stripe and uppertail. **VOICE:** Emphatic, coarsely whistled *wheep*. **STATUS AND RANGE:** Fairly common but very local resident in southern and central Bahamas, Hispaniola, Puerto Rico, Virgin Islands, and Guadeloupe (Petite Terre). Rare and local, primarily outside breeding season, in northernmost Bahamas, Cuba, and Lesser Antilles. Vagrant elsewhere. **HABITAT:** Rocky headlands, stony beaches, offshore islands, and cays.

● **BLACK-NECKED STILT** *Himantopus mexicanus* 34–39cm (13.5–15.5in). Large, with long pink legs, black upperparts, and white underparts. **FLIGHT:** Black wings; white underparts, tail, and lower back, extending as 'V' on back. **VOICE:** Loud, raucous *wit, wit, wit, wit, wit.* **STATUS AND RANGE:** Widespread throughout West Indies. Common breeding resident March through October in southern and central Bahamas, Greater Antilles, and Virgin and Cayman Islands. Uncommon to rare breeding resident in northernmost Bahamas; uncommon in northern Lesser Antilles south to Guadeloupe; rare elsewhere. **HABITAT:** Mud flats, salt ponds, and open mangrove swamps.

● **AMERICAN AVOCET** *Recurvirostra americana* 40–51cm (16–20in). Large, black and white, with sharply upturned bill. **NON-BREEDING:** Head and neck gray. **BREEDING:** Head and neck cinnamon. **VOICE:** High-pitched, melodious *klee*. **STATUS AND RANGE:** Very rare non-breeding resident in Bahamas and Cuba primarily July through January and in April. Vagrant elsewhere. **HABITAT:** Shallow wetland borders.

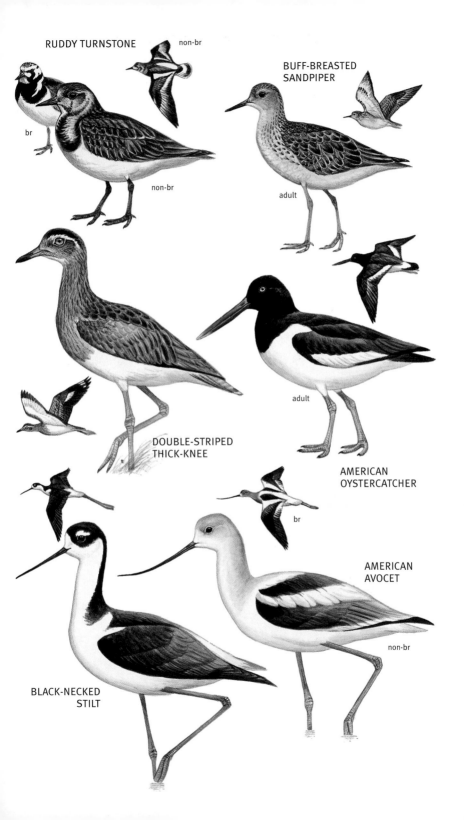

RUDDY TURNSTONE
non-br
br
non-br

BUFF-BREASTED
SANDPIPER
adult

DOUBLE-STRIPED
THICK-KNEE

AMERICAN
OYSTERCATCHER
adult

AMERICAN
AVOCET
br
non-br

BLACK-NECKED
STILT

● **SOLITARY SANDPIPER** *Tringa solitaria* 19–23cm (7.5–9in). Dark above; bars on white-edged tail; underwings dark. Wingbeats deep; erratic flight. (*See also* Plate 15.)

● **STILT SANDPIPER** *Calidris himantopus* 20–22cm (8–8.5in). White rump; whitish tail. (*See also* Plate 15.)

● **WILSON'S SNIPE** *Gallinago delicata* 27–29cm (10.5–11.5in). Zig-zag flight uttering call note. (*See also* Plate 15.)

● **SHORT-BILLED DOWITCHER** *Limnodromus griseus* 26–30cm (10–12in). White rump patch extends well up back. Distinguished from Long-billed Dowitcher by voice. (*See also* Plate 15.)

● **RED KNOT** *Calidris canutus* 25–28cm (9.75–11in). Barred above; pale gray rump; white wing stripe; pale gray wing linings. (*See also* Plate 17.)

● **DUNLIN** *Calidris alpina* 20–23cm (8–9in). White wing stripe; white rump divided by black bar. (*See also* Plate 16.)

● **SEMIPALMATED SANDPIPER** *Calidris pusilla* 14–16.5cm (5.5–6.5in). Fine white wing stripe; white rump divided by black bar. (*See also* Plate 16.)

● **LEAST SANDPIPER** *Calidris minutilla* 12.5–16.5cm (5–6.5in). Dark above; very faint wing stripe. (*See also* Plate 16.)

● **PECTORAL SANDPIPER** *Calidris melanotos* 20–24cm (8–9.5in). Sharp breast demarcation; fine white wing stripe; white rump divided by black bar. (*See also* Plate 16.)

● **WHITE-RUMPED SANDPIPER** *Calidris fuscicollis* 18–20cm (7–8in). White rump. Fine white wing stripe. (*See also* Plate 16.)

● **SANDERLING** *Calidris alba* 18–22cm (7–8.5in). White wing stripe; pale gray upperparts. (*See also* Plate 17.)

● **SPOTTED SANDPIPER** *Actitis macularia* 18–20cm (7–8in). Shallow, rapid wingbeats; white wing stripe. (*See also* Plate 17.)

● **LESSER YELLOWLEGS** *Tringa flavipes* 25–28cm (9.75–11in). Dark above; white uppertail-coverts. (*See also* Plate 19.)

● **RED-NECKED PHALAROPE** *Phalaropus lobatus* 18cm (7in). White wing stripe; white stripes on back. (*See also* Plate 19.)

● **WILSON'S PHALAROPE** *Phalaropus tricolor* 23cm (9in). White rump; dark upperparts. (*See also* Plate 19.)

● **RED PHALAROPE** *Phalaropus fulicarius* 21cm (8in). Unstreaked pale gray above; white wing stripe. (*See also* Plate 19.)

SOLITARY
SANDPIPER

STILT
SANDPIPER

WILSON'S
SNIPE

SHORT-BILLED
DOWITCHER

RED KNOT

DUNLIN

LEAST
SANDPIPER

WHITE-
RUMPED
SANDPIPER

MIPALMATED
SANDPIPER

PECTORAL
SANDPIPER

SANDERLING

SPOTTED
SANDPIPER

LESSER
YELLOWLEGS

RED-NECKED
PHALAROPE

WILSON'S
PHALAROPE

RED
PHALAROPE

ZAPATA RAIL *Cyanolimnas cerverai* 29cm (11.5in). Medium-sized; almost without stripes or spots. Long green bill, red at base; red legs and eye. **VOICE:** Resembles Bare-legged Owl, like bouncing ball *cutucutu-cutucutu-cutucutu.* **STATUS AND RANGE:** Endemic to Cuba: rare, confined to Zapata Swamp area. Endangered. **HABITAT:** Sawgrass savannas with tussocks.

SORA *Porzana carolina* 22cm (8.5in). Small, brownish-gray, with stubby, yellow bill. **ADULT:** Blackish face, throat and breast. **IMMATURE:** Black absent. **VOICE:** Clear, descending whinny and plaintive, rising whistle *ker-wee.* **STATUS AND RANGE:** Non-breeding resident throughout West Indies primarily October through April. Common in Cuba; fairly common in Bahamas; uncommon and local in Jamaica, Hispaniola, Puerto Rico, Virgin and Cayman Islands; rare in Lesser Antilles. **HABITAT:** Rice fields, dense vegetation of freshwater swamps.

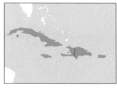

YELLOW-BREASTED CRAKE *Porzana flaviventer* 14cm (5.5in). Tiny, pale yellowish-brown, with blackish crown and white eyebrow stripe. **VOICE:** Medium-pitched *tuck* and high-pitched, whistled *peep.* **STATUS AND RANGE:** Uncommon and local resident in Cuba, Jamaica, and Puerto Rico; rare on Hispaniola. **HABITAT:** Short vegetation of swamps and canals.

KING RAIL *Rallus elegans* 38–48cm (15–19in). Chicken-like; bill long and slender. Flanks strongly banded black and white. **ADULT:** Throat, breast, and wing-coverts reddish-brown. **IMMATURE:** Grayer; lacks reddish-brown. (Clapper Rail less reddish, especially wings and neck; less distinct barring on flanks; occurs primarily in mangroves.) **VOICE:** Shorter, more musical than Clapper Rail. **STATUS AND RANGE:** Common resident in Cuba. Vagrant in Jamaica. **HABITAT:** Freshwater wetlands with tall, dense vegetation. Sometimes brackish marshes.

CLAPPER RAIL *Rallus longirostris* 36cm (14in). Gray, chicken-like, with long slender bill. Stalks among mangroves. **VOICE:** Loud, grating cackle *kek-kek-kek-kek...*, slowing at end. **STATUS AND RANGE:** Common resident in Bahamas, Cuba, and Puerto Rico; locally so in Jamaica, Hispaniola, Virgin Islands, and Barbuda; rare and local in St Christopher, Guadeloupe, and Martinique. Vagrant elsewhere. **HABITAT:** Salt marshes and mangroves.

SPOTTED RAIL *Pardirallus maculatus* 28cm (11in). Medium-sized, with long red legs. Long, greenish-yellow bill, red at base. **ADULT:** Spotted, barred black and white. **IMMATURE:** Browner, less spotting. **STATUS AND RANGE:** Rare and local resident in Cuba and Hispaniola. Very rare and local in Jamaica. Critically endangered in West Indies. **HABITAT:** Freshwater swamps with emergent vegetation. Also rice fields.

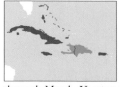

BLACK RAIL *Laterallus jamaicensis* 14cm (5.5in). Nocturnal, tiny, with short black bill, white spots on back, dark reddish-brown hindneck. (Downy young gallinules, coots, and rails are black, but lack these marks.) **VOICE:** Whistled *ki-ki-kurr*, last note lower. **STATUS AND RANGE:** Rare and local breeding resident in Hispaniola; rare non-breeding resident in Cuba; very rare and local in Bahamas, Jamaica, and Puerto Rico, primarily October through March. Vagrant elsewhere. **HABITAT:** Wet grassy marsh edges, saline and fresh.

VIRGINIA RAIL *Rallus limicola* 23cm (9in). **ADULT:** Breast, belly, and wing-coverts reddish-brown. Cheek gray; bill long, reddish. (King and Clapper Rails are about twice as big, with bill and wings usually less red.) **IMMATURE:** Mottled gray or blackish below; bill dark. **VOICE:** Metallic *kid-ik* or *ticket-ticket.* **STATUS AND RANGE:** Rare non-breeding resident September through April on Grand Bahama (Bahamas). Vagrant elsewhere. **HABITAT:** Primarily freshwater marshes with dense vegetation, also brackish and saltwater wetlands.

ZAPATA RAIL

SORA

imm

adult

KING RAIL

adult

YELLOW-BREASTED CRAKE

SPOTTED RAIL

adult

CLAPPER RAIL

VIRGINIA RAIL

adult

BLACK RAIL

imm

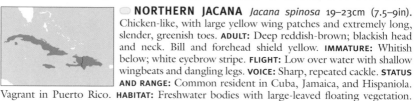

NORTHERN JACANA *Jacana spinosa* 19–23cm (7.5–9in). Chicken-like, with large yellow wing patches and extremely long, slender, greenish toes. **ADULT:** Deep reddish-brown; blackish head and neck. Bill and forehead shield yellow. **IMMATURE:** Whitish below; white eyebrow stripe. **FLIGHT:** Low over water with shallow wingbeats and dangling legs. **VOICE:** Sharp, repeated cackle. **STATUS AND RANGE:** Common resident in Cuba, Jamaica, and Hispaniola. Vagrant in Puerto Rico. **HABITAT:** Freshwater bodies with large-leaved floating vegetation.

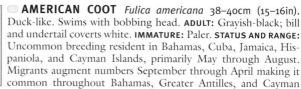

AMERICAN COOT *Fulica americana* 38–40cm (15–16in). Duck-like. Swims with bobbing head. **ADULT:** Grayish-black; bill and undertail coverts white. **IMMATURE:** Paler. **STATUS AND RANGE:** Uncommon breeding resident in Bahamas, Cuba, Jamaica, Hispaniola, and Cayman Islands, primarily May through August. Migrants augment numbers September through April making it common throughout Bahamas, Greater Antilles, and Cayman Islands during these months. Uncommon and occasionally breeds in Virgin Islands; rare or vagrant in Lesser Antilles, but breeds on several islands. **HABITAT:** Open freshwater.

CARIBBEAN COOT *Fulica caribaea* 38–40cm (15–16in). Duck-like. Swims with bobbing head. Grayish-black; white undertail coverts and frontal shield extending well up onto the crown. (American Coot lacks white frontal shield extending onto crown.) **STATUS AND RANGE:** Uncommon and local resident in Hispaniola and Puerto Rico; rare resident in Jamaica and Virgin Islands; rare wanderer in Lesser Antilles; very rare non-breeding transient in Cuba. Threatened. **HABITAT:** Primarily open fresh water.

PURPLE GALLINULE *Porphyrio martinica* 33cm (13in). **ADULT:** Bluish-purple; yellow legs; bluish-white frontal shield. **IMMATURE:** Golden-brown, bluish wings. **VOICE:** High-pitched, melodious *klee-klee*. **STATUS AND RANGE:** Common resident in Cuba and Hispaniola; uncommon in Jamaica, Puerto Rico, the Cayman Islands, and San Andrés. In Bahamas, uncommon migrant on larger northern islands August through October and March through May; rare and local on remainder. Rare resident on St Bartholomew, Montserrat, Martinique, and Barbados. Vagrant elsewhere. **HABITAT:** Freshwater bodies with dense vegetation.

COMMON MOORHEN Gallinula chloropus 34cm (13.5in). Duck-like. Swims with bobbing head. **ADULT:** Red bill tipped yellow, red frontal shield; white line down flank. **IMMATURE:** Gray and brown; bill lacks red. **VOICE:** Piercing, laugh-like cackle, slowing at end: *ki-ki-ki-ka-, kaa, kaaa*. **STATUS AND RANGE:** Generally common resident throughout West Indies. **HABITAT:** Most wetlands with water plants.

LEAST GREBE Tachybaptus dominicus 23–26cm (9–10in). Small, blackish, with thin bill and yellow-orange eye. White wing patch not always visible. **VOICE:** Rising, reed-like *week*. **STATUS AND RANGE:** Common resident in Bahamas, Cuba, and Jamaica; uncommon and local in Hispaniola and Puerto Rico; rare in Virgin Islands and Montserrat. Rare non-breeding wanderer to Cayman Islands. **HABITAT:** Primarily freshwater cattail swamps and small ponds with plant cover.

PIED-BILLED GREBE Podilymbus podiceps 30–38cm (12–15in). Grayish-brown, duck-like, with conical bill. **BREEDING ADULT:** Black throat; bill with black band. **NON-BREEDING ADULT:** White throat; bill lacks black band. **IMMATURE:** Head mottled brown and white. **VOICE:** Harsh cackle breaking into distinctive *kowp, kowp, kowp*, slowing at end. **STATUS AND RANGE:** Throughout West Indies. Common resident on larger islands, less common on medium-sized islands, and rare or absent from smallest ones. **HABITAT:** Primarily fresh water, but also brackish and hypersaline lagoons.

NORTHERN JACANA

imm

adult

AMERICAN
COOT

adult

CARIBBEAN
COOT

adult

imm

PURPLE
GALLINULE

adult

imm

COMMON
MOORHEN

adult

LEAST GREBE

non-br adult

br

PIED-BILLED GREBE

non-br adult

imm

br

DOVEKIE *Alle alle* 21cm (8in). Small, stout seabird with short, thick neck, large head, and short, black stubby bill. **NON-BREEDING ADULT:** Black above; white below extending well around neck. **BREEDING ADULT:** Head and breast entirely black. **FLIGHT:** Wingbeats blurringly rapid. **STATUS AND RANGE:** Vagrant in West Indies October through December. **HABITAT:** At sea.

COMMON LOON *Gavia immer* 70–100cm (27–40in). Large waterbird, similar to goose in size. Bill long, straight. **NON-BREEDING:** Dark above, light below. **BREEDING:** Dark head; upperparts with large white flecks. **FLIGHT:** Head lower than body, legs extend beyond tail. **STATUS AND RANGE:** Very rare migrant in Cuba late November through December. **HABITAT:** Coastal wetlands.

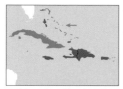

DOUBLE-CRESTED CORMORANT *Phalacrocorax auritus* 74–89cm (29–35in). Large, with long neck and hooked bill. Sits with wings spread. (Shorter tail than Neotropic Cormorant, especially noticeable in flight.) **BREEDING ADULT:** Black. Small ear-tufts sometimes visible. **NON-BREEDING ADULT:** Lacks ear-tufts. **IMMATURE:** Brown; paler below. **STATUS AND RANGE:** Common resident in Cuba, and San Salvador (Bahamas). Uncommon non-breeding resident locally elsewhere in Bahamas and very rare wanderer through Greater Antilles to Virgin and Cayman Islands. Expanding range eastward. **HABITAT:** Inland and calm coastal waters. Frequents salt water more than Neotropic Cormorant.

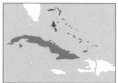

NEOTROPIC CORMORANT *Phalacrocorax brasilianus* 63–69cm (25–27in). Large, black, with long neck and hooked bill. Sits with wings spread. **BREEDING ADULT:** Throat pouch edged white. **NON-BREEDING ADULT:** White edge on throat pouch reduced or absent. **IMMATURE:** Brown, paler below. **STATUS AND RANGE:** Common resident in Cuba, and locally in Bahamas. Non-breeding birds range more broadly. Expanding range eastward. **HABITAT:** Inland and calm coastal waters. Frequents fresh water more than Double-crested.

ANHINGA *Anhinga anhinga* 85cm (34in). Large, with long neck, long tail, pointed bill, large whitish patches on back and upperwing. **ADULT MALE:** Glossy black. **ADULT FEMALE:** Head to breast light brown. **IMMATURE:** Brown above; tan below. Resembles cormorant, but neck more snake-like, tail longer, and bill longer and pointed. **STATUS AND RANGE:** Common resident in Cuba, vagrant elsewhere. **HABITAT:** Shallow calm waters.

TUNDRA SWAN *Cygnus columbianus* 122–140cm (48–55in). Huge, with long neck and short legs. **ADULT:** White; bill black, sometimes yellow on lores. **IMMATURE:** Pale grayish-brown; bill pinkish. **STATUS AND RANGE:** Vagrant to West Indies. **HABITAT:** Shallow ponds and lagoons.

ORINOCO GOOSE *Neochen jubata* 61–67cm (24–26.5in). Large, with pale gray head and neck. Reddish-brown body; dark wings with white speculum. **STATUS AND RANGE:** Vagrant to West Indies. Recorded from Barbados and Jamaica. **HABITAT:** Freshwater marshes and wet savannas.

GREATER WHITE-FRONTED GOOSE *Anser albifrons* 66–86.5cm (26–34in). Medium-sized. **ADULT:** Brownish-gray above; white rump; pink or orange bill has white edge; belly barred black. **IMMATURE:** Uniform dark brown. **STATUS AND RANGE:** Vagrant to West Indies. Recorded from Cuba. **HABITAT:** Ponds and lagoons.

SNOW GOOSE *Chen caerulescens* 58–71cm (23–28in). **ADULT:** Two color phases. White phase—Entirely white; black primaries; pink bill and legs. Dark phase—Bluish-gray; white head and upper neck; pink bill and legs. **STATUS AND RANGE:** Rare migrant in northern Bahamas and Cuba October through March. Vagrant elsewhere. Numbers increasing. **HABITAT:** Borders of freshwater ponds and swamps, flooded uplands, croplands.

CANADA GOOSE *Branta canadensis* 64–110cm (25–43in). Distinctive black head and neck, with white band on cheeks and throat. **FLIGHT:** Dark wings with white band across the uppertail-coverts. **STATUS AND RANGE:** Vagrant October through April to Bahamas, Cuba, Jamaica, Hispaniola, Puerto Rico, and Cayman Islands. **HABITAT:** Wetland borders.

DOVEKIE

non-br adult

br

NEOTROPIC CORMORANT

non-br adult

br

COMMON LOON

non-br adult

br

br adult

Imm

adult ♀

ANHINGA

non-br adult

DOUBLE-CRESTED CORMORANT

imm

br

adult ♀

TUNDRA SWAN

imm

adult

GREATER WHITE-FRONTED GOOSE

adult

imm

ORINOCO GOOSE

dark phase

imm

white phase

imm

CANADA GOOSE

adult

Illustrations not to scale

SNOW GOOSE

NORTHERN SHOVELER *Anas clypeata* 43–53cm (17–21in). Unusually large bill. **MALE:** Green head, white breast, reddish-brown sides and belly. **FEMALE:** Mottled brown. **STATUS AND RANGE:** Non-breeding resident throughout West Indies primarily October through May. Common in Cuba; uncommon in Bahamas, Hispaniola, Puerto Rico, and Cayman Islands; rare in Jamaica; very rare in Virgin Islands. Generally rare in Lesser Antilles. **HABITAT:** Shallow wetlands. (*See also* Plate 28.)

NORTHERN PINTAIL *Anas acuta* Male: 69–74cm (27–29in); Female: 54–56cm (21–22in). **FEMALE AND NON-BREEDING MALE:** Mottled brown; pointed tail; long, slender neck; gray bill. **BREEDING MALE:** Brown head; white breast and neck stripe; long, pointed tail. **STATUS AND RANGE:** Common non-breeding resident in Cuba; uncommon in Puerto Rico; rare in Bahamas, Hispaniola, Virgin and Cayman Islands, St Bartholomew, and Barbados. Occurs September through April. **HABITAT:** Shallow wetlands. (*See also* Plate 28.)

AMERICAN BLACK DUCK *Anas rubripes* 53–64cm (21–25in). Dark brown with purple speculum. **MALE:** Bill yellow. **FEMALE:** Bill olive, mottled black. **STATUS AND RANGE:** Vagrant in West Indies. **HABITAT:** Shallow waters. (*See also* Plate 28.)

MALLARD *Anas platyrhynchos* 51–71cm (20–28in). Large, with blue speculum edged white. **NON-BREEDING MALE AND IMMATURE:** Mottled brown, olive bill. **ADULT FEMALE:** Bill orange with black markings. **BREEDING MALE:** Green head, yellow bill, maroon breast. **STATUS AND RANGE:** Very rare non-breeding resident October through April in northern Bahamas and Cuba. **HABITAT:** Shallow waters. (*See also* Plate 28.)

EURASIAN WIGEON *Anas penelope* 42–52cm (16.5–20in). **MALE:** Dark reddish-brown head; cream-colored crown stripe; pinkish breast. **FEMALE:** Gray phase—Brownish; gray head; light blue bill. Red phase—Similar; reddish tint to head and neck. **STATUS AND RANGE:** Vagrant to West Indies October through February. **HABITAT:** Freshwater ponds. (*See also* Plate 28.)

AMERICAN WIGEON *Anas americana* 46–56cm (18–22in). **MALE:** White crown, light blue bill, green eye-patch. **FEMALE:** Brownish; gray head; light blue bill. **STATUS AND RANGE:** Non-breeding resident throughout West Indies principally October through April. Common in Cuba; fairly common in Hispaniola; uncommon in Bahamas, Puerto Rico, Virgin and Cayman Islands; rare in Jamaica and Lesser Antilles. **HABITAT:** Shallow wetlands. (*See also* Plate 28.)

GADWALL *Anas strepera* 46–57cm (18–22.5in). White speculum. **MALE:** Mottled gray; rump black; head dark brown. **FEMALE:** Mottled brown; whitish belly; bill slightly orange with dark gray ridge. **STATUS AND RANGE:** Rare non-breeding resident in Bahamas; very rare in Cuba. Increasing in numbers. Occurs October to March. **HABITAT:** Freshwater wetlands. (*See also* Plate 28.)

BLUE-WINGED TEAL *Anas discors* 38–40cm (15–16in). Small, with blue forewing. **FEMALE AND NON-BREEDING MALE:** Mottled brown; speculum green; very similar to female and non-breeding male Green-winged Teal, but Blue-winged has light spot on lores, darker belly, and lacks pale patch beneath tail. **BREEDING MALE:** White face crescent. **STATUS AND RANGE:** Most common non-breeding duck in West Indies, primarily October through April. **HABITAT:** Shallow wetlands. (*See also* Plate 28.)

CINNAMON TEAL *Anas cyanoptera* 38–40cm (15–16in). **FEMALE AND NON-BREEDING MALE:** Mottled brown; speculum green. **BREEDING MALE:** Cinnamon-colored head and underparts. **STATUS AND RANGE:** Vagrant in West Indies. **HABITAT:** Shallow ponds. (*See also* Plate 28.)

GREEN-WINGED TEAL *Anas crecca* 33–39cm (13–15.5in). Small, with green speculum; lacks blue in forewing. **FEMALE AND NON-BREEDING MALE:** Mottled brown; dark lores; whitish belly; pale patch beneath tail. **BREEDING MALE:** Green eye-patch and speculum; reddish-brown head; white vertical bar in front of wing. **STATUS AND RANGE:** Uncommon non-breeding resident in northern Bahamas; rare in southern Bahamas, Greater Antilles, Virgin and Cayman Islands, and Barbados; vagrant in Lesser Antilles. Occurs October through March. **HABITAT:** Shallow fresh water. (*See also* Plate 28.)

NORTHERN SHOVELER

♀

♂

NORTHERN PINTAIL

♀ & non-br ♂

br ♂

AMERICAN BLACK DUCK

♀

♂

non-br ♂

adult ♀

br ♂

MALLARD

EURASIAN WIGEON

♀

♂

AMERICAN WIGEON

♀

♂

GADWALL

♀

♂

BLUE-WINGED TEAL

♀ & non-br ♂

br ♂

CINNAMON TEAL

♀ & non-br ♂

br ♂

GREEN-WINGED TEAL

♀ & non-br ♂

br ♂

CANVASBACK *Aythya valisineria* 51–61cm (20–24in). Sloping forehead profile. (Similarly patterned Redhead lacks sloping forehead.) **MALE:** Reddish-brown head and neck. **FEMALE:** Brown head and neck; less contrast in plumage. **STATUS AND RANGE:** Very rare non-breeding resident in Cuba October through March; vagrant elsewhere. **HABITAT:** Large, deep lagoons. (*See also* Plate 29.)

REDHEAD *Aythya americana* 46–56cm (18–22in). Steep forehead; blue bill tipped black. **MALE:** Pale gray back and black neck contrast with rounded reddish head. Black breast and rump. **FEMALE:** Dull brown. **STATUS AND RANGE:** Very rare non-breeding resident in Bahamas, Cuba, and Barbados November through March. Vagrant elsewhere. **HABITAT:** Ponds and lagoons. (*See also* Plate 29.)

RING-NECKED DUCK *Aythya collaris* 40–46cm (16–18in). **MALE:** White bill-ring, black back and white vertical bar in front of wing. **FEMALE:** Light bill-ring and eye-ring, sometimes a trailing white streak between cheek and crown. **STATUS AND RANGE:** Common non-breeding resident on Cuba, locally common in northern Bahamas; uncommon in Jamaica, Hispaniola, Puerto Rico, and Virgin Islands; rare in southern Bahamas, Cayman Islands, Barbados, and San Andrés; vagrant elsewhere. Occurs October through March. **HABITAT:** Open fresh water. (*See also* Plate 29.)

GREATER SCAUP *Aythya marila* 38–51cm (15–20in). **MALE:** Head appears smoothly rounded or slightly flat-topped. Head iridescent green, appearing black at distance. Bill pale blue with wide black nail on tip. (Adult male Lesser Scaup has more peaked head profile, deep purple iridescence on head, a narrow black-tipped bill, and white confined to the secondaries in flight.) **FEMALE:** White around base of bill reaches forehead. Dark brown sides and rump. **STATUS AND RANGE:** Very rare southbound migrant in Bahamas, Virgin Islands (St Croix), and Barbados September through February. **HABITAT:** Open bays. (*See also* Plate 29.)

LESSER SCAUP *Aythya affinis* 38–46cm (15–18in). **MALE:** Dark head, breast, and tail; whitish back and flanks. **FEMALE:** Brown; large white mark behind bill. (Greater Scaup has rounder head and broader bill tip.) **STATUS AND RANGE:** Fairly common, but local non-breeding resident in Bahamas and Cuba; uncommon in Jamaica, Hispaniola, Puerto Rico, and Cayman Islands. Rare in Virgin Islands and San Andrés; very rare in Lesser Antilles south to Barbados. Occurs November through March. **HABITAT:** Open bays. (*See also* Plate 29.)

BUFFLEHEAD *Bucephala albeola* 33–38cm (13–15in). Small. **MALE:** Large white head patch; white forewing; plumage primarily white. **FEMALE:** Browner; white facial stripe. **STATUS AND RANGE:** Very rare in Cuba. Vagrant elsewhere. Occurs October through March. **HABITAT:** Open bays. (*See also* Plate 29.)

HOODED MERGANSER *Lophodytes cucullatus* 40–48cm (16–19in). Crest; slender, hooked bill. **MALE:** Crest has large white patch. **FEMALE:** Dark plumage and bill; bill dull orange near base. (Larger but similar female Red-breasted Merganser has darker face, bill, and back.) **STATUS AND RANGE:** Uncommon to rare non-breeding resident in Bahamas. Very rare in Cuba, Hispaniola, Puerto Rico, Virgin Islands, Martinique, and Barbados. Occurs November through February. **HABITAT:** Inland ponds, lagoons. (*See also* Plate 29.)

RED-BREASTED MERGANSER *Mergus serrator* 51–64cm (20–25in). Crest; slender, hooked bill. **MALE:** Green head, white collar, dark breast. **FEMALE:** Reddish-brown head and bill; whitish chin, foreneck and breast; gray back. Differs from Hooded Merganser by lighter face and back, reddish bill. **STATUS AND RANGE:** Very rare non-breeding resident in Bahamas, most of Greater Antilles, and Cayman Islands in November and March. **HABITAT:** Open bays, ocean near shore, inland lagoons. (*See also* Plate 29.)

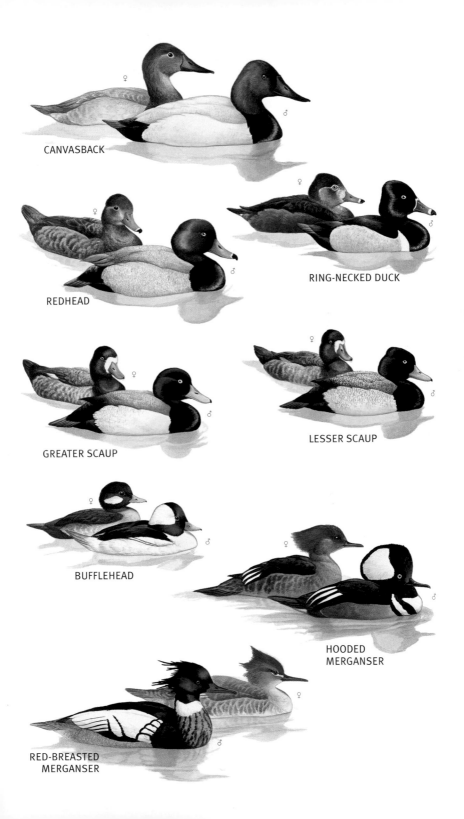

CANVASBACK

REDHEAD

RING-NECKED DUCK

GREATER SCAUP

LESSER SCAUP

BUFFLEHEAD

HOODED
MERGANSER

RED-BREASTED
MERGANSER

WEST INDIAN WHISTLING-DUCK *Dendrocygna arborea* 48–56cm (19–22in). Deep brown; white abdomen with black markings; erect stance. **VOICE:** Shrill whistle: *chiriria*. **STATUS AND RANGE:** Locally common resident in Cuba and Cayman Islands; uncommon in Bahamas and Dominican Republic; rare and local in Jamaica, Puerto Rico, Virgin Islands, and Antigua. Endangered. These islands comprise entire range. **HABITAT:** Mangroves, savannas, wooded swamps, lagoons. (*See also* Plate 30.)

FULVOUS WHISTLING-DUCK *Dendrocygna bicolor* 46–51cm (18–20in). Pale yellowish-brown with thin white side stripe, white uppertail-coverts, erect stance. **VOICE:** Squealing whistle *puteow*. **STATUS AND RANGE:** Common year-round in Cuba; locally common in Hispaniola; uncommon in Puerto Rico. Rare non-breeding resident or wanderer elsewhere in West Indies. Extending range eastward. **HABITAT:** Fresh water with emergent plants, rice fields. (*See also* Plate 30.)

WHITE-FACED WHISTLING-DUCK *Dendrocygna viduata* 44cm (17in). **ADULT:** White face. **IMMATURE:** Paler; face beige. **VOICE:** High-pitched 3-note whistle. **STATUS AND RANGE:** Vagrant to West Indies. **HABITAT:** Open wetlands. (*See also* Plate 30.)

BLACK-BELLIED WHISTLING-DUCK *Dendrocygna autumnalis* 46–53cm (18–21in). **ADULT:** White wing patch; black belly; reddish bill and legs. **VOICE:** Shrill, chattering whistle. **STATUS AND RANGE:** Recent breeding on Barbados. Very rare wanderer through West Indies. **HABITAT:** Freshwater and brackish lagoons. (*See also* Plate 30.)

WHITE-CHEEKED PINTAIL *Anas bahamensis* 38–48cm (15–19in). Red bill mark; white cheek. Speculum green, edged buff. **STATUS AND RANGE:** Locally common resident in Bahamas, Cuba, Virgin Islands, and Antigua; locally uncommon on Hispaniola and Puerto Rico; uncommon to rare in most northern Lesser Antilles and Barbados. Threatened. **HABITAT:** Calm, shallow waters. (*See also* Plate 30.)

RUDDY DUCK *Oxyura jamaicensis* 35–43cm (14–17in). Tail often erect. **MALE:** Overall reddish-brown; white cheek patch; blue bill. **FEMALE AND IMMATURE:** Mostly brown; single brown stripe below eye. (Female Masked Duck has 2 dark facial stripes.) **STATUS AND RANGE:** Locally common resident on New Providence in Bahamas and Greater Antilles; uncommon and local elsewhere in Bahamas; rare in Virgin Islands and Barbados. **HABITAT:** Deep, open freshwater bodies; also brackish lagoons. (*See also* Plate 30.)

MASKED DUCK *Nomonyx dominicus* 30–36cm (12–14in). Erect tail; white wing patch. **BREEDING MALE:** Black face; reddish-brown coloration; blue bill. **NON-BREEDING MALE, FEMALE, AND IMMATURE:** 2 brown facial stripes; white wing patch. **STATUS AND RANGE:** Fairly common but local resident in Cuba; uncommon in Jamaica, Hispaniola, and St Lucia; rare in Puerto Rico, Marie Galante off Guadeloupe, Martinique, and Barbados. Very rare elsewhere. Threatened. **HABITAT:** Dense vegetation of freshwater swamps and rice fields. (*See also* Plate 30.)

WOOD DUCK *Aix sponsa* 43–51cm (17–20in). Crest. **MALE:** Unusual facial pattern. **FEMALE:** Asymmetrical eye-ring. **VOICE:** Male—Short call 3–4 times. Female—Wavering note, like woodpecker. **STATUS AND RANGE:** Cuba: uncommon resident. Northern Bahamas: rare migrant and non-breeding resident October to March. **HABITAT:** Canals, lagoons and impoundments. (*See also* Plate 30.)

WEST INDIAN WHISTLING-DUCK

FULVOUS WHISTLING-DUCK

WHITE-FACED WHISTLING-DUCK

adult

BLACK-BELLIED WHISTLING-DUCK

WHITE-CHEEKED PINTAIL

♀ & imm

non-br ♂

non-br ♂, ♀ & imm

br ♂

RUDDY DUCK

br ♂

MASKED DUCK

♀

♂

WOOD DUCK

NORTHERN SHOVELER *Anas clypeata* 43–53cm (17–21in). Large bill; green speculum; blue patch on forewing. **MALE:** Green head; white breast; reddish-brown sides and belly. **FEMALE:** Mottled brown. (*See also* Plate 25.)

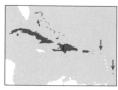

NORTHERN PINTAIL *Anas acuta* Male: 69–74cm (27–29in); Female: 54–56cm (21–22in). Long slender neck, pointed tail. **FEMALE AND NON-BREEDING MALE:** White border on trailing edge of brown speculum; gray underwing contrasts with white belly. **BREEDING MALE:** Greenish speculum, pale tan inner border; white trailing edge. (*See also* Plate 25.)

AMERICAN BLACK DUCK *Anas rubripes* 53–64cm (21–25in). White underwings contrast with dark body; purple speculum. (*See also* Plate 25.)

MALLARD *Anas platyrhynchos* 51–71cm (20–28in). Blue speculum with white borders. **ADULT FEMALE:** Mottled brown. **BREEDING MALE:** Green head; maroon breast. (*See also* Plate 25.)

EURASIAN WIGEON *Anas penelope* 42–52cm (16.5–20in). White patches on forewing; green speculum; white belly; blackish flecks on wingpits. **MALE:** Dark reddish-brown head; cream-colored crown stripe. **FEMALE:** Brownish; gray or reddish head. (*See also* Plate 25.)

AMERICAN WIGEON *Anas americana* 46–56cm (18–22in). White patch on forewing; green speculum; white belly. (*See also* Plate 25.)

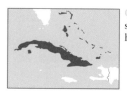

GADWALL *Anas strepera* 46–57 cm (18–22.5in). White speculum. **MALE:** Mottled gray above; black rump; dark brown head. **FEMALE:** Mottled brown; white belly. (*See also* Plate 25.)

BLUE-WINGED TEAL *Anas discors* 38–40cm (15–16in). Small, with blue forewing; green speculum. **FEMALE AND NON-BREEDING MALE:** Mottled brown; darkish belly. **BREEDING MALE:** White crescent on face. (*See also* Plate 25.)

CINNAMON TEAL *Anas cyanoptera* 38–40cm (15–16in). Light blue forewing; green speculum. **BREEDING MALE:** Cinnamon head and underparts. **FEMALE AND NON-BREEDING MALE:** (Not illustrated) Similar to female Blue-winged Teal. (*See also* Plate 25.)

GREEN-WINGED TEAL *Anas crecca* 33–39cm (13–15.5in). Small. Green speculum; lacks blue in forewing. **FEMALE AND NON-BREEDING MALE:** Mottled brown; whitish belly. **BREEDING MALE:** Green eye-patch; reddish-brown head; whitish belly. (*See also* Plate 25.)

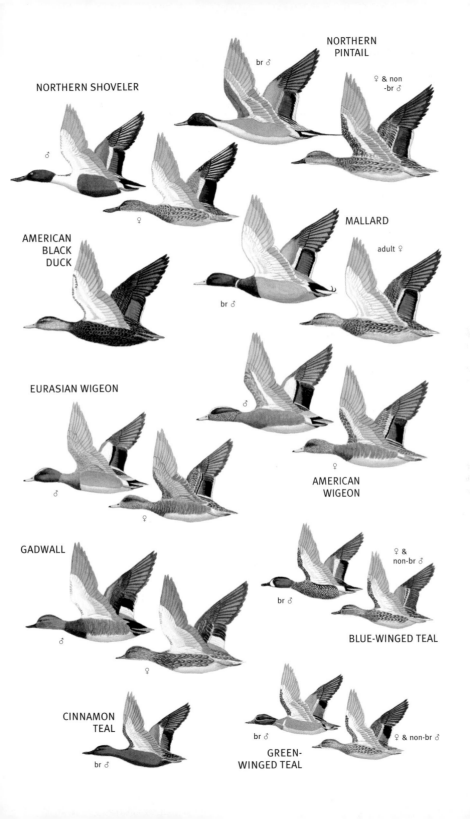

NORTHERN PINTAIL

br ♂

♀ & non -br ♂

NORTHERN SHOVELER

♂

♀

MALLARD

adult ♀

br ♂

AMERICAN BLACK DUCK

EURASIAN WIGEON

♂

♀

♂

♀

AMERICAN WIGEON

GADWALL

♂

♀

♀ & non-br ♂

br ♂

BLUE-WINGED TEAL

CINNAMON TEAL

br ♂

br ♂

♀ & non-br ♂

GREEN-WINGED TEAL

● **CANVASBACK** *Aythya valisineria* 51–61cm (20–24in). Elongated appearance. **MALE:** White belly and underwings sandwiched between black breast and tail. **FEMALE:** Whitish belly and underwings contrast with dark breast and tail. (*See also* Plate 26.)

● **REDHEAD** *Aythya americana* 46–56cm (18–22in). **MALE:** Gray back and black neck contrast with reddish head. **FEMALE:** Dull brown; white eye-ring; blue band around black-tipped bill. (*See also* Plate 26.)

● **RING-NECKED DUCK** *Aythya collaris* 40–46cm (16–18in). Dark upperwing-coverts contrast with pale gray secondaries. **MALE:** Underparts contrast black and white. **FEMALE:** Underparts contrast brown and white. (*See also* Plate 26.)

● **GREATER SCAUP** *Aythya marila* 38–51cm (15–20in). White secondaries and inner primaries. White belly and abdomen. **MALE:** Black breast. **FEMALE:** Brown breast. (*See also* Plate 26.)

● **LESSER SCAUP** *Aythya affinis* 38–46cm (15–18in). White secondaries and black primaries. White belly and abdomen. **MALE:** Black breast. **FEMALE:** Brown breast. (*See also* Plate 26.)

● **BUFFLEHEAD** *Bucephala albeola* 33–38cm (13–15in). **MALE:** Large white head patch, white forewing. **FEMALE:** Browner; white facial stripe. (*See also* Plate 26.)

● **HOODED MERGANSER** *Lophodytes cucullatus* 40–48cm (16–19in). Crest; dark upperparts; small white patch on secondaries. **MALE:** Pale forewing. (*See also* Plate 26.)

● **RED-BREASTED MERGANSER** *Mergus serrator* 51–64cm (20–25in). Crest. **MALE:** White secondaries and forewing, crossed by 2 bars. **FEMALE:** White secondaries, crossed by 1 bar. (*See also* Plate 26.)

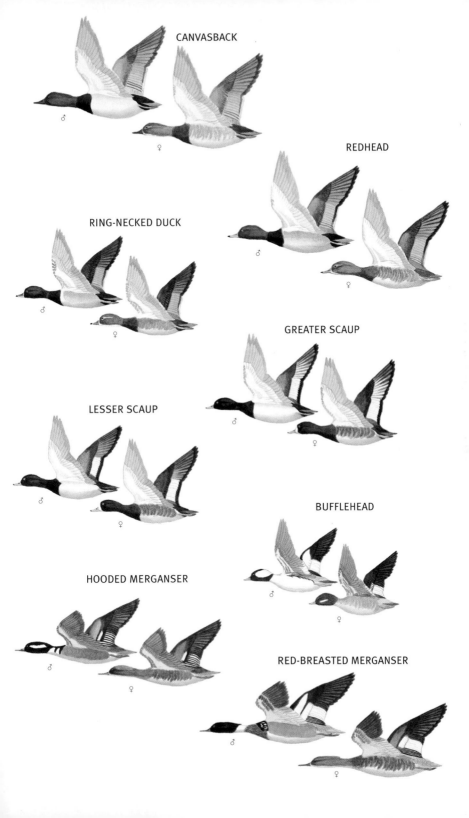

CANVASBACK

REDHEAD

RING-NECKED DUCK

GREATER SCAUP

LESSER SCAUP

BUFFLEHEAD

HOODED MERGANSER

RED-BREASTED MERGANSER

● **BLACK-BELLIED WHISTLING-DUCK** *Dendrocygna autumnalis* 46–53cm (18–21in). Large, white upperwing patch; black belly, reddish bill and legs. Head and feet droop; feet trail beyond tail. (*See also* Plate 27.)

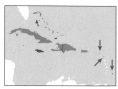

● **FULVOUS WHISTLING-DUCK** *Dendrocygna bicolor* 46–51cm (18–20in). Pale yellowish-brown; white stripe at wing base; white rump; dark wings; reddish-brown upperwing-coverts. Head and feet droop; feet extend beyond tail. (*See also* Plate 27.)

● **WEST INDIAN WHISTLING-DUCK** *Dendrocygna arborea* 48–56cm (19–22in). Dark overall; black and white abdomen; gray upperwing-coverts. Head and feet droop; feet extend beyond tail. (*See also* Plate 27.)

● **WHITE-FACED WHISTLING-DUCK** *Dendrocygna viduata* 44cm (17in). White face. Wings dark above and below; no white markings except on head. Head and feet droop; feet extend beyond tail. (*See also* Plate 27.)

● **WOOD DUCK** *Aix sponsa* 43–51cm (17–20in). Long, squared tail; large head; bill tilted down. **MALE:** White throat. **FEMALE:** White eye-patch. (*See also* Plate 27.)

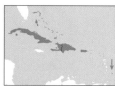

● **WHITE-CHEEKED PINTAIL** *Anas bahamensis* 38–48cm (15–19in). Red bill mark, white cheek; green speculum edged buff. (*See also* Plate 27.)

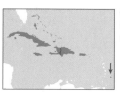

● **RUDDY DUCK** *Oxyura jamaicensis* 35–43cm (14–17in). Chunky body; long tail; dark upperwings. **BREEDING MALE:** White cheek. **FEMALE AND IMMATURE:** Cheek stripe. (*See also* Plate 27.)

● **MASKED DUCK** *Nomonyx dominicus* 30–36cm (12–14in). Chunky body; white wing patch; long tail. **BREEDING MALE:** Reddish-brown with black face. **NON-BREEDING MALE, FEMALE, AND IMMATURE:** Brown; 2 dark stripes on face. (*See also* Plate 27.)

BLACK-BELLIED WHISTLING-DUCK

FULVOUS WHISTLING-DUCK

WEST INDIAN WHISTLING-DUCK

WHITE-FACED WHISTLING-DUCK

WHITE-CHEEKED PINTAIL

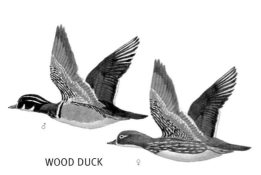
♂

WOOD DUCK   ♀

br ♂   MASKED DUCK

non-br ♂, ♀, & imm

br ♂

♀ & imm
RUDDY DUCK

SHARP-SHINNED HAWK *Accipiter striatus* 25–35cm (10–14in). A small forest hawk. Short, rounded wings; small head; long, narrow, squared-off tail, boldly barred with black. (Gundlach's Hawk is much larger and more robust.) **ADULT:** Dark steel-blue above; narrow reddish bars below. **FEMALE:** Larger than male. **IMMATURE:** Brown above; buffish below, streaked dark brown. **VOICE:** Leisurely, high-pitched *que-que-que-que....* **STATUS AND RANGE:** Uncommon and increasingly local resident in Cuba and Hispaniola; rare and very local in Puerto Rico. Migrants occur in Bahamas, Cuba, and Jamaica February through April. Endangered. **HABITAT:** Mature mountain forests; sometimes coastal forests in Cuba. (*See also* Plate 34.)

MERLIN *Falco columbarius* 25–34cm (10–13.5in). Small. Upperparts dark gray in male, dark brown in female. Underparts heavily streaked, tail barred black. Pale eyebrow stripe. **FLIGHT:** Fast and agile. Pointed wings; long, narrow tail. **STATUS AND RANGE:** Migrant throughout West Indies primarily in October. Somewhat scarcer as non-breeding resident until March. Common in Bahamas, uncommon in Greater Antilles, Virgin and Cayman Islands, rare in Lesser Antilles. **HABITAT:** Coastal lakes and lagoons where shorebirds abound, also woodlands and forests.

PEREGRINE FALCON *Falco peregrinus* 38–51cm (15–20in). Large, with pointed wings and long narrow tail. Rapid pigeon-like flight; mask-like head pattern. **ADULT:** Dark gray above; cream-colored with dark bars below. **IMMATURE:** Brown above; underparts cream-colored with heavy brown streaks. **STATUS AND RANGE:** Uncommon to rare and local non-breeding resident throughout West Indies primarily October through April. A few breed. **HABITAT:** Offshore cays and rocks with seabirds, wetlands with shorebirds or waterfowl. Sometimes inland including high buildings and church steeples.

GUNDLACH'S HAWK *Accipiter gundlachi* 43–51cm (17–20in). Chunky, medium-sized forest hawk. Relatively short, rounded wings. Long narrow tail, rounded at tip, is boldly barred with black. **ADULT:** Upperparts dark steel-blue; underparts lightly barred gray-red. **IMMATURE:** Brown above; lighter and heavily streaked dark brown below. **VOICE:** Loud, harsh, cackling *kek-kek-kek-kek....* **STATUS AND RANGE:** Endemic to Cuba; rare, but widely distributed. Endangered. **HABITAT:** Forest borders, swamps, wooded coasts, mangroves, and mountains below 800m (2600ft). (*See also* Plate 34.)

NORTHERN HARRIER *Circus cyaneus* 46–61cm (18–24in). Large, with long wings and tail; white rump. **ADULT MALE:** Grayish-blue. **ADULT FEMALE:** Brown above; white below, heavily streaked with brown. **IMMATURE:** Brown above; entirely reddish-brown below with dark brown streaks on breast. **FLIGHT:** Low over ground with heavy flaps and distinctive tilting glides, narrow wings held well above horizontal. **STATUS AND RANGE:** Uncommon and local non-breeding resident primarily October through April in Bahamas, Cuba, Hispaniola, and Puerto Rico. Uncommon only as migrant in Cayman Islands; rare in Virgin Islands and Lesser Antilles. **HABITAT:** Marshes, swamps, open savannas, and rice fields.

AMERICAN KESTREL *Falco sparverius* 23–30cm (9–12in). Small, with reddish-brown back (except dark phase of Cuban race *F. s. sparveroides* which is dark gray). Reddish tail with broad, black terminal band; 2 black facial bars. Underparts vary between races from white to reddish-brown. **ADULT MALE:** Blue-gray wings. **ADULT FEMALE:** Reddish-brown wings. **IMMATURE:** Dark breast streaks. **VOICE:** High-pitched *killi-killi-killi.* **STATUS AND RANGE:** Common resident in Bahamas, Greater Antilles, Virgin Islands and Lesser Antilles south to St Lucia. Rare further south. Fairly common migrant to Cayman Islands. **HABITAT:** Dry, open lowlands with adequate perches and palm savannas. Also towns and forest edges in mountains.

imm

adult

Puerto Rico race

SHARP-SHINNED HAWK

♀

MERLIN

♂

imm

adult

PEREGRINE
FALCON

imm

adult

GUNDLACH'S
HAWK

adult
♂

adult ♀

adult ♂

NORTHERN
HARRIER

adult ♀ Hispaniola race

Cuba,
Bahamas,
Jamaica race

adult ♀

Hispaniola race

AMERICAN
KESTREL

adult ♂

HOOK-BILLED KITE *Chondrohierax uncinatus* 38–43cm (15–17in). Chunky. Bill large and deeply hooked; large oval wings prominently barred beneath; long, banded tail. Plumage variable. **ADULT MALE:** Light phase—Dark gray; gray or finely gray-barred underparts. **ADULT FEMALE:** Light phase—Dark brown; reddish-brown barring below; tan hindneck. **ADULT MALE AND FEMALE:** Black phase—Solid black; tail with 1 broad white band. **IMMATURE:** Light phase—White cheeks, hindneck and underparts; breast, thighs, and tail barred. Black phase—Dark blue above, dark brown wings flecked white, streaked breast. **VOICE:** 2–3 whistled notes, also shrill scream. **STATUS AND RANGE:** Critically endangered resident in southwest and northeast Grenada. **HABITAT:** Dry scrub. (*See also* Plate 34.)

CUBAN KITE *Chondrohierax wilsonii* 38–43cm (15–17in). Large and robust, with massive, yellowish hooked bill and long, banded tail. **ADULT MALE:** Typically dark gray with gray or finely gray-barred underparts. **ADULT FEMALE:** Generally dark brown; underparts coarsely barred, reddish; tan hindneck. **IMMATURE:** Bi-colored black above, white below, white hindneck. **STATUS AND RANGE:** Endemic to Cuba where confined to northeast. Nearly extinct. **HABITAT:** Tall trees of forests bordering rivers below 500m (1640ft). (*See also* Plate 34.)

SWALLOW-TAILED KITE *Elanoides forficatus* 51–66cm (20–26in). Bi-colored; long, deeply forked tail. White head and underparts contrast with black back, wings, and tail. **STATUS AND RANGE:** Rare migrant in Cuba and Cayman Islands; very rare in northern Bahamas. Primarily occurs August through October. **HABITAT:** Coastal swamps, savannas, and river mouths.

SNAIL KITE *Rostrhamus sociabilis* 43–48cm (17–19in). White rump; slender bill conspicuously hooked. Red legs, eyes, and lores. (Similar Northern Harrier has long, narrower wings and gliding, tilting flight.) **ADULT MALE:** Blackish. **ADULT FEMALE:** Brown above; white below, heavily streaked with brown; white eyebrow stripe. **VOICE:** Raspy, ratchet-like *ge-ge-ge-ge*. **STATUS AND RANGE:** Common resident in Cuba. **HABITAT:** Freshwater marshes, open swamps, reservoirs, rice fields, and canals. (*See also* Plate 34.)

COMMON BLACK-HAWK *Buteogallus anthracinus* 51–58cm (20–23in). Large, stocky, relatively inactive chocolate-brown (Cuba) or black (St Vincent) hawk with broad wings. **ADULT:** Single broad white tail band. **IMMATURE:** Underparts white to buffish, heavily streaked black; tail has several narrow pale bands. **VOICE:** Nasal, whistled *ba-tis-taa*, and a harsh *haaaah*. **STATUS AND RANGE:** Common and widely distributed resident in Cuba; uncommon on St Vincent. **HABITAT:** Cays, coastal forests, and open areas near swamps and beaches in Cuba. Mountain forests in St Vincent. (*See also* Plate 34.)

BROAD-WINGED HAWK *Buteo platypterus* 35–41cm (14–16in). Medium-sized, chunky. Soars. **ADULT:** Tail boldly banded black and white; underparts barred reddish-brown. (Red-tailed Hawk much larger; white breast with dark belly streaks.) **IMMATURE:** Underparts white, streaked dark brown; tail bands more numerous, but less distinct. **VOICE:** Thin, shrill squeal *pweeeeeeeee*. **STATUS AND RANGE:** Common resident in Cuba, Antigua, and Dominica south to Grenada; rare and very local in Puerto Rico; uncommon on St Christopher; several recent records from Hispaniola. **HABITAT:** Dense broadleaved, mixed, and plantation forests at all elevations, less frequently open woodlands. Open woodlands and towns in Antigua. (*See also* Plate 34.)

HOOK-BILLED KITE

♀

♂

CUBAN KITE

adult ♀

adult ♂

SWALLOW-TAILED KITE

SNAIL KITE

adult ♂

adult ♀

COMMON BLACK-HAWK

St Vincent race

Cuba race

adult

imm

BROAD-WINGED HAWK

Puerto Rico race

adult

imm

RIDGWAY'S HAWK *Buteo ridgwayi* 36–41cm (14–16in). **ADULT:** Dark brownish-gray upperparts; underparts gray washed with brownish-red; thighs reddish-brown; tail barred black and white. **ADULT MALE:** Grayer than female with bright reddish-brown bend of wing. **ADULT FEMALE:** Browner overall; drab brown bend of wing; lighter breast with more barring, more heavily barred tail. **VOICE:** Whistled *kleeah*. **STATUS AND RANGE:** Endemic to Hispaniola. Endangered. **HABITAT:** Forested foothills, wet limestone forest and mixed savannah-woodland-palm habitat. (*See also* Plate 34.)

RED-TAILED HAWK *Buteo jamaicensis* 48–64cm (19–25in). Large. **ADULT:** Dark brown above; white below, dark belly stripes; tail reddish. **IMMATURE:** Tail faintly barred grayish-brown; more heavily streaked underparts. **VOICE:** Raspy *keeer-r-r-r*, slurring downward. **STATUS AND RANGE:** Common resident on larger islands of northern Bahamas, Greater Antilles, Virgin Islands, St Bartholomew, Saba, St Christopher, and Nevis; rare on St Eustatius. Vagrant elsewhere. **HABITAT:** Open country, woodlands, forests, towns, at all elevations. (*See also* Plate 34.)

CRESTED CARACARA *Caracara cheriway* 50–63cm (19.5–25in). Large, crested head; large beak with reddish facial skin. **ADULT:** Breast whitish and barred. **IMMATURE:** Browner overall; breast buffish and streaked. **FLIGHT:** Contrasting white patches near wingtips. Flies like a crow. Often on ground with vultures. **VOICE:** Harsh rattling *ca-ca-ca-ca*. **STATUS AND RANGE:** Rare and local but widespread resident in Cuba. **HABITAT:** Semi-arid open country, including palm savannas, cut-over areas, and pastures.

BLACK VULTURE *Coragyps atratus* 58–68cm (23–26.5in). Large, black, with very short tail. **FLIGHT:** Labored, alternating rapid flapping with brief glides. Wings held horizontal; white wing patches. (Turkey Vulture lacks white wing patches, has a longer tail and rocks as it soars, flapping only occasionally, with wings held well above the horizontal.) **STATUS AND RANGE:** Rare migrant to Cuba. Vagrant in Bahamas. **HABITAT:** Open lowlands; also urban areas.

 **TURKEY VULTURE** *Cathartes aura* 68–80cm (27–32in). Large, blackish-brown, with small bare head. **FLIGHT:** Soars. Dark two-toned wings held well above horizontal in broad 'V'. **STATUS AND RANGE:** Common and widespread resident in Cuba and Jamaica; common, but local, in large northern Bahamas (Grand Bahama, Abaco, and Andros), northeastern Hispaniola (where range is expanding), and southwestern Puerto Rico. Rare non-breeding resident in Cayman Islands (Cayman Brac). Vagrant elsewhere. **HABITAT:** Open areas at all elevations.

 **OSPREY** *Pandion haliaetus* 53–61cm (21–24in). Widespread migratory race (*P. h. carolinensis*)—White head, dark bar behind eye, contrast of primarily white underparts and dark upperparts. Resident race (*P. h. ridgwayi*)—Whiter head, only trace of eye-stripe. **FLIGHT:** Wings characteristically bent at wrist, dark wrist patch. **VOICE:** Piercing whistles. **STATUS AND RANGE:** Non-breeding resident throughout West Indies primarily September through April. Common in Bahamas, Greater Antilles, Virgin and Cayman Islands; uncommon in Lesser Antilles. Breeds in Bahamas and Cuba. **HABITAT:** All calm fresh- or saltwater bodies.

RIDGWAY'S HAWK

imm

adult

RED-TAILED HAWK

adult

imm

CRESTED CARACARA

adult

BLACK VULTURE

TURKEY VULTURE

imm

adult

OSPREY

migratory race

resident race

○ **COMMON BLACK-HAWK** *Buteogallus anthracinus* 51–58cm (20–23in). Large white patch at base of primaries; long legs dangle during flap and glide flight. Cuba and St Vincent. (*See also* Plate 32.)

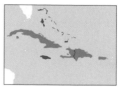

○ **SHARP-SHINNED HAWK** *Accipiter striatus* 25–35cm (10–14in). Short, rounded wings; long, narrow, squared-off tail. Flight rapid, alternately flapping and gliding. (*See also* Plate 31.)

○ **GUNDLACH'S HAWK** *Accipiter gundlachi* 43–51cm (17–20in). Short, rounded wings; long, narrow tail, rounded at tip; flight rapid, alternating quick wingbeats with glides. (*See also* Plate 31.)

○ **SNAIL KITE** *Rostrhamus sociabilis* 43–48cm (17–19in). White rump; coursing flight, low to water. Cuba. (*See also* Plate 32.)

○ **CUBAN KITE** *Chondrohierax wilsonii* 38–43cm (15–17in). Large oval wings heavily barred beneath; long, banded tail. Cuba. (*See also* Plate 32.)

○ **RIDGWAY'S HAWK** *Buteo ridgwayi* 36–41cm (14–16in). Broad, rounded wings; fan-shaped tail; soars; light 'wing windows'. Hispaniola. (*See also* Plate 33.)

○ **HOOK-BILLED KITE** *Chondrohierax uncinatus* 38–43cm (15–17in). Large oval wings heavily barred beneath; long, banded tail. Grenada. (*See also* Plate 32.)

○ **RED-TAILED HAWK** *Buteo jamaicensis* 48–64cm (19–25in). Soars on broad, rounded wings and fanned tail. **ADULT:** Reddish tail; white underparts; dark belly band. **IMMATURE:** Lightly barred tail; dark belly band less distinct. (*See also* Plate 33.)

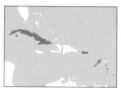

○ **BROAD-WINGED HAWK** *Buteo platypterus* 35–41cm (14–16in). Alternates soaring and flapping on broad, rounded wings. **ADULT:** Boldly banded tail. **IMMATURE:** Tail with finer bars; underparts streaked. (*See also* Plate 32.)

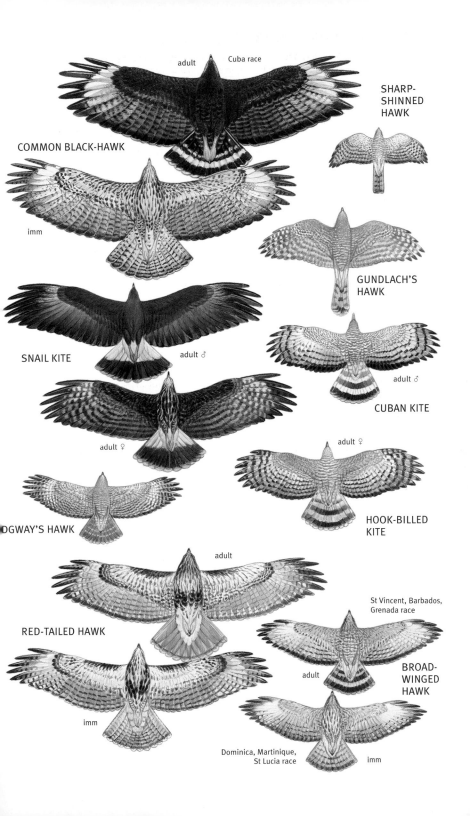

SHARP-
SHINNED
HAWK

COMMON BLACK-HAWK

adult   Cuba race

imm

GUNDLACH'S
HAWK

SNAIL KITE

adult ♂

adult ♂

CUBAN KITE

adult ♀

HOOK-BILLED
KITE

adult ♀

DGWAY'S HAWK

RED-TAILED HAWK

adult

St Vincent, Barbados,
Grenada race

adult

BROAD-
WINGED
HAWK

imm

Dominica, Martinique,
St Lucia race   imm

RUFOUS-VENTED CHACHALACA *Ortalis ruficauda* 55cm (22in). Large, long-tailed, primarily terrestrial, chicken-like bird. Olive-brown upperparts; gray head and hindneck; bronze-colored tail tipped with reddish-brown; gray underparts; reddish-brown flanks and undertail coverts and bare red throat. VOICE: Repeated *cocrico, cocrico....* STATUS AND RANGE: Uncommon resident in Grenadines. HABITAT: Scrub and woodlands.

RING-NECKED PHEASANT *Phasianus colchicus* 76–92cm (30–36in). Large, chicken-like bird with long, pointed tail. MALE: Iridescent green head with crest; red face wattle; very long tail; incomplete white neck band. FEMALE: Mottled brown; tail shorter. STATUS AND RANGE: Introduced widely in West Indies, but failed to survive on most islands. Rare on Eleuthera in Bahamas, and in Dominican Republic; locally common in Cuba on Isle of Youth. HABITAT: Brush and hedgerows.

HELMETED GUINEAFOWL *Numida meleagris* 53cm (21in). Terrestrial. Unusual body shape; dark gray feathering with white spots; nearly naked head and neck. Forms flocks. VOICE: Wild cackles. STATUS AND RANGE: Introduced in West Indies where widespread domestically in farmyards, but locally feral. In feral state, fairly common locally in Dominican Republic; rare in Cuba, Puerto Rico, Virgin Islands (St Croix), St Martin (Isle Pinel), and Barbuda. HABITAT: Primarily dry scrubland.

RED JUNGLEFOWL *Gallus gallus* Male: 71cm (28in); Female: 43cm (17in). MALE (ROOSTER): Resplendently plumaged; red comb head wattle; long, bushy tail. FEMALE (HEN): Smaller comb and wattle; brownish plumage. VOICE: Universally recognized *cockadoodledoo*. STATUS AND RANGE: Well known, introduced; feral very locally in Dominican Republic, Puerto Rico, and Grenadines. Domesticated birds common on farms throughout West Indies. HABITAT: Dry and moist forests.

NORTHERN BOBWHITE *Colinus virginianus* 25cm (10in). Small terrestrial bird resembling small chicken. Flocks. Does not flush until underfoot. MALE: White throat and eyebrow stripe. FEMALE: Tan throat and eyebrow stripe. VOICE: Clear, whistled *bob, bob-white*, rising at end, repeated. STATUS AND RANGE: Common resident in Cuba. Introduced and now common in northern Bahamas; uncommon in Hispaniola; rare and local in Puerto Rico. Introductions on other islands unsuccessful. HABITAT: Scrubland and pasture with dense cover.

CRESTED BOBWHITE *Colinus cristatus* 18cm (8in). Small terrestrial bird with short tail and long, pointed crest. Flocks. MALE: Throat and eyebrow stripe reddish-brown, crest and ear-patch white; underparts spotted with white. FEMALE: Lacks male's distinctive facial coloration. STATUS AND RANGE: Introduced to Grenadines (Mustique), Puerto Rico, and Virgin Islands (St Thomas); extirpated from last two. Status in Grenadines uncertain. HABITAT: Cultivated areas, hedgerows, and scrubland.

COMMON PEAFOWL *Pavo cristatus* Male: 250cm (100in); Female: 100cm (40in). MALE: Peacock. Primarily blue; magnificent, huge tail raises to broad fan. FEMALE: Peahen. Grayish-brown; white belly and face; greenish neck and breast; distinctive crest. VOICE: Loud scream, "*My arm!*" STATUS AND RANGE: Widely introduced in West Indies to farmyards and gardens. Feral and fairly common on Little Exuma in Bahamas. HABITAT: Thick broadleaf coppice.

RUFOUS-VENTED CHACHALACA

RING-NECKED
PHEASANT

♂

♀

HELMETED
GUINEAFOWL

RED
JUNGLEFOWL

♂

♀

NORTHERN
BOBWHITE ▶ ♀

♂

CRESTED
BOBWHITE

♀

COMMON PEAFOWL

♂

♀

● **RING-TAILED PIGEON** *Columba caribaea* 41cm (16in). Large, with black band across uppertail; lacks white in wings. Arboreal. **VOICE:** Throaty *cru-cru-crooooo*, last note lower. Also mournful, soft *uhu-cooo*, repeated, last syllable louder and more emphatic. **STATUS AND RANGE:** Endemic to Jamaica where fairly common locally, particularly Cockpit Country, Blue and John Crow Mountains. **HABITAT:** Forested inland hills and mountains. Descends to lower elevations in cooler months.

● **PLAIN PIGEON** *Columba inornata* 38–40cm (15–16in). Paler than other large pigeons; white edge to wing-coverts, reddish-brown on wings and breast. Arboreal, gregarious. **FLIGHT:** Thin white band across wing. **VOICE:** Deep, deliberate *whoo, wo-oo* or *who, oo-oo.* **STATUS AND RANGE:** Greater Antilles where common but local resident in Hispaniola, particularly Dominican Republic; rare and local in Cuba, Jamaica, and Puerto Rico. These islands comprise entire range. **HABITAT:** Savannas, open woodlands, coastal scrub, dry limestone forests and forest edges in lowlands, also to moderate elevations.

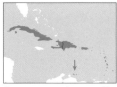

● **SCALY-NAPED PIGEON** *Columba squamosa* 36–40cm (14–16in). Arboreal, gregarious. **ADULT:** Appears slate-gray. **VOICE:** Sounds like *"Who are you!"* **STATUS AND RANGE:** Resident through much of West Indies. Common in Puerto Rico, Virgin Islands, and much of Lesser Antilles; fairly common only locally in Hispaniola. In Cuba, uncommon in east and rare in west. These islands comprise nearly entire range. **HABITAT:** Typically mountain forests; sometimes well-wooded lowlands; on St Christopher and Barbados occurs in towns and villages.

● **WHITE-CROWNED PIGEON** *Columba leucocephala* 33–36cm (13–14in). Dark gray with white crown. Arboreal, gregarious. **VOICE:** *"Who took two?"* (Faster and less deliberate than Scaly-naped Pigeon.) Second syllable rises. **STATUS AND RANGE:** Common breeding resident generally year-round in Bahamas, Cuba, Jamaica, and Antigua; locally common in Hispaniola, Puerto Rico, Virgin Islands, San Andrés and Providencia. Uncommon in Cayman Islands, Anguilla, and St Bartholomew; rare on St Martin and Guadeloupe. Very rare elsewhere. These islands comprise nearly entire range. **HABITAT:** Coastal woodlands and mangroves when breeding, sometimes mountains when not breeding.

● **ROCK DOVE** *Columba livia* 33–36cm (13–14in). Very variable. Often gray with black tail band and white rump. **VOICE:** Gentle cooing. **STATUS AND RANGE:** Introduced. Common through much of West Indies. **HABITAT:** Tame resident of city streets.

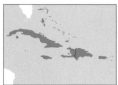

● **WHITE-WINGED DOVE** *Zenaida asiatica* 28–30cm (11–12in). Large, white central wing patch. Tail tips white. Gregarious. **VOICE:** Single pitch, like *"Two bits for two"*. Also yodel-like cooing between two notes. **STATUS AND RANGE:** Generally common resident in southern Bahamas, Cuba, Jamaica, Hispaniola, Grand Cayman in Cayman Islands, San Andrés, and Providencia. Uncommon in northern Bahamas and Puerto Rico; rare in Virgin Islands and remaining Cayman Islands. Expanding eastward through West Indies. **HABITAT:** Scrubland, mangroves, open woodlands, and urban gardens. Primarily coastal.

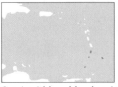

● **EARED DOVE** *Zenaida auriculata* 22–25cm (8.5–10in). **ADULT:** Grayish-brown above with few small black spots on scapulars. Underparts brown to undertail coverts and reddish-brown tips to outer feathers of short tail. Lacks white in wings or tail. **VOICE:** Like Zenaida Dove but shorter. **STATUS AND RANGE:** Fairly common resident on St Lucia and common on St Vincent, the Grenadines, and Grenada. Very local on Barbados. **HABITAT:** Semi-arid brushlands primarily in lowlands.

PLAIN PIGEON

RING-TAILED
PIGEON

SCALY-NAPED
PIGEON

imm

adult ♂

WHITE-
CROWNED
PIGEON

ROCK DOVE

EARED DOVE

WHITE-WINGED DOVE

CRESTED QUAIL-DOVE *Geotrygon versicolor* 31cm (12in). Plump, ground-dwelling dove, with short but distinct crest, primarily gray head and underparts, bronze-colored hindneck and reddish-brown upper back and much of wings. Pumps head and bobs tail while walking. **VOICE:** Mournful 2- to 3-syllabled *woof-woo-wooo*, first note sharp with following notes softer and lower in pitch. **STATUS AND RANGE:** Endemic to Jamaica. Fairly common locally, particularly Blue Mountains and Cockpit Country. **HABITAT:** Wet forest undergrowth of mountains and limestone hills.

BLUE-HEADED QUAIL-DOVE *Starnoenas cyanocephala* 30–33cm (12–13in). The largest Cuban quail-dove. Conspicuous light blue head; white facial stripe; and mark on throat. **VOICE:** 2 similar notes: *uuuu-up, uuuu-up*, the last syllable rising and stopping quickly. **STATUS AND RANGE:** Endemic to Cuba. Fairly rare and very local. Principal areas include Guanahacabibes Peninsula, Pinares de La Güira, and Zapata Swamp area. Endangered. **HABITAT:** Deciduous forests with a dense canopy, open understory, and stony forest floor, particularly with ample leaf-litter.

RUDDY QUAIL-DOVE *Geotrygon montana* 25cm (10in). Plump, ground-dwelling dove. Predominantly reddish-brown with light buff stripe beneath eye. **VOICE:** Mournful *coo* gradually fading in strength and sometimes pitch, like blowing across mouth of bottle. Very ventriloquial. **STATUS AND RANGE:** Fairly common resident in Puerto Rico; locally common in Cuba, Jamaica, and Hispaniola; uncommon on large, forested islands of Lesser Antilles. Very rare in Virgin Islands (St John and St Croix). **HABITAT:** Primarily dense forests and plantations of shade coffee in hills and mountains, also locally on the coast.

BRIDLED QUAIL-DOVE *Geotrygon mystacea* 30cm (12in). White streak below eye; brown upperparts (except for crown and neck); reddish-brown limited to patch on wing. Underparts buffish-brown. Terrestrial. **VOICE:** Mournful *who-whooo*, on one pitch or descending towards the end, loudest in middle of 2nd syllable and then trailing off. Sometimes 1st syllable omitted. Similar to Key West Quail-dove. **STATUS AND RANGE:** Generally uncommon to rare resident in Lesser Antilles and larger, forested Virgin Islands. Extremely rare and local in Puerto Rico. These islands comprise entire range. **HABITAT:** Dense mountain forests with thick undergrowth; sometimes coastal forests.

KEY WEST QUAIL-DOVE *Geotrygon chrysia* 28–30cm (11–12in). White line under eye; reddish-brown back and wings, primarily white underparts. (Bridled Quail-dove has browner upperparts and is much darker below. Ruddy Quail-dove has more reddish-brown underparts and a duller streak below eye.) **VOICE:** Moan on one pitch, gradually increasing in volume and then fading rapidly. Very ventriloquial. Similar to call of Bridled Quail-dove. **STATUS AND RANGE:** Fairly common resident locally in northern Bahamas, Cuba, and Hispaniola; uncommon in southern Bahamas (Caicos Islands) and locally in Puerto Rico. These islands comprise entire range. **HABITAT:** Dense woods and scrubby thickets with ample leaf-litter, primarily arid and semi-arid zones, but also in moist and wet mountain forests with undisturbed understory.

GRAY-HEADED QUAIL-DOVE *Geotrygon caniceps* 28cm (11in). Pigeon-like, ground-dwelling dove, with metallic purplish-blue sheen on back. Hispaniola: distinctive white forehead; Cuba: completely gray crown. Displays peculiar neck and tail movements. **VOICE:** Continuous, low *uup-uup-uup-uup* without pauses. Hispaniola: prolonged *coo-o-o*. **STATUS AND RANGE:** Known only from Cuba and Hispaniola. Cuba: rare and very local, mainly in western and central portions of island. Hispaniola: only in Dominican Republic where rare and very local. Endangered on Hispaniola, threatened on Cuba. **HABITAT:** Cuba: low elevation wet forests bordering swamps and middle altitudes in dense, moist woods. Dominican Republic: primarily dense mountain forests and shade coffee, sometimes near sea level.

CRESTED QUAIL-DOVE

BLUE-HEADED QUAIL-DOVE

RUDDY QUAIL-DOVE

BRIDLED
QUAIL-DOVE

KEY WEST QUAIL-DOVE

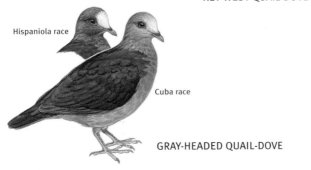

Hispaniola race

Cuba race

GRAY-HEADED QUAIL-DOVE

EURASIAN COLLARED-DOVE Streptopelia decaocto 28–30cm (11–12in). Medium-sized dove, gray with dark primaries and black hindneck. Larger and browner than Domestic Ringed Turtle-dove (*Streptopelia risoria*) (not illustrated), with gray, rather than whitish, undertail coverts, and much darker primaries. **VOICE:** Repeated 3-syllable *kuk-koooooó-kook*, with brief pauses between phrases. Harsh, nasal *mew* in flight or upon landing. (Domestic Ringed Turtle-dove has 2-syllable, throaty call.) **STATUS AND RANGE:** Introduced. Common resident in northern Bahamas; locally common and spreading in Cuba, Guadeloupe, and Martinique. Entire West Indies may soon be colonized. **HABITAT:** Urban areas.

SPOTTED DOVE Streptopelia chinensis 30cm (12in). **ADULT:** Black hindneck spotted white; long tail broadly tipped with white; light gray bend of wing. **IMMATURE:** Lacks neck pattern. **VOICE:** Coarse *ooo-hoo-ooo-hurrrrp*, with rising inflection. **STATUS AND RANGE:** Introduced. Was very local around Estate Canaan in Virgin Islands (St Croix). May have been wiped out by Hurricane Hugo in 1989. **HABITAT:** Gardens and open woodland.

COMMON GROUND-DOVE Columbina passerina 15–18cm (5.75–7in). The only tiny dove in West Indies. Plumage varies among islands. **FLIGHT:** Flashes reddish-brown wing patch. **VOICE:** Monotonous, often repeated call, either of single or double notes, *coo, coo, coo, coo...* or *co-coo, co-coo, co-coo...* or *hoop, hoop, hoop...* in staccato fashion. **STATUS AND RANGE:** Very common resident throughout West Indies. **HABITAT:** Most lowland habitats except heavily wooded areas.

CARIBBEAN DOVE Leptotila jamaicensis 30–33cm (12–13in). A plump, ground-dwelling dove. White face and underparts; long, red legs; cinnamon-colored underwings; gray crown; white-tipped outertail feathers. Other ground-dwelling woodland doves have darker underparts. **VOICE:** High-pitched, plaintive *cu-cu-cu-oooo,* "Who cooks for you?" or "What's that to you-oo?" Last note drawn out, accented, descending, and broken into 2 syllables. **STATUS AND RANGE:** Locally common resident in Jamaica; uncommon resident on Grand Cayman; fairly common on San Andrés; introduced in Bahamas (New Providence). Now uncommon and local. **HABITAT:** Primarily lowlands and foothills from open areas and gardens to dense secondary forests.

GRENADA DOVE Leptotila wellsi 31cm (12in). **ADULT:** Unmarked gray-brown upperparts; white forehead to crown; buffish cinnamon-colored breast; white belly; no markings on wings; outertail feathers tipped with white. **FLIGHT:** Cinnamon-colored underwings. **VOICE:** Distinctive, descending *hoooo,* repeated at 8-second intervals virtually like clockwork. **STATUS AND RANGE:** Endemic to Grenada: very rare. Restricted to southwestern peninsula where best found around Mount Hartman Estate and Halifax Harbor. Critically endangered. **HABITAT:** Lowlands and hillsides with mature dry scrub forest. Favors mixture of closed canopy, dense scrub, and large areas of bare ground.

ZENAIDA DOVE Zenaida aurita 25–28cm (10–11in). White band on trailing edge of secondaries; white-tipped, rounded tail. (Mourning Dove lacks white in wing and has longer, pointed tail.) **VOICE:** Gentle cooing, almost identical to Mourning Dove, *coo-oo, coo, coo, coo,* 2nd syllable rising sharply. Rendered as *"Mar-y boil brown rice."* **STATUS AND RANGE:** Common resident throughout West Indies, though slightly less abundant in southern Lesser Antilles where Eared Dove is more common. **HABITAT:** Open areas, gardens, and hotel grounds. Also open woodlands, scrub thickets, and pine woods with dense understory. Primarily coastal.

MOURNING DOVE Zenaida macroura 28–33cm (11–13in). Long, wedge-shaped tail fringed with white. Lacks white in wing. (Zenaida and White-winged Doves have white wing markings. Spotted Dove has black hindneck spotted with white, and less pointed tail.) **VOICE:** Mournful cooing almost identical to Zenaida Dove, *coo-oo, coo, coo, coo,* 2nd syllable rising sharply. **STATUS AND RANGE:** Locally common resident in Bahamas and Greater Antilles. Rare migrant in Cayman Islands. Expanding range in West Indies. **HABITAT:** Primarily lowland open country, dry coastal forests, and agricultural lands, often near fresh water. Also agricultural areas in mountains.

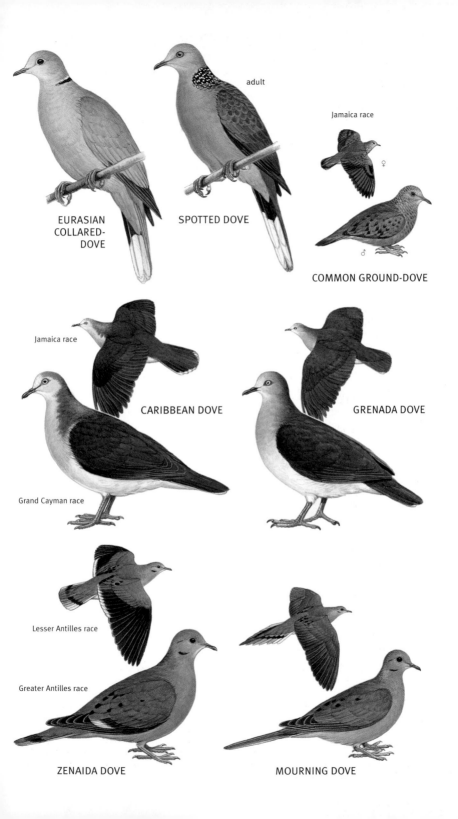

EURASIAN
COLLARED-
DOVE

SPOTTED DOVE

adult

Jamaica race

COMMON GROUND-DOVE

♀

♂

Jamaica race

CARIBBEAN DOVE

GRENADA DOVE

Grand Cayman race

Lesser Antilles race

Greater Antilles race

ZENAIDA DOVE

MOURNING DOVE

● YELLOW-BILLED PARROT *Amazona collaria* 28–31cm (11–12in). Yellow bill; white forehead and eye-ring; bluish forecrown and ear-coverts; maroon throat and base of tail; blue primaries and secondaries. **FLIGHT:** Wingbeats shallow, below plane of back. **VOICE:** Perched—High-pitched *tah-tah-eeeeep*; Flight—Bugling *tuk-tuk-tuk-taaah*, lower pitched, and last syllable more drawn out, than in Black-billed Parrot. **STATUS AND RANGE:** Endemic to Jamaica: locally common and more widespread than Black-billed Parrot. **HABITAT:** Primarily mid-elevation wet forests of hills and mountains.

● ST LUCIA PARROT *Amazona versicolor* 42–46cm (16.5–18in). Large, with violet-blue forehead, cheeks, and forecrown; red band across throat extending down center of breast; wings green with violet-blue primaries and a red patch. **VOICE:** Raucous squawks. **STATUS AND RANGE:** Endemic to St Lucia: uncommon and local. Numbers slowly increasing. Endangered. **HABITAT:** Primarily moist mountain forests. Also secondary forests and cultivated areas.

● BLACK-BILLED PARROT *Amazona agilis* 26cm (10in). Blackish bill and eye-ring. Flight feathers primarily blue. Some have red patch in wing visible in flight. Base of tail red. **VOICE:** Perched—*rrak* and *muh-weep*; Flight—*tuh-tuk*. Also a sharp screech. Calls are higher pitched than Yellow-billed Parrot's. **STATUS AND RANGE:** Endemic to Jamaica: fairly common, particularly Mount Diablo and Cockpit Country. **HABITAT:** Mid-level moist forests of hills and mountains.

● ST VINCENT PARROT *Amazona guildingii* 41–46cm (16–18in). Large and dramatically patterned, with variable coloration. Two major color phases—one predominantly green, the other golden-brown. Intermediates occur. Creamy white forehead shades to orange-yellow on hindcrown; violet-blue cheeks; black wings with yellow-orange patches conspicuous in flight. Tail orange at base with wide central band of violet and broad yellow tip. **VOICE:** Loud, un-parrot-like *gua, gua, gua...* in flight. **STATUS AND RANGE:** Endemic to St Vincent: uncommon and critically endangered. Occurs primarily in upper reaches of Buccament, Cumberland, and Wallilibou valleys. **HABITAT:** Mature moist mountain forests.

● IMPERIAL PARROT *Amazona imperialis* 46–51cm (18–20in). Large, with dark maroon-purple head. Dark violet band on hindneck appears black in low light. Wings green with red speculum, primaries dull violet-blue. Underparts purple-violet from breast to abdomen. **VOICE:** Flight—Distinctive, trumpeting, metallic *eeeee-er* that descends at end; Perched—Shrieks, squawks, whistles and bubbly trills. More shrill and metallic than Red-necked Parrot. **STATUS AND RANGE:** Endemic to Dominica where uncommon and local, primarily on Morne Diablotin in Northern Forest Reserve. Numbers slowly increasing. Critically endangered. **HABITAT:** Mid–high elevation wet forests.

● RED-NECKED PARROT *Amazona arausiaca* 33–36cm (13–14in). Blue crown, face, and chin; bright red spot on throat; red wing patch. Smaller of the two parrots on Dominica. **VOICE:** 2-syllable *rrr-eee*, like a drawn out hiccup. **STATUS AND RANGE:** Endemic to Dominica where critically endangered, but increasing in numbers. Locally common in Northern Forest Reserve. **HABITAT:** Moist primary rain forests, generally at mid-elevations.

YELLOW-BILLED
PARROT

BLACK-BILLED
PARROT

ST LUCIA
PARROT

adult

ST VINCENT
PARROT

adult

IMPERIAL PARROT

RED-NECKED
PARROT

● **YELLOW-HEADED PARROT** *Amazona oratrix* 36cm (14in). Large, with yellow on head covering most of face or entire head. **FLIGHT:** Red wing patch and blue primaries. **VOICE:** Raucous squawks. **STATUS AND RANGE:** Puerto Rico: introduced. Rare and very local along northern coast. **HABITAT:** Lowland second-growth forests.

● **YELLOW-CROWNED PARROT** *Amazona ochrocephala* 36cm (14in). Large, with yellow crown. **VOICE:** Raucous squawks. **STATUS AND RANGE:** Very local in Cayman Islands (Grand Cayman). Not well established. **HABITAT:** Woodlands and areas with fruiting trees.

● **HISPANIOLAN PARROT** *Amazona ventralis* 28–31cm (11–12in). White forehead, dark ear-spot, and maroon belly. **FLIGHT:** Bright blue primaries and secondaries. **VOICE:** Flight— Loud bugling; Perched—Loud squawks and screeches. **STATUS AND RANGE:** Endemic to Hispaniola: locally common only in major forest reserves. Threatened. Introduced to Puerto Rico where locally common. **HABITAT:** Hispaniola: all elevations in forests, woodlands, and scrub. Puerto Rico: forests and woodlands of foothills.

● **PUERTO RICAN PARROT** *Amazona vittata* 30cm (12in). White eye-ring, red forehead, and two-toned blue primaries. **VOICE:** Raucous squawks including distinct bugling flight call. **STATUS AND RANGE:** Endemic to Puerto Rico: rare and very local. Critically endangered. **HABITAT:** Mid-elevation wet forests of eastern Puerto Rico.

● **RED-CROWNED PARROT** *Amazona viridigenalis* 30–33cm (12–13in). Red forecrown and light green cheeks. **FLIGHT:** Orange-red wing patch and blue primaries. (Puerto Rican Parrot has red only on forehead and lacks orange-red wing patch.) **VOICE:** Distinctive, not as raspy and raucous as most parrots, *keet, kau-kau-kau-kau.* **STATUS AND RANGE:** Puerto Rico: introduced. Very local around the coast. **HABITAT:** Lowland moist forests and scrub.

● **ORANGE-WINGED PARROT** *Amazona amazonica* 32cm (12.5in). Yellow cheeks and crown; blue lores and eyebrow stripe. **FLIGHT:** Orange-red wing patch and blue primaries. **VOICE:** Call *kweet, kweet, kweet, kweet* is higher pitched, weaker and less raucous than most other parrots in West Indies. **STATUS AND RANGE:** Introduced. Puerto Rico: uncommon very locally. Martinique: moderately widespread in center of island. Grenada: rare very locally. **HABITAT:** Lowland second-growth forests and urban areas with ornamental trees.

 ● **ROSE-THROATED PARROT** *Amazona leucocephala* 28–33cm (11–13in). Chin, throat, and lower face pale red. Forehead and eye-ring white, primaries blue. Variable among islands. **VOICE:** Noisy squawks. In flight, harsh *squawk-squawk.* Calls vary among populations. **STATUS AND RANGE:** Bahamas, Cuba, and Cayman Islands only. Bahamas: only on Abaco and Great Inagua where fairly common. Cuba: locally common. Cayman Islands: fairly common on Grand Cayman and Cayman Brac. Threatened. **HABITAT:** Forests at all elevations and palm savannas.

YELLOW-HEADED
PARROT

YELLOW-CROWNED
PARROT

HISPANIOLAN
PARROT

PUERTO RICAN
PARROT

RED-CROWNED
PARROT

Cayman
Islands race

ROSE-
THROATED
PARROT

Bahamas race

ORANGE-WINGED PARROT

Cuba race

HISPANIOLAN PARAKEET *Aratinga chloroptera* 30–33cm (12–13in). Large parakeet with long, pointed tail, white eye-ring, red edge along bend of wing. **FLIGHT:** Red underwing-coverts. **VOICE:** Screeches. **STATUS AND RANGE:** Endemic to Hispaniola. Locally common, but rapidly declining. Dominican Republic: primarily Sierra de Baoruco and Sierra de Neiba. Haiti: common in Massif de la Selle and la Citadelle area in Massif du Nord. Uncommon elsewhere in Haiti. Introduced to Puerto Rico and Guadeloupe where very local. Threatened. **HABITAT:** Forests and woodlands at all elevations.

CUBAN PARAKEET *Aratinga euops* 24–27cm (9.5–10.5in). Long, pointed tail; scattered red feathers on head, sides of neck, and bend of wing. **FLIGHT:** Red underwing-coverts. **VOICE:** Loud, characteristic *crick-crick-crick*. **STATUS AND RANGE:** Endemic to Cuba: fairly common locally in Zapata Swamp, Trinidad Mountains, Sierra de Najasa, and eastern part of island. Endangered. **HABITAT:** Woodlands, forest edges, riverine forests, savannas, and tree stumps near swamps.

BLACK-HOODED PARAKEET *Nandayus nenday* 36cm (14in). Large, with black head, red thighs, and long, pointed tail. **VOICE:** Raucous squawks. **STATUS AND RANGE:** Introduced. Puerto Rico: rare and local primarily along northeastern coast. **HABITAT:** Sparse woodlands, palm groves and pastures with thickets.

ORANGE-FRONTED PARAKEET *Aratinga canicularis* 23–24cm (9–9.5in). Medium-sized, with orange forehead, white eye-ring, long, pointed tail, and blue primaries. **VOICE:** Raspy squawks. **STATUS AND RANGE:** Introduced. Uncommon and local in Puerto Rico. **HABITAT:** Wooded pastures and urban areas with ornamental trees.

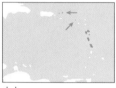

BROWN-THROATED PARAKEET *Aratinga pertinax* 23–28cm (9–11in). Fairly large, with yellowish-orange face and forehead. Long, pointed tail; throat and breast dull yellowish-brown; primaries blue. **VOICE:** Raucous squawks. **STATUS AND RANGE:** Introduced. Virgin Islands: fairly common resident on St Thomas, particularly eastern end, reports from Tortola and St John. Saba and Dominica: uncommon. Guadeloupe and Martinique: recent reports. **HABITAT:** On St Thomas, wooded thickets in hills.

MONK PARAKEET *Myiopsitta monachus* 28cm (11in). Fairly large, with gray crown, throat, and breast. Long, pointed tail; flight feathers blue. **VOICE:** Raucous squawks. **STATUS AND RANGE:** Introduced. Puerto Rico: common locally on coast. Cayman Islands: George Town on Grand Cayman. Guadeloupe: rare. **HABITAT:** Coastal palm groves, and urban gardens.

OLIVE-THROATED PARAKEET *Aratinga nana* 30.5cm (12in). Small, with long, pointed tail. Dark brownish-olive underparts; pale eye-ring and bill. (Hispaniolan Parakeet has red on bend of wing.) **VOICE:** Screeches. **STATUS AND RANGE:** Common and widespread resident on Jamaica. Introduced to Dominican Republic where increasing. **HABITAT:** Scrub, woodlands, forests, croplands, and gardens from coast to lower mountains.

WHITE-WINGED PARAKEET *Brotogeris versicolurus* 23cm (9in). Small, but larger than Budgerigar. Ivory-colored bill; yellow band bordering wing. Tail long and pointed. **FLIGHT:** Wings flash large whitish-yellow triangular patches. **VOICE:** High-pitched squawks. **STATUS AND RANGE:** Introduced. Locally common in Puerto Rico; reported in Dominican Republic, but status unknown. **HABITAT:** Woodlands from coast to foothills. Also towns and urban areas.

GREEN-RUMPED PARROTLET *Forpus passerinus* 13cm (5in). Very small, with short tail and pale bill. **MALE:** Greenish-blue rump and wings. **FEMALE:** Lacks blue in wing. Yellower breast. **VOICE:** Shrill, squeaky chattering. **STATUS AND RANGE:** Introduced. Common and widespread in Jamaica; rare in Barbados. **HABITAT:** Primarily open country, particularly drier lowlands and hills.

BUDGERIGAR *Melopsittacus undulatus* 18cm (7in). The typical pet shop parakeet or 'budgie'. Natural coloration green below, yellow head, and back heavily barred with black. **VOICE:** Sharp screech. **STATUS AND RANGE:** Introduced. Regular escapee on Puerto Rico in San Juan area. Small flocks in Grand Cayman (Cayman Islands); occasional escapee elsewhere. **HABITAT:** Open areas with short grass.

HISPANIOLAN PARAKEET

CUBAN PARAKEET

BROWN-
THROATED
PARAKEET

imm

BLACK-HOODED
PARAKEET

adult

MONK
PARAKEET

ORANGE-
FRONTED
PARAKEET

OLIVE-
THROATED
PARAKEET

WHITE-WINGED
PARAKEET

GREEN-RUMPED
PARROTLET

BUDGERIGAR

● **YELLOW-BILLED CUCKOO** *Coccyzus americanus* 28–32cm (11–12.5in). White underparts; long tail; down-curved bill, yellow at base. Reddish-brown wing patch. **VOICE:** Throaty *ka-ka-ka-ka-ka-ka-ka-ka-ka-kow, kow, kow, kow*; volume increases and slows at end. **STATUS AND RANGE:** Uncommon breeding resident May through August in Cuba, Hispaniola, and Puerto Rico; rarely in Jamaica and Virgin Islands. Migrates September–October and March–April. Variable status. Generally common in southern Bahamas, Cuba, Hispaniola, and Puerto Rico; uncommon in northern Bahamas, Cayman Islands, and Jamaica; rare in Virgin Islands; uncommon to rare in Lesser Antilles. **HABITAT:** Lowland scrub and dry forests.

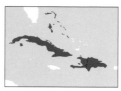

● **BLACK-BILLED CUCKOO** *Coccyzus erythropthalmus* 30cm (12in). White underparts; long tail; dark, down-curved bill; reddish eye-ring. **VOICE:** *Cu-cu-cu-cu.* **STATUS AND RANGE:** Rare migrant in Cuba and Hispaniola; very rare in northern Bahamas. Occurs September through November and April through May. **HABITAT:** Scrublands, lowland forests.

● **MANGROVE CUCKOO** *Coccyzus minor* 28–30cm (11–12in). Black ear-patch and buff-colored abdomen. Slender; long tail; long, down-curved bill, yellow at base. **VOICE:** Slower, more nasal than Yellow-billed Cuckoo. **STATUS AND RANGE:** Fairly common resident throughout West Indies. In Cuba, occurs primarily in east where uncommon. **HABITAT:** Dry scrub, mangroves, thickets.

● **HISPANIOLAN LIZARD-CUCKOO** *Saurothera longirostris* 41–46cm (16–18in). Large, with pale gray breast, long tail, and straight, slender bill. Reddish-brown wing patch. **VOICE:** Throaty *ka-ka-ka-ka-ka-ka-ka-ka-kau-kau-ko-ko*, descending. **STATUS AND RANGE:** Endemic to Hispaniola: common at all elevations. **HABITAT:** Forests.

● **PUERTO RICAN LIZARD-CUCKOO** *Saurothera vieilloti* 40–48cm (16–19in). Large, with long tail and two-toned underparts. **VOICE:** Emphatic *ka-ka-ka-ka...* accelerating, becoming louder. **STATUS AND RANGE:** Endemic to Puerto Rico: fairly common at all elevations. **HABITAT:** Dense forests.

● **JAMAICAN LIZARD-CUCKOO** *Saurothera vetula* 38cm (15in). Fairly large, with long tail and long, straight bill. Lower underparts pale reddish-brown. Reddish-brown wing patch, red eye-ring. **VOICE:** Rapid, low, trailing *cak-cak-cak-ka-ka-ka-k-k.* **STATUS AND RANGE:** Endemic to Jamaica: common and widespread. **HABITAT:** Moist or wet mid-elevation forests, woodlands, and wooded ravines.

● **CHESTNUT-BELLIED CUCKOO** *Hyetornis pluvialis* 48–56cm (19–22in). Large, with long tail and down-curved bill. Primarily reddish underparts; pale gray throat and upper breast. **VOICE:** Throaty, accelerating *quawk-quawk-ak-ak-ak-ak-ak.* **STATUS AND RANGE:** Endemic to Jamaica: common. **HABITAT:** Open, wet forests at mid-elevations. Also open woodlands, dense second-growth forests, and gardens.

● **GREAT LIZARD-CUCKOO** *Saurothera merlini* 44–55cm (17–22in). Large, with long tail and bill. **VOICE:** Long, increasingly loud *ka-ka-ka....* **STATUS AND RANGE:** Cuba: common and widespread. Bahamas: uncommon and limited to Andros, Eleuthera, and New Providence. These islands comprise entire range. **HABITAT:** Dense woods.

● **BAY-BREASTED CUCKOO** *Hyetornis rufigularis* 43–51cm (17–20in). Large, with dark reddish-brown throat and breast; thick, curved bill. Reddish-brown wing patch; long tail. **VOICE:** Strong *cua*, followed by guttural, accelerating *u-ak-u-ak-ak-ak-ak-ak-ak-ak.* **STATUS AND RANGE:** Endemic to Hispaniola: rare and local. **HABITAT:** All forests.

● **SMOOTH-BILLED ANI** *Crotophaga ani* 30–33cm (12–13in). Large, with black, parrot-like bill and long tail. Occurs in flocks. **VOICE:** Loud, squawky whistle *a-leep.* **STATUS AND RANGE:** Common resident in Bahamas, Greater Antilles, Virgin and Cayman Islands, Dominica, St Vincent, Grenada, and Providencia. Uncommon in Martinique and Guadeloupe. Rare or absent in other Lesser Antilles. Rare in San Andrés. **HABITAT:** Open lowlands.

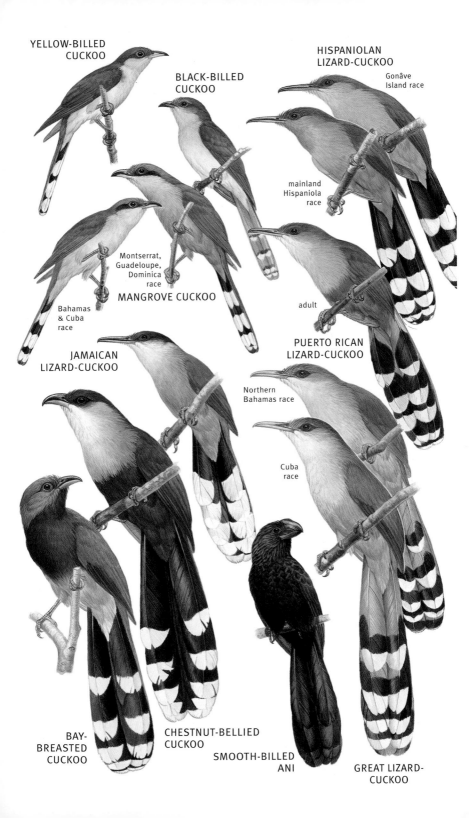

YELLOW-BILLED
CUCKOO

BLACK-BILLED
CUCKOO

HISPANIOLAN
LIZARD-CUCKOO

Gonâve
Island race

mainland
Hispaniola
race

Montserrat,
Guadeloupe,
Dominica
race

MANGROVE CUCKOO

Bahamas
& Cuba
race

adult

PUERTO RICAN
LIZARD-CUCKOO

JAMAICAN
LIZARD-CUCKOO

Northern
Bahamas race

Cuba
race

BAY-
BREASTED
CUCKOO

CHESTNUT-BELLIED
CUCKOO

SMOOTH-BILLED
ANI

GREAT LIZARD-
CUCKOO

○**ASHY-FACED OWL** *Tyto glaucops* 35cm (14in). Nocturnal. Reddish-brown; long-legged; with silver-gray, heart-shaped face. **VOICE:** Hissing, prefaced by high-pitched, ratchety clicks. **STATUS AND RANGE:** Endemic to Hispaniola: fairly widespread and common locally. **HABITAT:** Open woodlands, scrub, dry and moist forests.

○**BARN OWL** *Tyto alba* 30–43cm (12–17in). Large, nocturnal owl with flat, heart-shaped face and large dark eyes. Greater Antilles birds paler. **VOICE:** Loud, hissing screech, and loud clicking sounds. **STATUS AND RANGE:** Common year-round in Cuba, Jamaica, Hispaniola, and Dominica. Uncommon in Bahamas and Cayman Islands. Rare in St Vincent, Grenadines, and Grenada. **HABITAT:** Relatively open areas from the coast to the mountains.

○**CUBAN SCREECH-OWL** *Otus lawrencii* 20–23cm (8–9in). Small, plump, nocturnal owl with big head and large brown eyes. Beige eyebrow stripe; short tail; long, bare, greenish legs. Brownish overall, speckled with white. **VOICE:** *Cu-cu-cu-cucucu,* in low and repeated sequence reminiscent of a bouncing ball. Sometimes harsh, plaintive screams. **STATUS AND RANGE:** Endemic to Cuba: common. **HABITAT:** Woods.

○**JAMAICAN OWL** *Pseudoscops grammicus* 31–36cm (12–14in). Medium-sized, nocturnal owl with short ear-tufts. **ADULT:** Mottled yellowish-brown above; paler with dark streaks below. **VOICE:** Guttural *whogh;* occasionally high-pitched quiver *whoooo.* **STATUS AND RANGE:** Endemic to Jamaica: common and widespread coast to mid-elevations, infrequent in high mountains. **HABITAT:** Forests, woodlands, forest edges, and gardens.

○**PUERTO RICAN SCREECH-OWL** *Otus nudipes* 23–25cm (9–10in). Nocturnal. Grayish- to reddish-brown above, white below marked with heavy brown streaks. **VOICE:** Tremulous trill; sometimes chatters, whoops, or maniacal laugh. **STATUS AND RANGE:** The only small owl in Puerto Rico and Virgin Islands. Endemic to Puerto Rico: common. Very rare in Virgin Islands. **HABITAT:** Forests and wooded areas.

○**BURROWING OWL** *Athene cunicularia* 23cm (9in). Small, diurnal owl with long legs; bobs when approached. **ADULT:** Underparts barred. **VOICE:** Soft, high-pitched, 2-note *coo-coooo.* Clucking chatter when alarmed. **STATUS AND RANGE:** Bahamas: generally fairly common resident. Cuba: locally common primarily in west. Hispaniola: common resident in Haiti and western Dominican Republic. **HABITAT:** Open scrub, sandy pine savannas, pastures, golf courses.

○**CUBAN PYGMY-OWL** *Glaucidium siju* 17.5cm (7in). Small owl with big head and yellow eyes. Short, feathered, yellow feet; short tail often twitched sideways; 2 dark spots on back of head. **VOICE:** Low, sporadically repeated *uh, uh, uh...,* syllables short and plaintive. Also *hui-hui-chiii-chiii-chi-chi-chi...,* increasing in strength. **STATUS AND RANGE:** Endemic to Cuba: fairly common. **HABITAT:** Woods and tree plantations.

○**STYGIAN OWL** *Asio stygius* 41–46cm (16–18in). Large nocturnal owl, dark with conspicuous ear-tufts. **VOICE:** Generally silent; occasionally loud, abrupt *hu!,* as if to scare someone. **STATUS AND RANGE:** Cuba: uncommon and local resident. Threatened. Hispaniola: generally very rare resident. Critically endangered. **HABITAT:** Dense deciduous and pine forests, from semi-arid to humid, all elevations.

○**SHORT-EARED OWL** *Asio flammeus* 35–43cm (14–17in). Large owl, tan below, breast heavily streaked. Yellow eyes; distinct facial disk. Perches on posts. **FLIGHT:** Erratic flaps and glides. Conspicuous black wrist patches on whitish underwings. Most active at dawn and dusk. **VOICE:** Short, emphatic *bow-wow.* Also distinct wing clap. **STATUS AND RANGE:** Locally common resident in Cuba and Hispaniola. Uncommon in Puerto Rico. Rare in Cayman Islands. **HABITAT:** Open lowlands.

ASHY-
FACED OWL

Lesser
Antilles
race

JAMAICAN
OWL

adult

BARN OWL

CUBAN
SCREECH-
OWL

Greater Antilles race

PUERTO RICAN
SCREECH-OWL

red phase

gray
phase

adult

CUBAN PYGMY-OWL

front
view

rear
view

Hispaniola race

BURROWING OWL

STYGIAN
OWL

Puerto Rico
race

SHORT-EARED
OWL

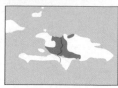

○ **LEAST POORWILL** *Siphonorhis brewsteri* 17–20cm (6.75–8in). The smallest nightjar in the West Indies. Darkly mottled. Nocturnal. **ADULT:** White neck band; narrow white terminal band on tail. **FLIGHT:** Like giant moth, erratic and floppy. **VOICE:** Guttural, repeated *torico, torico*. Also rising whistle. **STATUS AND RANGE:** Endemic to Hispaniola: somewhat common locally in southwestern Dominican Republic, and occurs between Arcahaie and Montruis north of Port-au-Prince in Haiti. Threatened. **HABITAT:** Semi-arid cactus and thorn scrub often associated with pine forests.

○ **JAMAICAN POORWILL** *Siphonorhis americanus* 24cm (9.5in). Small, mottled dark brown with narrow white chin band; reddish-brown hindneck spotted black and white. Nocturnal. **MALE:** Long tail tipped white. **FEMALE:** Buffish, narrow tail markings. **STATUS AND RANGE:** Endemic to Jamaica: critically endangered; perhaps extinct. **HABITAT:** Open forest in semi-arid lowlands such as Hellshire Hills.

○ **WHITE-TAILED NIGHTJAR** *Caprimulgus cayennensis* 20–23cm (8–9in). Nocturnal. **ADULT MALE:** Reddish-brown collar; distinct white eye-line; white outertail feathers; white bar on outer primaries. **ADULT FEMALE:** Duller; lacks collar; white outertail feathers and outer primaries. **VOICE:** High whistle. **STATUS AND RANGE:** Very rare and local resident on Martinique in south and Caravelle Peninsula. **HABITAT:** Grassy fields.

○ **WHIP-POOR-WILL** *Caprimulgus vociferus* 23–26cm (9–10in). Nocturnal. **ADULT MALE:** Mottled grayish-brown; blackish throat; narrow white throat stripe; outertail feathers broadly tipped white. **ADULT FEMALE:** Duller; throat stripe buff; outertail feathers narrowly tipped buff. **VOICE:** Repeated *whip-poor-will*. Usually not vocal in West Indies. **STATUS AND RANGE:** Vagrant in western Cuba and Jamaica. **HABITAT:** Dry, open woodlands.

○ **PUERTO RICAN NIGHTJAR** *Caprimulgus noctitherus* 22cm (8.5in). Small nightjar, mottled gray, brown, and black. Black throat edged with pale band. Nocturnal. **MALE:** White throat band and portion of outertail feathers. **FEMALE:** Buff throat band and tips of outertail feathers. Identical to but smaller than Whip-poor-will. **VOICE:** Emphatic, repeated whistle *whip, whip, whip....* Also emphatic clucking. **STATUS AND RANGE:** Endemic to Puerto Rico: locally common on southwest coast. Endangered. **HABITAT:** Dry semi-deciduous forests with open understory and dense leaf-litter.

○ **RUFOUS NIGHTJAR** *Caprimulgus rufus* 28cm (11in). Medium-sized nightjar. Motttled reddish-brown with white throat band; short, rounded wings. Nocturnal. Nearly identical to Chuck-will's-widow. **VOICE:** Loud rendition of local name *Jacques-pas-papa-pouw*, emphasis on last syllable. Calls mostly at dusk and only during breeding season. **STATUS AND RANGE:** Locally common resident in northeastern St Lucia. Endangered. **HABITAT:** Relatively undisturbed dry scrub forests.

○ **CHUCK-WILL'S-WIDOW** *Caprimulgus carolinensis* 31cm (12in). Large nightjar, mottled reddish-brown; breast primarily blackish; white throat band. Nocturnal. **MALE:** White inner webs of outertail feathers. **FEMALE:** Outertail feathers tipped buff, blend to dark. **VOICE:** Whistles name. Seldom calls in West Indies. **STATUS AND RANGE:** Rare breeding resident in Bahamas. Non-breeding residents occur September through May where common in Hispaniola; uncommon in Bahamas, Cuba, Jamaica, and Saba; rare in Puerto Rico, Virgin and Cayman Islands. **HABITAT:** Woodlands from coast to mid-elevations; also cave entrances.

○ **GREATER ANTILLEAN NIGHTJAR** *Caprimulgus cubanensis* 28cm (11in). Mottled dark gray overall; breast spotted white. Nocturnal. **MALE:** Outertail feathers tipped white. **FEMALE:** Lacks white in tail. **VOICE:** Plaintive, repeated *gua-by-ro*. **STATUS AND RANGE:** Unique to Cuba and Hispaniola. Common and widespread in parts of Cuba. Fairly common in western Dominican Republic. **HABITAT:** Cuba: moderately dense forests, particularly bordering wooded swamps. Hispaniola: forests, especially semi-arid.

LEAST POORWILL

JAMAICAN POORWILL

WHITE-TAILED NIGHTJAR

WHIP-POOR-WILL/PUERTO RICAN NIGHTJAR

RUFOUS NIGHTJAR/CHUCK-WILL'S-WIDOW

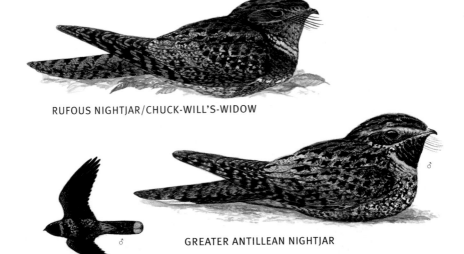

GREATER ANTILLEAN NIGHTJAR

○ **NORTHERN POTOO** *Nyctibius jamaicensis* 43–46cm (17–18in). Large with long tail. Eye yellow, but appears reddish in light. Nocturnal, arboreal. Perches upright on stump or post. **VOICE:** Guttural *kwah, waugh, waugh, waugh, kwaah*. Also hoarse *waark-cucu*. **STATUS AND RANGE:** Fairly common resident in Jamaica where widespread primarily below 1000m (3300ft). Generally rare in Hispaniola. **HABITAT:** Arid and humid forests and scrublands adjacent to open areas. Also palm groves, pastures, and cattle corrals. In Jamaica, also on golf courses.

○ **ANTILLEAN NIGHTHAWK** *Chordeiles gundlachii* 20–25cm (8–10in). Dark, hawk-like, with slender, pointed wings and conspicuous white wing patch. Erratic flight. Nearly identical to Common Nighthawk; distinguished with certainty only by call. **VOICE:** Loud, raspy, *que-re-be-bé*. Active dawn and dusk. **STATUS AND RANGE:** Common breeding resident in Bahamas, Cuba, Cayman Islands, Jamaica, and Hispaniola primarily May through August. Locally common breeding bird in Puerto Rico, Virgin Islands, and Guadeloupe during same months. Generally rare migrant through Lesser Antilles. **HABITAT:** Open fields, pastures, pine barrens, savannas, and coastal fringes.

○ **COMMON NIGHTHAWK** *Chordeiles minor* 20–25cm (8–10in). Virtually identical to Antillean Nighthawk which has tan, rather than blackish, wing linings and is sometimes buffer below and paler above, but these are not consistent field marks. Identified with certainty only by call. **VOICE:** Distinctive, nasal *neet*. Rarely calls during migration. **STATUS AND RANGE:** Migrant throughout West Indies September through October and April through May. Abundance uncertain. **HABITAT:** Open areas including human settlements.

NIGHTJAR TAILS

Chuck-will's-widow ♂

Chuck-will's-widow ♀

Rufous Nightjar ♂

Rufous Nightjar ♀

White-tailed Nightjar uppertail, ♂

White-tailed Nightjar uppertail, ♀

Greater Antillean Nightjar Hispaniola race, ♂

Greater Antillean Nightjar Cuba race, ♂

White-tailed Nightjar lower tail, ♂

White-tailed Nightjar lower tail, ♀

Whip-poor-will ♂

Whip-poor-will ♀

Puerto Rican Nightjar ♀

NORTHERN POTOO

ANTILLEAN NIGHTHAWK/
COMMON NIGHTHAWK

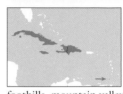

● **WHITE-COLLARED SWIFT** *Streptoprocne zonaris* 20–22cm (8–8.5in). Large swift, black with distinctive white collar. Aerial, in flocks. **VOICE:** High-pitched *screee-screee* or rapid *chip-chip-chip-chip*. **STATUS AND RANGE:** Common resident in Jamaica and Hispaniola. Declining on Haiti. Fairly common resident locally in Cuba, in eastern mountains and Sierra del Escambray. Uncommon wanderer to Grenada. **HABITAT:** Primarily over foothills, mountain valleys, and forests, including open areas. Less regularly over lowlands.

● **BLACK SWIFT** *Cypseloides niger* 15–18cm (5.75–7in). Fairly large, black swift, with slightly forked tail. Aerial, in flocks. Most similar swifts smaller, with shorter tails, more darting flight, and quicker wingbeats. **STATUS AND RANGE:** Widespread in West Indies. Locally common resident in Jamaica and Hispaniola; rare and local in Cuba. Common breeding resident April through September in Guadeloupe, Dominica, and Martinique; uncommon in Puerto Rico, St Lucia, and St Vincent; rare on Montserrat, Barbados, and Grenada. Migrates infrequently in Virgin Islands and Lesser Antilles. **HABITAT:** Mountains; less frequently lowlands.

● **ALPINE SWIFT** *Apus melba* 20cm (8in). Large swift, grayish-brown above, whitish below; dark bar across breast. Aerial. **STATUS AND RANGE:** Vagrant in West Indies. **HABITAT:** Open areas and fields.

● **CHIMNEY SWIFT** *Chaetura pelagica* 12–14cm (4.75–5.5in). Medium-sized; dark; pale brown chin and throat. Short, rounded tail barely visible in flight. Aerial, in flocks. (Black Swift larger; more conspicuous, slightly forked tail.) **VOICE:** Loud, rapid, twittering. **STATUS AND RANGE:** Uncommon migrant in Cayman Islands, decidedly uncommon and local in Bahamas and very rare in Cuba, Jamaica, Hispaniola, and Virgin Islands (St Croix). Occurs August through October and April through May. **HABITAT:** Above cities and towns. Also above open fields and woodlands.

● **SHORT-TAILED SWIFT** *Chaetura brachyura* 10cm (4in). Small. Pale gray rump and undertail coverts contrast with blackish plumage. Tail very short. Aerial, in flocks. (Other small Lesser Antillean swifts are more uniform in color and have longer tails.) **STATUS AND RANGE:** Common breeding resident in St Vincent March through September; apparently departs after breeding. Vagrant elsewhere in West Indies. **HABITAT:** Over towns, open areas, and forests in lowlands and hills.

● **GRAY-RUMPED SWIFT** *Chaetura cinereiventris* 11cm (4.25in). Small, with black upperparts and triangular gray rump patch. Black, longish tail gives slender appearance; gray underparts. Aerial, in flocks. **STATUS AND RANGE:** Locally common in Grenada; probably only seasonal. Primarily in mountains, but also Halifax Harbor in lowlands. **HABITAT:** Typically over forests.

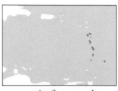

● **LESSER ANTILLEAN SWIFT** *Chaetura martinica* 11cm (4.25in). Small swift, with dull brownish-gray upperparts, gray rump, dark gray underparts, and short gray tail. Aerial, in flocks. (Gray-rumped Swift nearly identical, but does not overlap range.) **STATUS AND RANGE:** Fairly common resident in Dominica, Martinique, St Lucia, and St Vincent. Uncommon in Guadeloupe. These islands compose entire range. **HABITAT:** Primarily over mountain forests, also over lowland forests and open areas.

● **ANTILLEAN PALM SWIFT** *Tachornis phoenicobia* 10–11cm (4–4.25in). Aerial, in flocks. **ADULT:** Small, with white rump, black breast band. (Bank Swallow lacks white rump.) **STATUS AND RANGE:** Common resident in Cuba, Jamaica, and Hispaniola. These islands comprise entire range. **HABITAT:** Open cultivated areas, sugarcane plantations, edges of palm savannas, and urban zones.

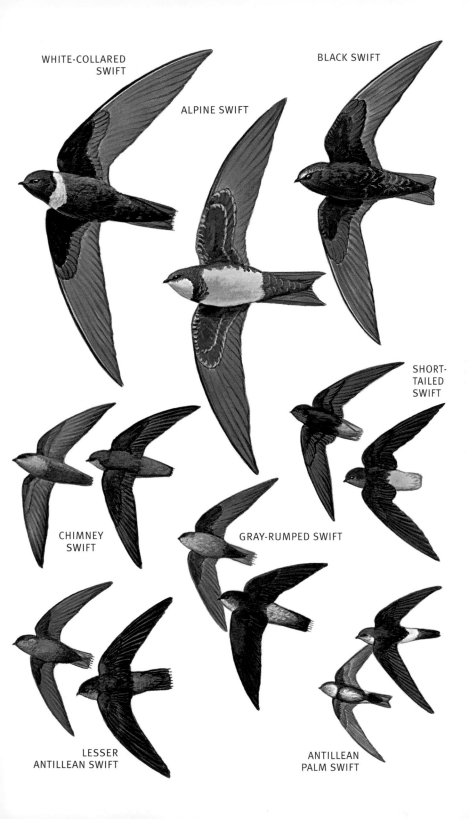

WHITE-COLLARED
SWIFT

BLACK SWIFT

ALPINE SWIFT

SHORT-
TAILED
SWIFT

CHIMNEY
SWIFT

GRAY-RUMPED SWIFT

LESSER
ANTILLEAN SWIFT

ANTILLEAN
PALM SWIFT

PUERTO RICAN EMERALD *Chlorostilbon maugaeus* 9–10cm (3.5–4in). Small hummer with forked tail and no crest. **MALE:** Green above and below with black tail and pinkish base of lower mandible. **FEMALE:** Underparts white, bill entirely black, outertail feathers tipped white. Tail may be forked, notched or even-edged. (Antillean Crested Hummingbird has crest and rounded tail.) **VOICE:** Series of *tic*s and a trill with buzz at end. **STATUS AND RANGE:** Puerto Rico: common in mountains, irregular on coast, particularly drier south coast. **HABITAT:** Forests and edges including shade coffee, also lowland wooded areas.

ANTILLEAN MANGO *Anthracothorax dominicus* 11–12.5cm (4.25–5in). Large hummer with down-curved black bill. **ADULT MALE:** Primarily black below; throat green. **FEMALE:** Whitish below and on tail tips. **IMMATURE MALE:** Black stripe down center of whitish underparts. **VOICE:** Unmusical, thin trill, quite loud. Also sharp, chipping notes. **STATUS AND RANGE:** Hispaniola: common resident at all elevations; Puerto Rico: common on southern coast and northern haystack hills. Nearly absent from east coast. Virgin Islands: increasingly rare. **HABITAT:** Clearings and scrub; also gardens and shade coffee plantations.

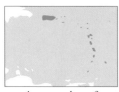

ANTILLEAN CRESTED HUMMINGBIRD *Orthorhyncus cristatus* 8.5–9.5cm (3.25–3.75in). Tiny. **ADULT MALE:** Pointed crest; underparts blackish. **ADULT FEMALE:** Crest less evident; underparts pale gray. **IMMATURE:** Lacks crest. **VOICE:** Emphatic notes. **STATUS AND RANGE:** Common resident throughout Lesser Antilles, Virgin Islands, and on Puerto Rico's northeastern coast. Range expanding in Puerto Rico. **HABITAT:** Primarily lowland openings, gardens, forest edges, and arid habitats; also mountain forests.

GREEN MANGO *Anthracothorax viridis* 11.5cm (4.5in). Large hummer with entirely emerald-green underparts, black, down-curved bill, and rounded tail. **VOICE:** Trill-like twitter; loud, harsh rattling or chattering notes; a hard *tic*. **STATUS AND RANGE:** Endemic to Puerto Rico: common in central and western mountains; decidedly uncommon in eastern mountains and on coast. **HABITAT:** Mountain forests and coffee plantations.

PURPLE-THROATED CARIB *Eulampis jugularis* 11.5cm (4.5in). Large hummer with purplish-red throat and breast, emerald-green wings, and down-curved bill. **FEMALE:** Longer, more sharply down-curved bill than male. **VOICE:** Sharp *chewp*, repeated rapidly when agitated. **STATUS AND RANGE:** Limited to Lesser Antilles. Fairly common resident on St Bartholomew, Saba, Guadeloupe, Dominica, Martinique, St Lucia, St Vincent, and Grenada; uncommon on St Eustatius, St Christopher, Nevis, Antigua, and Montserrat. Vagrant elsewhere. **HABITAT:** Mountain forests and banana plantations; occasionally sea level.

GREEN-THROATED CARIB *Eulampis holosericeus* 10.5–12cm (4–4.75in). Large hummer with green breast and slightly down-curved bill. Blue breast mark visible in good light. **VOICE:** Sharp *chewp* and loud wing rattle. **STATUS AND RANGE:** Common resident throughout Lesser Antilles, Virgin Islands, and northeastern Puerto Rico. **HABITAT:** Gardens and rain forests at all elevations in Lesser Antilles. In Puerto Rico, primarily coastal.

BLUE-HEADED HUMMINGBIRD *Cyanophaia bicolor* 9.5cm (3.75in). **MALE:** Head, throat, upper breast, and tail violet-blue. **FEMALE:** Shiny green above with bronze sheen on mantle; grayish-white below with flecks of green on sides; blackish ear-patch. **VOICE:** Shrill, metallic notes, rapidly descending. **STATUS AND RANGE:** Common resident of Dominica and Martinique. Usually mid-elevations. **HABITAT:** Moist open areas in mountain forests, along mountain streams, and wooded edges of fields.

RUFOUS-BREASTED HERMIT *Glaucis hirsuta* 12.5cm (5in). Long down-curved bill, yellow lower mandible; white-tipped, rounded tail. **MALE:** Upperparts dull green. **FEMALE:** Upperparts more reddish. **VOICE:** High *sweep,* sometimes repeated. Less frequently *sweep, sweeswee.* **STATUS AND RANGE:** Fairly common resident in Grenada in mountains above 450m (1500ft). **HABITAT:** Mountain forests, forest edges, and banana, cocoa, and nutmeg plantations.

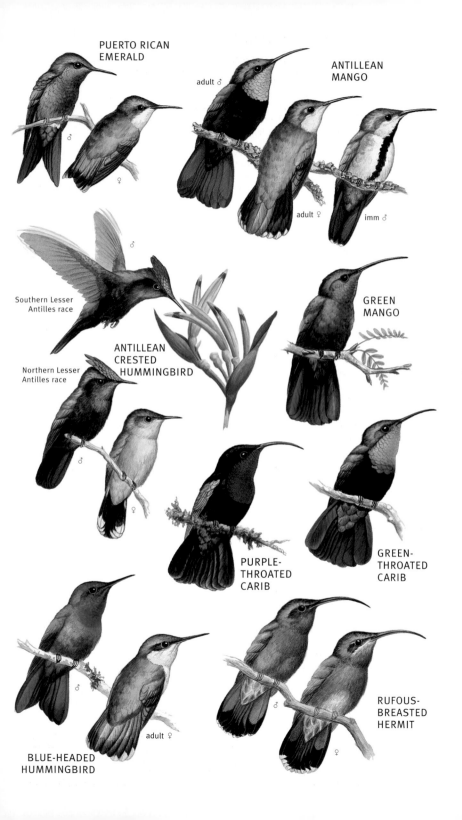

PUERTO RICAN
EMERALD

♂

♀

ANTILLEAN
MANGO

adult ♂

adult ♀

imm ♂

Southern Lesser
Antilles race

♂

ANTILLEAN
CRESTED
HUMMINGBIRD

GREEN
MANGO

Northern Lesser
Antilles race

♂

♀

PURPLE-
THROATED
CARIB

GREEN-
THROATED
CARIB

♂

adult ♀

♂

♀

BLUE-HEADED
HUMMINGBIRD

RUFOUS-
BREASTED
HERMIT

CUBAN EMERALD *Chlorostilbon ricordii* 9–10.5cm (3.5–4in). Medium-sized hummer with long, forked tail and long thin bill, pinkish below. **VOICE:** Short, squeaking twitter. **STATUS AND RANGE:** Common, widespread resident in Cuba. In Bahamas, common on Grand Bahama, Abaco, and Andros; absent elsewhere. **HABITAT:** All habitats from coast to mid-elevations.

BEE HUMMINGBIRD *Mellisuga helenae* 5.5cm (2.25in). The world's smallest bird. Short, white-tipped tail. **MALE:** Iridescent red throat plumes. **FEMALE:** Inconspicuous white spot behind eye; black spot on lores. **VOICE:** Twitter, long and quite high. Also low warbling notes. **STATUS AND RANGE:** Endemic to Cuba: rare and local. Threatened. **HABITAT:** Primarily coastal forests and forest edges, also mountain valleys, forests of interior, swamplands, and gardens.

VERVAIN HUMMINGBIRD *Mellisuga minima* 6cm (2.5in). Tiny hummer with straight black bill. Chin and throat sometimes flecked; sides and flanks dull green. **ADULT MALE:** Tail deeply notched. **ADULT FEMALE:** Tail rounded, tipped white. **VOICE:** Loud, rhythmic, high-pitched, metallic squeaks. Also throaty buzz. **STATUS AND RANGE:** Unique to Jamaica and Hispaniola: common and widespread. **HABITAT:** Open areas, open woodlands, and shade coffee.

HISPANIOLAN EMERALD *Chlorostilbon swainsonii* 10.5cm (4in). Tiny hummer with straight bill. **MALE:** Green overall, dull black breast spot, deeply forked tail, lower mandible pinkish. **FEMALE:** Dull grayish below, metallic green sides, whitish outertail tips. (Female Antillean Mango larger, bill darker.) **VOICE:** Sharp, metallic *tic*s. **STATUS AND RANGE:** Generally common in Hispaniola, though threatened in Haiti. **HABITAT:** Moist forests and shade coffee plantations in mountains, hills, and karst. Also clearings.

BLACK-BILLED STREAMERTAIL *Trochilus scitulus* Male (with tail plumes) 22–24cm (8.5–9.5in); Female 10.5cm (4in). Similar to Red-billed Streamertail, but bill completely black. **VOICE:** Similar to Red-billed Streamertail. **STATUS AND RANGE:** Endemic to Jamaica: common, but occurs only in extreme east of island from Port Antonio and Morant River eastward. **HABITAT:** Humid forests, banana plantations, and gardens.

RED-BILLED STREAMERTAIL *Trochilus polytmus* Male (with tail plumes) 22–25cm (8.5–10in); Female 10.5cm (4in). **ADULT MALE:** 2 long tail feathers. **Adult FEMALE:** Bill red at base, sometimes appearing black. **VOICE:** Loud, metallic *ting* or *teet* and prolonged *twink-twink-twink...* dropping in pitch. In flight, male's streamers hum. **STATUS AND RANGE:** Endemic to Jamaica: widespread. Absent from extreme east. **HABITAT:** Primarily middle- and high-elevation forests and gardens; seasonal on coast.

JAMAICAN MANGO *Anthracothorax mango* 13cm (5in). Large hummer with black underparts; reddish-purple cheeks and sides of neck. **ADULT MALE:** Underparts velvet-black. **ADULT FEMALE:** Duller. **VOICE:** Sharp, raspy *tic*s. **STATUS AND RANGE:** Endemic to Jamaica: Widespread and common. **HABITAT:** Forest edges, banana plantations, and gardens.

RUBY-THROATED HUMMINGBIRD *Archilochus colubris* 8–9.5cm (3–3.75in). **MALE:** Red throat; moderately forked tail. **FEMALE:** Buffish sides; dark bill; rounded, white-tipped tail. Often has white spot behind eye. (Female Cuban and Hispaniolan Emeralds have paler bills, more conspicuous white stripe behind eye, and greenish sides.) **VOICE:** Peculiar twitter, similar to mouse. **STATUS AND RANGE:** Rare migrant to northern Bahamas and Cuba March and April, very rare November through February. Vagrant elsewhere. **HABITAT:** Gardens, wood edges, and clusters of trees.

GREEN-BREASTED MANGO *Anthracothorax prevostii* 12.5cm (5in). **ADULT MALE:** Blended black, green, and violet-blue underparts. **ADULT FEMALE:** Slightly paler. **IMMATURE:** Underparts have black median stripe. **STATUS AND RANGE:** Common resident on Providencia and San Andrés. **HABITAT:** Primarily open coastal areas with scattered trees and bushes.

BAHAMA WOODSTAR *Calliphlox evelynae* 9–9.5cm (3.5–3.75in). **ADULT MALE:** Deeply forked tail with reddish-brown inner feathers. Reddish-violet throat, lower underparts reddish-brown. **ADULT FEMALE:** White throat and breast; rounded, reddish-brown tail and lower underparts. **VOICE:** Sharp *tit, titit, tit, tit, titit,* often speeding to rapid rattle. **STATUS AND RANGE:** Endemic to Bahamas where common throughout. **HABITAT:** Gardens, scrub, woodlands, forest edges, clearings, and mixed pine forests.

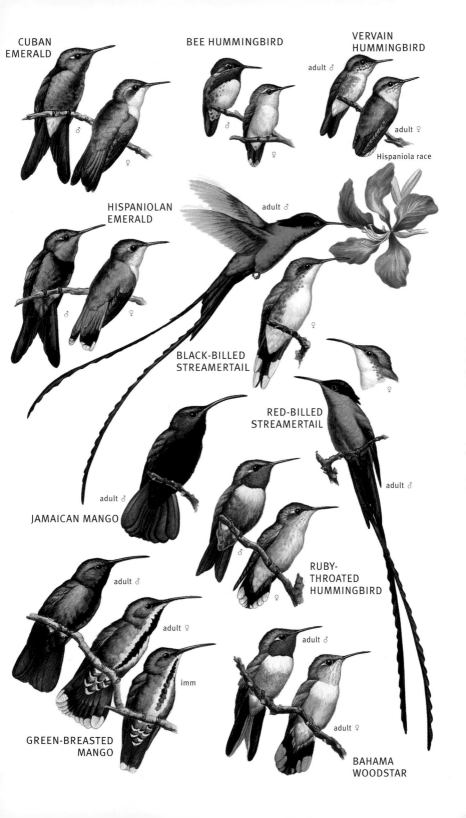

CUBAN
EMERALD

♂

♀

BEE HUMMINGBIRD

♂

♀

VERVAIN
HUMMINGBIRD

adult ♂

adult ♀

Hispaniola race

HISPANIOLAN
EMERALD

♂

♀

adult ♂

♀

♀

BLACK-BILLED
STREAMERTAIL

RED-BILLED
STREAMERTAIL

adult ♂

JAMAICAN MANGO

adult ♂

adult ♂

♀

adult ♂

RUBY-
THROATED
HUMMINGBIRD

adult ♀

♀

imm

adult ♂

GREEN-BREASTED
MANGO

adult ♀

BAHAMA
WOODSTAR

● PUERTO RICAN TODY *Todus mexicanus* 11cm (4.25in). Tiny; chunky; bright green above; red throat; long, broad, reddish bill. **VOICE:** Loud, nasal *beep* or *bee-beep*. Wing rattles in flight. **STATUS AND RANGE:** Endemic to Puerto Rico: common and widespread from coast to mountains. **HABITAT:** Forested areas from wet to dry including dense thickets.

● JAMAICAN TODY *Todus todus* 9cm (3.5in). Tiny; chunky; bright green above; red throat; long, broad reddish bill. Flanks pink; abdomen and sides of breast pale yellow. **VOICE:** Almost silent during non-breeding season. Calls include a loud *beep* and a rapid guttural 'throat-rattling' given during territorial displays while perched. **STATUS AND RANGE:** Endemic to Jamaica: widespread and common from coast to mountains. **HABITAT:** All forest types, from arid to wet.

● CUBAN TODY *Todus multicolor* 11cm (4.25in). Small, stubby, primarily green, with big head, no neck, large flat bill, and red throat. Flanks pink; sides of throat blue; undertail coverts yellow. **FLIGHT:** Characteristic wing rattle. **VOICE:** Typically a soft *pprreeee-pprreeee*. Sometimes a peculiar short *tot-tot-tot-tot*. **STATUS AND RANGE:** Common and widespread in Cuba. **HABITAT:** Wooded and semi-wooded areas, forests, stream edges, and areas with earthen embankments at all elevations.

● BROAD-BILLED TODY *Todus subulatus* 11–12cm (4.25–4.75in). Bright green above; grayish-white tinted yellow below; pink sides; red throat. Lower mandible entirely reddish. (Narrow-billed Tody is whiter below and usually has black-tipped bill. Best distinguished by voice.) **VOICE:** Monotonous, often repeated whistle *terp, terp, terp*, uttered in complaining tone. Single-note call of same tone contrasts with Narrow-billed Tody's 2-note call. **STATUS AND RANGE:** Endemic to Hispaniola: common in lowlands. **HABITAT:** Semi-arid areas from lowlands to 1700m (5600ft) in forests, including pine; also scrub, shade coffee plantations and some mangroves. Frequents ravines.

● NARROW-BILLED TODY *Todus angustirostris* 11cm (4.25in). Tiny; chunky; brilliant green upperparts; red throat; whitish underparts tinted with yellow; pinkish sides. Lower mandible reddish, usually with black tip. (Broad-billed Tody grayish-white below with entirely red lower mandible. Since Narrow-billed Tody sometimes lacks black tip on lower mandible, best distinguished by voice.) **VOICE:** Frequently repeated, 2-part *chip-chee*, accented on the 2nd syllable. Also chattering, trilly *chippy-chippy-chippy-chip*, dropping in pitch, but not in tone. **STATUS AND RANGE:** Endemic to Hispaniola: common primarily at higher elevations. Threatened in Haiti. **HABITAT:** Dense, wet forests, including pine, chiefly at high elevations, but locally at lower elevations. Frequents ravines and earthen embankments.

● CUBAN TROGON *Priotelus temnurus* 25–28cm (10–11in). Red belly; green back; blue crown; short, broad bill; long, peculiar tail with much white on underside. Distinctive posture. **VOICE:** Very varied. Most commonly a repeated *toco-toco-tocoro-tocoro*…. Also a low, short mournful call, difficult to locate. **STATUS AND RANGE:** Cuba: widely distributed and common. **HABITAT:** Wet and dry forests at all altitudes. Primarily shady areas.

●HISPANIOLAN TROGON *Priotelus roseigaster* 27–30cm (10.5–12in). Glossy green upperparts, red belly, yellow bill, gray throat and breast. Long, dark blue tail heavily marked with white below. **MALE:** Wings with fine black-and-white barring. **FEMALE:** Lacks fine wing markings. **VOICE:** *Toca-loro; coc, ca-rao* or *cock-craow*, repeated several times. Also cooing and puppy-like whimpering. **STATUS AND RANGE:** Hispaniola. In Dominican Republic still locally common in undisturbed habitat. During non-breeding season, descends to lower elevations. Locally abundant in Haiti (Massif de la Hotte), but declining and considered threatened. **HABITAT:** Mountain forests, including mature pine and broadleaf forests. Local in mangroves.

PUERTO
RICAN TODY

adult

imm

JAMAICAN
TODY

CUBAN
TODY

BROAD-
BILLED
TODY

NARROW-BILLED
TODY

CUBAN TROGON

♀

♂

HISPANIOLAN
TROGON

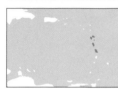

RINGED KINGFISHER *Ceryle torquata* 38–41cm (15–16in). Large, with crest and large bill; primarily reddish-brown underparts. **FEMALE:** Blue breast band. **FLIGHT:** Distinctive reddish underwing-coverts. Hovers and dives for fish. (Belted Kingfisher smaller, with white lower belly and underwing-coverts.) **VOICE:** Loud, harsh rattle. **STATUS AND RANGE:** Fairly common resident in Dominica and Martinique; uncommon and local in Guadeloupe. **HABITAT:** Edges of large streams, lakes, and reservoirs.

BELTED KINGFISHER *Ceryle alcyon* 28–36cm (11–14in). Large bill; crest. **MALE:** Blue breast band. **FEMALE:** 1 blue and 1 orange breast band. Hovers and dives for fish. (Ringed Kingfisher is larger, heavier-billed, and has more extensive reddish-brown underparts and reddish underwing-coverts.) **VOICE:** Loud, harsh rattle. **STATUS AND RANGE:** Generally fairly common non-breeding resident throughout West Indies September through April; records from every month. **HABITAT:** Calm bodies of water, both saline and fresh.

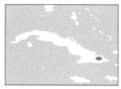

IVORY-BILLED WOODPECKER *Campephilus principalis* 45–50cm (17.5–19.5in). By far the largest West Indian woodpecker. Crow-sized with prominent crest, black-and-white plumage, and large ivory-colored bill. **MALE:** Red crest. **FEMALE:** Black crest. **VOICE:** Soft, toy trumpet-like call *tut-tut-tut-tut;* unusual for the bird's large size. **STATUS AND RANGE:** On verge of extinction. May survive south of Moa. **HABITAT:** Pine woods, mixed with deciduous forests.

WEST INDIAN WOODPECKER *Melanerpes superciliaris* 26cm (10in). Upperparts and wings barred black and white, underparts buff-cinnamon to brownish-gray, abdomen red. **ADULT MALE:** Crown to hindneck red. **ADULT FEMALE:** Top of head black or tan; only back of crown and hindneck red. **VOICE:** Distinctive loud, high-pitched *krruuu-krruu-kruu...*, frequently repeated. **STATUS AND RANGE:** Known only from Bahamas, Cuba, and Cayman Islands. Cuba: common and widespread. Bahamas: common on Abaco, uncommon on San Salvador, nearly extirpated from Grand Bahama. Cayman Islands: only Grand Cayman, where fairly common. Grand Bahama race endangered. **HABITAT:** Primarily dry forest, scrub, coastal forests, and palm groves. On Abaco, settlements.

YELLOW-BELLIED SAPSUCKER *Sphyrapicus varius* 20–23cm (8–9in). Large. White wing patch shows as white wing-coverts in flight. **ADULT:** Red forehead and crown, rarely black. Black-and-white facial pattern, black breast band. **ADULT MALE:** Red throat. **ADULT FEMALE:** White throat. **IMMATURE:** Pale brown plumage, lightly spotted. Faint facial stripes. **STATUS AND RANGE:** Non-breeding resident in West Indies, primarily October through April. Common in Bahamas and Cuba; uncommon in Jamaica, Hispaniola, Cayman Islands, and San Andrés. Rare in Puerto Rico and Virgin Islands. **HABITAT:** Forests, forest edges, woodlands, and gardens, from coast to mountains.

NORTHERN FLICKER *Colaptes auratus* 30–32cm (12–12.5in). Fairly large, with conspicuous black bar across breast. Yellow underwings and undertail; beige underparts with black spots; large white rump patch spotted with black; red patch on hindneck. **ADULT MALE:** Black mustache stripe. **ADULT FEMALE:** Lacks mustache stripe. **VOICE:** Long cackle *pic-pic-pic-pic-pic-pic.* (Can be confused with Fernandina's Flicker.) Also, softer and lower *fli-quer, fli-quer.* **STATUS AND RANGE:** Fairly common year-round resident in Cayman Islands (Grand Cayman) and locally in Cuba. **HABITAT:** All areas with trees from forests to gardens.

HAIRY WOODPECKER *Picoides villosus* 20–23cm (8–9in). Upperparts mostly black with white on back; underparts mostly white. Black eye-line and mustache stripe on otherwise white face; white outertail feathers. **ADULT MALE:** Red patch on back of head, **ADULT FEMALE:** Lacks red head patch. **VOICE:** Loud *keek.* **STATUS AND RANGE:** Fairly common year-round resident in northern Bahamas (Grand Bahama, Abaco, Andros, and New Providence). **HABITAT:** Primarily pine woods.

♀ hovering

BELTED
KINGFISHER

♂

♂

RINGED
KINGFISHER

♀

♀

IVORY-BILLED
WOODPECKER

Grand Cayman race

adult ♀

adult ♂

♀

Abaco race

♂

adult ♀
Cuba race

adult ♂

WEST INDIAN
WOODPECKER

adult ♀

imm

♀

YELLOW-BELLIED
SAPSUCKER

adult ♀

♂

HAIRY
WOODPECKER

adult ♂

NORTHERN
FLICKER

GUADELOUPE WOODPECKER *Melanerpes herminieri* 25–29cm (10–11.5in). **ADULT:** Black overall with reddish wash on throat and belly, most noticeable in breeding season. **MALE:** Bill about 20% longer than female's. **FLIGHT:** Direct, unlike most other woodpeckers. **VOICE:** *wa-uh*, or *wa-ah*, and staccato *cht-cht-cht-cht-cht-cht-cht-cht*. **STATUS AND RANGE:** Endemic to Guadeloupe: common and widespread. **HABITAT:** Sea level to tree line at 1000m (3300ft) in every forest type including semi-deciduous and evergreen forests, coconut palms, and mangroves.

CUBAN GREEN WOODPECKER *Xiphidiopicus percussus* 21–25cm (8–10in). Small, with noticeable crest. Green on upperparts, yellowish underparts; white face with black stripe behind eye; red patch on breast. **MALE:** Red crown. **FEMALE:** Black crown. **VOICE:** Short, low and harsh *jorr-jorr-jorr....* Also higher-pitched, shorter *eh-eh-eh*. **STATUS AND RANGE:** Endemic to Cuba: common and widespread. **HABITAT:** Many forest types including wet and dry, open and dense, mountains and lowlands; also mangroves.

ANTILLEAN PICULET *Nesoctites micromegas* 13–16cm (5–6.25in). Tiny, chunky, atypical woodpecker. Criss-crosses along twigs and vines. **ADULT:** Olive above, pale yellowish with heavy dark spots below. Yellow on crown. **ADULT MALE:** Red patch in center of crown. **VOICE:** Staccato *kuk-ki-ki-ki-ke-ku-kuk*, surprisingly loud. **STATUS AND RANGE:** Endemic to Hispaniola: common, especially in east. Occurs from lowlands to mountains, not usually at highest elevations. Threatened in Haiti. **HABITAT:** Dry and humid forests, including pines mixed with broadleaved trees, thorn forests, and dense second growth, semi-arid areas, and mangroves.

HISPANIOLAN WOODPECKER *Melanerpes striatus* 22–25cm (8.5–10in). Medium-sized, with white and black patches on hindneck; red hindcrown and uppertail-coverts; whitish to yellow eye. **MALE:** Larger and longer-billed. **VOICE:** Strong, variable including loud, rolling call interrupted with throaty noises. Call notes *wup* and *ta-a*. Short *bdddt* with 3–5 distinct notes. **STATUS AND RANGE:** Endemic to Hispaniola: common and widespread. **HABITAT:** Primarily hilly, partly cultivated and partly wooded areas, and in palms scattered among cultivated fields. From coast to humid mountain forests.

JAMAICAN WOODPECKER *Melanerpes radiolatus* 24cm (9.5in). Red hindcrown and hindneck; whitish face; black upperparts; wings finely streaked with white. **MALE:** Red crown. **FEMALE:** Brownish-olive crown. **VOICE:** Loud, rollicking *chee-ee-urp* cry, similar to Olive-throated Parakeet. Call variable: single note or rapid series of 3 or more *churp-chur-churp* notes. **STATUS AND RANGE:** Endemic to Jamaica: common and widespread. The only woodpecker in Jamaica, except for the uncommon Yellow-bellied Sapsucker. **HABITAT:** Coastal coconut groves to forested mountain summits, including both dry and wet forests, forest edges, woodlands, shade coffee plantations, and gardens.

PUERTO RICAN WOODPECKER *Melanerpes portoricensis* 23–27cm (9–10.5in). Red throat and breast; white rump and forehead; blackish upperparts. **ADULT MALE:** Underparts primarily red with buffish sides. **ADULT FEMALE AND IMMATURE:** Less red on underparts. **FLIGHT:** Undulating. **VOICE:** Wide variety of calls, most commonly *wek, wek, wek-wek-wek-wek-wek...* becoming louder and faster. **STATUS AND RANGE:** Endemic to Puerto Rico: common and widespread. **HABITAT:** Coastal plantations to mountain forests, but primarily hills and lower mountains including shade coffee.

FERNANDINA'S FLICKER *Colaptes fernandinae* 33–35cm (13–14in). The largest Cuban woodpecker except for Ivory-billed. Almost entirely yellowish-tan with fine black barring. No red on head. Underwings yellow. **MALE:** Black mustache stripe. **FEMALE:** Lacks mustache stripe. **VOICE:** Loud *pic-pic-pic-pic-pic-pic*, slightly slower and deeper than Northern Flicker. Also loud, short *ch-ch-ch*, with nasal resonance. **STATUS AND RANGE:** Endemic to Cuba where rare and local. Less rare in central provinces and near Camagüey. Endangered. **HABITAT:** Savanna edges and open forests with scattered trees and dense leaf-litter.

ANTILLEAN
PICULET

CUBAN GREEN
WOODPECKER

♂

♀

♂

♀

GUADELOUPE
WOODPECKER

HISPANIOLAN
WOODPECKER

♂

♀

JAMAICAN
WOODPECKER

♂

♀

♀

PUERTO RICAN
WOODPECKER

♂

♂

♀

FERNANDINA'S
FLICKER

● **RUFOUS-TAILED FLYCATCHER** *Myiarchus validus* 24cm (9.5in). Large, with rusty tail and primaries. Belly and abdomen yellow. **VOICE:** Fast, rolling, descending *pree-ee-ee-ee-ee*, like horse's neigh. Also *chi-chi-chiup*. **STATUS AND RANGE:** Endemic to Jamaica where fairly common, primarily middle elevations. **HABITAT:** Forests, primarily moist.

● **SAD FLYCATCHER** *Myiarchus barbirostris* 16.5cm (6.5in). **ADULT:** Relatively small, with dark crown and yellow underparts, except for chin and throat. Faint wing bars. **VOICE:** Emphatic *pip, pip-pip*. Sometimes *pip-pip-pireee*, rising at end. **STATUS AND RANGE:** Endemic to Jamaica where widespread and common. **HABITAT:** Primarily forests and woodlands from lowlands to middle elevations. Less frequent in semi-arid lowlands and in fairly open forests at higher elevations.

● **GREAT CRESTED FLYCATCHER** *Myiarchus crinitus* 18–20.5cm (7–8in). **ADULT:** Wings and tail with reddish-brown; whitish wing bars; throat and breast gray; belly bright yellow. **VOICE:** Loud, harsh *wheeep* with rising inflection. **STATUS AND RANGE:** Rare migrant and non-breeding resident in Cuba September through April. Very rare in northern Bahamas. **HABITAT:** Forests.

● **STOLID FLYCATCHER** *Myiarchus stolidus* 20cm (8in). Medium-sized, with 2 pale white wing bars. Primaries heavily fringed white. Throat and breast whitish; abdomen and belly pale yellow; bill black, moderately heavy. **VOICE:** Rolling *whee-ee-ee, swee-ip, bzzrt*. Also plaintive *jui* in Hispaniola. **STATUS AND RANGE:** Common resident throughout Jamaica and Hispaniola, its entire range. **HABITAT:** Lowland forests and edges, including arid woodlands, scrub, and mangroves. Less frequent in wet mid-elevation forests. On Hispaniola, also pine woods.

● **JAMAICAN BECARD** *Pachyramphus niger* 18cm (7in). Heavy set; large head; stubby bill; short tail; behaves like flycatcher. **VOICE:** 2 hoarse *queeck*s followed by musical *"Co-ome and Tell me what you hee-ear"*; gradually rises, then falls. **STATUS AND RANGE:** Endemic to Jamaica: widespread and fairly common locally. **HABITAT:** Tall open forests and edges in hills and lower mountains. Also closed forests, woodlands, pastures with trees, and gardens.

● **LA SAGRA'S FLYCATCHER** *Myiarchus sagrae* 19–22cm (7.5–8.5in). Medium-sized, with unusual leaning posture and flat-headed appearance. Long, usually all-black bill, 2 inconspicuous white wing bars. **VOICE:** 2-syllable whistle *tra-hee*. Also short, plaintive whistle *huit*. **STATUS AND RANGE:** Common resident in northern Bahamas, Cuba, and Cayman Islands (Grand Cayman). Generally uncommon in southern Bahamas and absent from Turks & Caicos. These islands comprise entire range. **HABITAT:** Pine woods, mixed woodlands, dense thickets, mangroves, and forests, at all elevations.

● **PUERTO RICAN FLYCATCHER** *Myiarchus antillarum* 18.5–20cm (7.25–8in). Medium-sized, with faint wing bars. Light brownish-gray underparts, lighter toward tail; lacks yellow wash. Best identified by call. **VOICE:** Plaintive whistle *whee*. Also, *whee-a-wit-whee*. **STATUS AND RANGE:** Puerto Rico: common resident. Virgin Islands: uncommon on St John; rare on St Thomas, Virgin Gorda, and Tortola. These islands comprise entire range. **HABITAT:** Wooded areas, including mangrove borders, arid scrub, coffee plantations, haystack hills, and mountain forests, except higher slopes.

● **GRENADA FLYCATCHER** *Myiarchus nugator* 20cm (8in). Slightly erectile crest; black bill with pinkish lower mandible; 2 pale brown wing bars; primaries with reddish edges; long tail with reddish edges. **VOICE:** Loud *quip* or harsh *queuk*. **STATUS AND RANGE:** Common resident known only from St Vincent, Grenadines, and Grenada at all elevations. **HABITAT:** Open areas around settlements and lowland scrub, especially near palms.

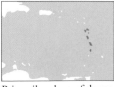

● **LESSER ANTILLEAN FLYCATCHER** *Myiarchus oberi* 19–22cm (7.5–8.5in). Mostly yellow underparts from upper belly to undertail coverts. Tail feathers with reddish inner webs. **VOICE:** Loud, plaintive whistle *peeu-wheeet*. Also short whistles *oo-ee, oo-ee* or *e-oo-ee*. **STATUS AND RANGE:** Common resident on Barbuda, St Christopher, Nevis, Dominica, Martinique, and St Lucia. Rare on Guadeloupe. These islands comprise its entire range. **HABITAT:** Primarily edges of dense woodlands, forests and tree plantations at or above 100m (330ft). Infrequently lower-altitude second growth or scrub.

RUFOUS-TAILED FLYCATCHER

GREAT CRESTED
FLYCATCHER

SAD FLYCATCHER

STOLID
FLYCATCHER

adult ♂

adult ♀ & imm

JAMAICAN BECARD

LA SAGRA'S
FLYCATCHER

LESSER
ANTILLEAN
FLYCATCHER

PUERTO RICAN
FLYCATCHER

GRENADA
FLYCATCHER

⬤ **TROPICAL KINGBIRD** *Tyrannus melancholicus* 23cm (9in). Fairly large, with primarily yellow underparts, pale gray crown, greenish back, and gray facial mask. Crown patch usually concealed. (Western Kingbird smaller, with white in outertail feathers.) **VOICE:** Similar to Gray Kingbird, but softer, less emphatic *pip-pri-pip-pri-pip-pri....* **STATUS AND RANGE:** Rare and irregular migrant on Grenada, breeds some years, but absent most years. Recorded all months. **HABITAT:** Open, semi-arid scrubland.

⬤ **WESTERN KINGBIRD** *Tyrannus verticalis* 21–24cm (8–9.5in). **ADULT:** Head and hindneck pale with dark gray line through eye; pale gray upper breast; yellow belly; conspicuous white edges to outertail feathers. **STATUS AND RANGE:** Very rare migrant in northern Bahamas south to Eleuthera primarily October and November. **HABITAT:** Open country.

⬤ **EASTERN KINGBIRD** *Tyrannus tyrannus* 22–23cm (8.5–9in). **ADULT:** Upperparts dark gray; head and tail black. White underparts; 2 indistinct wing bars; tail with terminal white band. Crown patch usually concealed. (Loggerhead Kingbird has heavier bill, brownish-gray back washed with olive, yellow wash on lower bill, and much less white on tail tip.) **STATUS AND RANGE:** Uncommon migrant in western Cuba and Cayman Islands (Grand Cayman). Rare in northern Bahamas, eastern Cuba, Jamaica, and San Andrés. Occurs most regularly September and October, less frequently April and early May. **HABITAT:** Semi-open woodlands including gardens in urban areas. Often perches in tall trees.

⬤ **GRAY KINGBIRD** *Tyrannus dominicensis* 22–25cm (8.5–10in). Gray above, pale gray-white below with distinct dark mask extending under eye; slightly notched tail. Crown patch rarely visible. **VOICE:** Emphatic *pi-tirr-ri.* **STATUS AND RANGE:** Conspicuous and common throughout West Indies. Resident from Hispaniola east through Lesser Antilles. Most breeding birds from Bahamas, Cuba, Jamaica, and Cayman Islands migrate off-island November through March. Some leave Lesser Antilles as well. **HABITAT:** Mountains and lowlands, in open areas with scattered trees. Usually on exposed perches.

⬤ **LOGGERHEAD KINGBIRD** *Tyrannus caudifasciatus* 24–26cm (9.5–10in). Distinctively two-toned: dark above and white below. Crown blackish, with rarely seen patch. Square tail has white trailing edge except in Hispaniola and Puerto Rico. Bill large. (Eastern Kingbird smaller; bill smaller; back blacker; tail whiter on tip.) **VOICE:** Variable, usually loud, mallet-like chattering, with *bzze-beep* or *bee-beep* elements. Song bubbling, repeated *p-p-q.* **STATUS AND RANGE:** Common and widespread resident through northern Bahamas, Greater Antilles, and Cayman Islands. These islands comprise entire range. **HABITAT:** Woodlands, pine and broadleaf forests, shade coffee, mangrove swamps, and open areas with scattered trees from lowlands to mid-elevations. Frequent exposed perches.

⬤ **GIANT KINGBIRD** *Tyrannus cubensis* 23cm (9in). Very large bill. Upperparts dark, especially crown; underparts white. Crown patch rarely visible. (Loggerhead Kingbird smaller, with smaller bill and darker crown with distinctive crest-like bulge towards back of head.) **VOICE:** Chatter resembling Loggerhead Kingbird, but louder, longer, deeper, and harsher. **STATUS AND RANGE:** Endemic to Cuba: rare and local, most abundant around Moa. Endangered. **HABITAT:** Forests and woodlands near rivers and swamps. Also pine barrens mixed with hardwoods and semi-open woodlands with tall trees. Frequents exposed perches.

⬤ **FORK-TAILED FLYCATCHER** *Tyrannus savana* 33–41cm (13–16in). **ADULT MALE:** Black head; pale gray back; blackish-brown wings; white underparts. Tail in breeding plumage very long with white-edged streamers; shorter during molt. **ADULT FEMALE AND IMMATURE:** Duller; tail shorter. **STATUS AND RANGE:** Very rare, local and irregular migrant in Grenada primarily July and August. Frequents vicinity of airport. Vagrant elsewhere in West Indies. **HABITAT:** Open savannas.

⬤ **SCISSOR-TAILED FLYCATCHER** *Tyrannus forficatus* 31–38cm (12–15in). Pale, with conspicuously long tail. Wings and tail blackish. (Fork-tailed Flycatcher has black cap and is white below, rather than pinkish-orange.) **STATUS AND RANGE:** Vagrant in West Indies late October through December. Recorded from Bahamas, western Cuba, Hispaniola, and Puerto Rico.

TROPICAL KINGBIRD

WESTERN KINGBIRD

GRAY KINGBIRD

EASTERN KINGBIRD

Puerto Rico race

Cuba race

GIANT KINGBIRD

LOGGERHEAD KINGBIRD

adult ♂

adult ♀ & imm

FORK-TAILED FLYCATCHER

adult

SCISSOR-TAILED FLYCATCHER

WILLOW FLYCATCHER *Empidonax trailli* 15cm (5.75in). Underparts grayish-white with almost no yellow; chin white. Lacks noticeable eye-ring; has whitish wing bars. (Eastern Wood-pewee has heavier, whitish wing bars. Acadian Flycatcher slightly yellower below, with more conspicuous eye-ring and greener back. Nearly indistinguishable from Least Flycatcher except by call.) **VOICE:** *Fi-bi-o,* cross between whistle and buzz. Also harsh *fitz.* **STATUS AND RANGE:** Very rare migrant in Cuba and Jamaica mid-September through mid-October. **HABITAT:** Wetland edges, woodlands, tree clumps, and gardens.

ACADIAN FLYCATCHER *Empidonax virescens* 12cm (4.75in). Yellowish eye-ring; 2 buffish or whitish wing bars; lower mandible yellowish; throat and belly white. (Yellow-bellied Flycatcher yellower below. Willow Flycatcher less yellow below, with less conspicuous eye-ring. Differences minimal.) **VOICE:** Usually silent during migration. **STATUS AND RANGE:** Rare migrant in Cuba and northern Bahamas September, October, and April. **HABITAT:** Open woodlands, forest edges, tree clumps, and gardens.

YELLOW-BELLIED FLYCATCHER *Empidonax flaviventris* 15cm (5.75in). Yellowish underparts including throat. Eye-ring broad and yellowish, 2 whitish or yellowish wing bars, lower mandible pale orange. (Acadian Flycatcher less yellow below; throat white.) **VOICE:** Usually silent during migration. **STATUS AND RANGE:** Very rare and irregular migrant on Cuba September, October, and April. **HABITAT:** Forests, woodlands, tree clumps, wetland edges, and gardens.

EULER'S FLYCATCHER *Lathrotriccus euleri* 13.5–14cm (5.25–5.5in). Buff or pale reddish-brown wing bars; underparts yellowish with grayish-olive breast band; whitish eye-ring. **VOICE:** Murmuring *pee, de-dee-dee-dee-dee,* first note higher. **STATUS AND RANGE:** Formerly very rare resident in Grenada where found near Grand Etang. Possibly extirpated. Critically endangered. **HABITAT:** Primarily moist mountain forests.

LEAST FLYCATCHER *Empidonax minimus* 13cm (5.25in). White eye-ring; 2 white wing bars; white chin; pale yellow belly. Best distinguished from other *Empidonax* by voice. **VOICE:** Sharp *weep* or *wit,* often repeated rapidly. **STATUS AND RANGE:** Vagrant in West Indies. **HABITAT:** Brush and open woodland.

JAMAICAN ELAENIA *Myiopagis cotta* 12.5cm (5in). Small, with whitish eyebrow stripe, small black bill, and yellowish primary edges. Lacks wing bars. Crown patch sometimes exposed. **VOICE:** Rapid, high-pitched *ti-si-si-sip* or *si-sip,* last note lower. **STATUS AND RANGE:** Endemic to Jamaica where uncommon, but widespread. **HABITAT:** Wet forests at moderate elevations. Also open woodlands, scrublands, shade coffee, and dry forests.

CARIBBEAN ELAENIA *Elaenia martinica* 15.5–18cm (6–7in). Throat and lower belly whitish with light yellowish wash; breast pale gray; lower mandible pinkish; 2 whitish wing bars. Slight crest; displays crown patch when agitated. **VOICE:** Repetitious *jui-up, wit-churr.* Song drawn-out *pee-wee-reereeree.* **STATUS AND RANGE:** Generally common and widespread resident in Cayman and Virgin Islands, Puerto Rico, and Lesser Antilles. Rare on Providencia and San Andrés. **HABITAT:** Woodlands, scrub, and forests. Primarily dry lowlands, but sometimes in mountains.

YELLOW-BELLIED ELAENIA *Elaenia flavogaster* 16.5cm (6.5in). Bill whitish-pink below; 2 white wing bars. Often raises crest slightly. (Caribbean Elaenia smaller, less prominent crest, less yellow on belly.) **VOICE:** Harsh, drawn-out *creup* or *creup-wi-creup.* **STATUS AND RANGE:** Fairly common resident in St Vincent, Grenadines, and Grenada. **HABITAT:** Primarily lowland forest edges, open woodlands, scrub, and gardens.

GREATER ANTILLEAN ELAENIA *Elaenia fallax* 15cm (5.75in). Faint dark eye-line; 2 distinct wing bars; small bill with pinkish base. Underparts pale gray, washed yellow. Neck and breast faintly streaked gray. **VOICE:** Harsh *pwee-chi-chi-chiup, see-ere, chewit-chewit.* Also trill. **STATUS AND RANGE:** Known only from Jamaica and Hispaniola. Locally common in mountains. **HABITAT:** Open country with scattered trees, wet and pine forests.

WILLOW
FLYCATCHER

ACADIAN
FLYCATCHER

YELLOW-BELLIED
FLYCATCHER

EULER'S
FLYCATCHER

LEAST
FLYCATCHER

JAMAICAN ELAENIA

CARIBBEAN
ELAENIA

YELLOW-
BELLIED
ELAENIA

GREATER
ANTILLEAN
ELAENIA

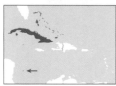

● **EASTERN WOOD-PEWEE** *Contopus virens* 16cm (6.25in). **ADULT:** 2 whitish wing bars; whitish underparts washed dark gray on sides and breast; sometimes complete breast bar. Generally lacks eye-ring. Dull orange lower mandible; undertail coverts sometimes yellowish. **VOICE:** Plaintive whistle *pee-a-wee,* slurring down, then up. **STATUS AND RANGE:** Rare migrant through Bahamas, Cuba, Cayman Islands, Providencia, and San Andrés. Most frequent September and October, less so March and April. Few December and January records. **HABITAT:** Mixed and coastal woodlands, forests, forest edges, scrub, open areas, and gardens.

● **WESTERN WOOD-PEWEE** *Contopus sordidulus* 15–17cm (5.75–6.75in). Only accurately distinguished from Eastern Wood-pewee by voice. **VOICE:** Nasal, descending *peeyee* or *peeer.* **STATUS AND RANGE:** Very rare migrant in Cuba September and October. **HABITAT:** Woodlands and river groves.

● **CRESCENT-EYED PEWEE** *Contopus caribaeus* 15–16.5cm (5.75–6.5in). Often erect crest. White crescent behind eye. Lacks wing bars. Flicks tail upon landing. **VOICE:** Prolonged, thin whistle. Sometimes feeble *vi-vi.* **STATUS AND RANGE:** Common in northern Bahamas and Cuba, its entire range. **HABITAT:** Pine forests, woods, forest edges, tree plantations, brushy scrub, swamp edges, and mangroves

● **HISPANIOLAN PEWEE** *Contopus hispaniolensis* 15–16cm (5.75–6.25in). Underparts gray with olive, yellow or brown wash; wing bars inconspicuous or absent. Lower mandible pale at base. Flicks tail upon landing. **VOICE:** Strong, mournful *purr, pip-pip-pip-pip.* Dawn song loud, rapid-fire volley with paired syllables rising in pitch. **STATUS AND RANGE:** Endemic to Hispaniola where common and widespread. **HABITAT:** Pine and broadleaf forests, forest edges, shade coffee, and orchards, at all elevations.

● **JAMAICAN PEWEE** *Contopus pallidus* 15cm (5.75in). Small flycatcher with dark olive-gray upperparts, darker on head. Underparts buffish-brown. Lower mandible orangish; wing bars absent or indistinct. Tail slightly notched. Flicks tail on landing. **VOICE:** Plaintive *pee.* Also, rising then falling *oéeoh.* Dawn song 2 alternating phrases. **STATUS AND RANGE:** Endemic to Jamaica where common and widespread. **HABITAT:** Mid-elevation forests; also high mountain forests.

● **PUERTO RICAN PEWEE** *Contopus portoricensis* 15cm (5.75in). Small flycatcher with brownish upperparts and blackish wings and tail. Underparts buffish-brown, lower mandible pale. **VOICE:** Sweet, high-pitched trill, sometimes rising. Also repetitive trill. **STATUS AND RANGE:** Endemic to Puerto Rico: fairly common in western two-thirds of island. **HABITAT:** Moist forests and woods at moderate to low elevation; also drier habitats and mangroves.

● **LESSER ANTILLEAN PEWEE** *Contopus latirostris* 15cm (5.75in). Small flycatcher with brownish-olive upperparts, yellowish-brown underparts, black wings and tail. Lower mandible pale at base. **VOICE:** Emphatic rising *pree-e-e* and high-pitched, repeated *peet-peet-peet.* **STATUS AND RANGE:** Fairly common but local resident known only from Guadeloupe, Dominica, and Martinique. Sporadic reports from St Christopher. **HABITAT:** Mountain forests and woods, sparingly drier forests, mangroves, and scrub near sea level.

● **ST LUCIA PEWEE** *Contopus oberi* 15cm (5.75in). Small flycatcher with dark olive-brown upperparts and reddish-brown underparts. Black wings and tail; bill has pale base to lower mandible. **VOICE:** Emphatic rising *pree-e-e* and high-pitched *peet-peet-peet.* **STATUS AND RANGE:** Endemic to St Lucia where fairly common. **HABITAT:** Moist forests at higher altitudes; scarce in lower, drier habitats.

● **EASTERN PHOEBE** *Sayornis phoebe* 16.5–18cm (6.5–7in). Dark head; no eye-ring; blackish wings; no wing bars. Often pumps its longish, dark tail. Underparts whitish with pale yellow wash, especially September and October. **STATUS AND RANGE:** Very rare migrant in Cuba and Bahamas mid-September to February. **HABITAT:** Woodland edges, fence lines, and hedgerows. Often near fresh water.

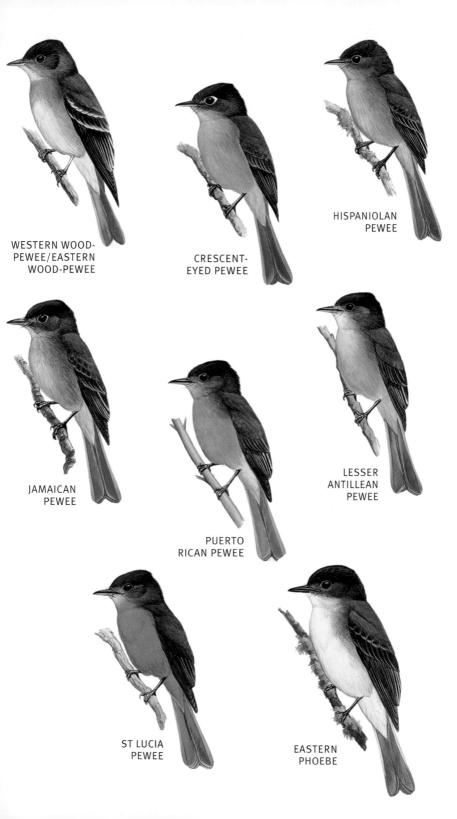

WESTERN WOOD-
PEWEE/EASTERN
WOOD-PEWEE

CRESCENT-
EYED PEWEE

HISPANIOLAN
PEWEE

JAMAICAN
PEWEE

PUERTO
RICAN PEWEE

LESSER
ANTILLEAN
PEWEE

ST LUCIA
PEWEE

EASTERN
PHOEBE

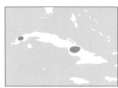

● **CUBAN PALM CROW** *Corvus minutus* 43cm (17in). Large, completely black, with faint violet sheen fading to dull brown-black in worn plumage. Nostrils covered by bristles. Arboreal; forms small flocks. Slightly smaller than Cuban Crow; neck appears shorter in flight. Identify by voice. Identical to Hispaniolan Palm Crow but ranges do not overlap. **VOICE:** Harsh *craaao*, initial abrupt rise in pitch, levels off, falls slightly at end. **STATUS AND RANGE:** Endemic to Cuba: rare and very local. Confined to northwestern part of Sierra de Los Organos in Pinar del Río Province and Camagüey Province. Endangered. **HABITAT:** Forests, scrub, and palm savannas.

● **HISPANIOLAN PALM CROW** *Corvus palmarum* 43cm (17in). Large, completely black, with purplish and bluish sheen fading to dull brown-black in worn plumage. Flicks tail downward. Forms flocks. Considerably smaller and less robust than White-necked Crow. Identify by voice. **FLIGHT:** Wings appear shorter than White-necked Crow's and wing flapping is steadier. **VOICE:** Harsh, nasal *aaar* (vowel sound as in "fast"). **STATUS AND RANGE:** Endemic to Hispaniola where common. **HABITAT:** Primarily mountain pine forests, irregular at lower elevations.

● **CUBAN CROW** *Corvus nasicus* 45–48cm (17.5–19in). Large, noisy black crow with purple sheen and conspicuous nostrils. Usually in flocks. **VOICE:** Much louder and noisier than parrots, especially in large flocks. Characteristic high-pitched call with nasal quality, *caah-caaah*. Also turkey-like gobbling, and diverse guttural phrases similar to parrots. **STATUS AND RANGE:** Cuba: common resident. Bahamas: common on North and Middle Caicos, rare on Providenciales. These islands comprise entire range. **HABITAT:** Primarily thin forests, but also palm plantations, treed borders of swamps, croplands, and garbage dumps.

● **WHITE-NECKED CROW** *Corvus leucognaphalus* 48–51cm (19–20in). Large, entirely black, with large bill. Upperparts have violet sheen; white at base of neck not seen except in display. Forms flocks. Identify from smaller Hispaniolan Palm Crow by voice. **VOICE:** Wide variety, including *caw*, clucking, gurgling, bubbling, and laugh-like calls and squawks. **STATUS AND RANGE:** Endemic and locally common in Hispaniola. Threatened. **HABITAT:** Primarily moist uplands, but occurs from semi-arid scrublands and open lowlands with scattered trees to mountain pine forests.

● **JAMAICAN CROW** *Corvus jamaicensis* 38cm (15in). Large, entirely dull black, with large bill. **FLIGHT:** Slow and labored. **VOICE:** Loud *craa-craa*, also semi-musical jabbering. **STATUS AND RANGE:** Endemic to Jamaica where locally common. Most frequent in Cockpit Country and John Crow Mountains. **HABITAT:** Primarily mid-elevations in undisturbed wet limestone forests. Less frequent in disturbed wooded areas and park-like country at mid-elevations.

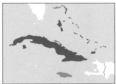

● **EUROPEAN STARLING** *Sturnus vulgaris* 22cm (8.5in). Glossy black, with short tail. Forms flocks. **BREEDING ADULT:** Bill yellow. **NON-BREEDING ADULT:** Underparts heavily flecked with white spots; dark bill. **FLIGHT:** Straight, unlike other black birds in region. Wings distinctively swept back. **VOICE:** Wide variety of whistles, squeaks, and raspy notes. **STATUS AND RANGE:** Introduced. Fairly common, but local. In Jamaica, and on Grand Bahama and Biminis in Bahamas. Rare elsewhere in Bahamas and eastern Cuba October through March. **HABITAT:** Primarily open lowlands, including pastures and gardens.

● **HILL MYNA** *Gracula religiosa* 30cm (12in). Black overall, with bright orange bill, yellow wattle on hindneck, and white wing patch. **VOICE:** Rich, somewhat plaintive, 3-syllabled whistle accented on 2nd note. One of the best mimics. **STATUS AND RANGE:** Introduced. Uncommon and very local in Puerto Rico along north and east coasts. **HABITAT:** Open woodlands with dead snags.

CUBAN/HISPANIOLAN
PALM CROW

CUBAN CROW

WHITE-NECKED CROW

JAMAICAN CROW

imm

non-br
adult ♂

EUROPEAN
STARLING

HILL
MYNA

br

● **PURPLE MARTIN** *Progne subis* 20–22cm (8–8.5in). **ADULT MALE:** Entirely bluish-purple. Indistinguishable from Cuban Martin. **ADULT FEMALE AND IMMATURE:** Scaled pattern on grayish-brown breast; light gray patches on sides of neck; indistinct border between darker breast and whitish belly. (Female Caribbean Martin has brown wash on breast, rather than scaled pattern.) **VOICE:** Gurgling, including high *twick-twick*. Also high, melodious warble. **STATUS AND RANGE:** Common migrant in Cuba and Cayman Islands (Grand Cayman); uncommon in Bahamas, primarily mid-August through mid-October, rare in March, infrequent in other months. Vagrant elsewhere. **HABITAT:** Towns and open areas.

● **CUBAN MARTIN** *Progne cryptoleuca* 20–22cm (8–8.5in). **MALE:** Bluish-purple overall. Indistinguishable from Purple Martin. **FEMALE:** White belly and abdomen contrast sharply with brown breast, sides, throat, and chin. (Female Purple Martin paler brown on breast; throat and chin blends gradually into whitish belly. Both sexes of Caribbean Martin similar to female Cuban Martin in underparts' pattern, but white below restricted to lower belly and abdomen. Also, female Caribbean Martin has less contrast between white and dark of underparts.) **VOICE:** Gurgling, including high-pitched *twick-twick*, like a vibrating wire. Also strong, melodious warble. **STATUS AND RANGE:** Common breeding resident on Cuba February through October. Vagrant in Bahamas. **HABITAT:** Cities and towns. Also swamp borders and open areas, particularly in lowlands.

 ● **CARIBBEAN MARTIN** *Progne dominicensis* 20cm (8in). Bicolored martin. **MALE:** Upperparts, head, and throat blue; belly and abdomen white. **FEMALE AND IMMATURE:** Blue of underparts replaced by brownish wash that blends into white of belly. **VOICE:** Gurgling, including high *twick-twick*. Also melodious warble and gritty *churr*. **STATUS AND RANGE:** Fairly common breeding resident in much of West Indies January to September. Vagrant in southern Bahamas and Cayman Islands and absent from northern Bahamas and Cuba. **HABITAT:** Towns, open areas, freshwater bodies, and coastal rock promontories.

 ● **NORTHERN ROUGH-WINGED SWALLOW** *Stelgidopteryx serripennis* 12.5–14cm (5–5.5in). Brown above, with white underparts blending to pale brown on throat. **STATUS AND RANGE:** Generally rare migrant and rarer non-breeding resident in Bahamas, Cuba, Jamaica, Hispaniola, and Cayman Islands August through April. Very rare in Virgin Islands. **HABITAT:** Open fields and wetlands.

● **GOLDEN SWALLOW** *Tachycineta euchrysea* 12.5cm (5in). Small swallow. **ADULT:** Iridescent bluish-green upperparts with golden sheen; white underparts; moderately forked tail. **FEMALE:** Duller, grayish on breast. **IMMATURE:** Duller above; gray breast band. (Tree Swallow has shallower tail notch, relatively shorter wings and no golden sheen on upperparts.) **VOICE:** Soft twittering. **STATUS AND RANGE:** Uncommon resident in Hispaniola. Increasingly rare and very local resident in Jamaica. Endangered. Hispaniola and Jamaica comprise entire range. **HABITAT:** In Hispaniola, relatively open country and pine forests of high mountains, also over rain forests. In Jamaica, open areas, such as sugarcane fields on northern fringe of Cockpit Country.

PURPLE MARTIN/
CUBAN MARTIN

adult ♂

CARIBBEAN
MARTIN

adult ♀

♀ & imm

CUBAN
MARTIN

PURPLE
MARTIN

NORTHERN ROUGH-
WINGED SWALLOW

GOLDEN
SWALLOW

TREE SWALLOW *Tachycineta bicolor* 12.5–15cm (5–5.75in). **ADULT:** Blue-green above, with entirely white underparts and slightly notched tail. Wing linings pale gray. **IMMATURE:** Brown upperparts. (Bahama Swallow has deeply forked tail and white wing linings.) **VOICE:** Mostly silent in West Indies. **STATUS AND RANGE:** Common non-breeding resident in Cuba and locally common in Cayman Islands primarily November through May, but occurring September through June. Uncommon in northern Bahamas and Jamaica; rare in Hispaniola, Puerto Rico, and Virgin Islands (St Croix); very rare in southern Bahamas. **HABITAT:** Swamps, marshes, rice fields, and other wetlands.

BAHAMA SWALLOW *Tachycineta cyaneoviridis* 15.5cm (6in). **ADULT:** Dark greenish above, with blue wings, white underparts including wing linings, and deeply forked tail. (Tree Swallow has slightly notched tail and pale gray wing linings.) **FEMALE:** Slightly duller. **IMMATURE:** Brownish upperparts; tail less forked. **VOICE:** Metallic *chep* or *chi-chep*. **STATUS AND RANGE:** Endemic to Bahamas: common on Grand Bahama, Abaco, and Andros, infrequent on other islands. Vagrant in eastern Cuba. **HABITAT:** Pine forests, towns, clearings, and near cliffs.

CAVE SWALLOW *Pterochelidon fulva* 12.5–14cm (5–5.5in). Dark reddish-brown rump; pale reddish-brown ear-patch, throat, breast, and sides; slightly notched tail. (Cliff Swallow has dark reddish-brown throat and ear-patch and lighter forehead.) **VOICE:** Chattering or twittering. Also rather musical *twit*. **STATUS AND RANGE:** Common breeding resident through Greater Antilles. Present year-round in Jamaica, Hispaniola, and Puerto Rico, but in Cuba most birds depart September through February. Rare breeding resident on South Andros (Bahamas). Rare migrant in Cayman and Virgin Islands. Vagrant elsewhere in West Indies. **HABITAT:** Principally over fields, wetlands, cliffs, and towns.

BARN SWALLOW *Hirundo rustica* 15–19cm (5.75–7.5in). **ADULT:** Primarily tan underparts; dark reddish-brown throat; deeply forked tail with white spots. **IMMATURE:** Throat and upper breast tan; remainder of underparts white; tail less deeply forked. **VOICE:** Thin, unmusical *chit*. **STATUS AND RANGE:** Generally common migrant throughout West Indies primarily September through October and April through May, but occurs every month. **HABITAT:** Open areas over fields and swamps, primarily along coast.

BANK SWALLOW *Riparia riparia* 12.5–14cm (5–5.5in). Dark breast band; dark brown upperparts. (Antillean Palm Swift has white rump; longer, narrower wings; more rapid, darting flight.) **STATUS AND RANGE:** Migrant through West Indies primarily September through December and April through May. Uncommon to rare. **HABITAT:** Primarily open coastal areas.

CLIFF SWALLOW *Pterochelidon pyrrhonota* 12.5–15cm (5–5.75in). Dark reddish-brown chin, throat, and ear-patch; buff-colored forehead and rump; slightly notched tail. (Cave Swallow has darker forehead and much paler ear-patch and throat.) **VOICE:** Short, melodious, repeated note. **STATUS AND RANGE:** Uncommon migrant in Cayman Islands, Barbados, and San Andrés; rare in Bahamas, Cuba, Virgin Islands, Guadeloupe, Dominica, and St Lucia; very rare or vagrant elsewhere in West Indies. Occurs late August through early December and late March through early May. **HABITAT:** Primarily along coast.

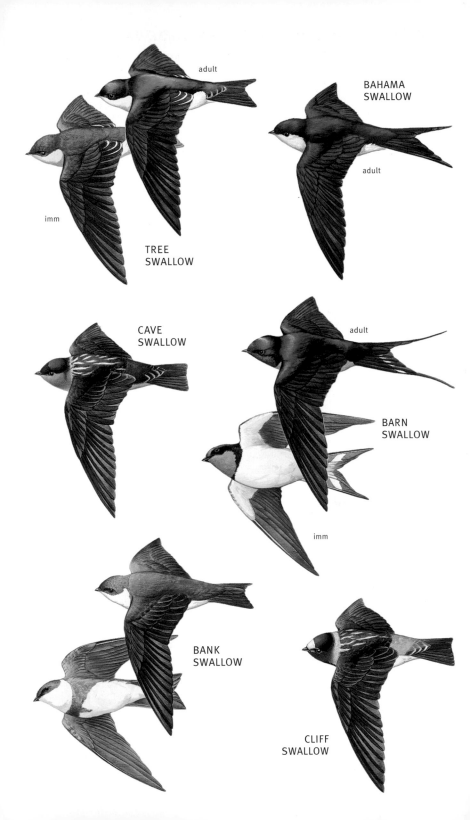

adult

BAHAMA
SWALLOW

adult

imm

TREE
SWALLOW

CAVE
SWALLOW

adult

BARN
SWALLOW

imm

BANK
SWALLOW

CLIFF
SWALLOW

PALMCHAT *Dulus dominicus* 20cm (8in). Dark brown above; underparts whitish and heavily streaked with brown. Arboreal; forms flocks. **VOICE:** Noisy, particularly around nest, producing array of strange call notes. **STATUS AND RANGE:** Endemic to Hispaniola: common, conspicuous, and widespread in lowlands to mid-elevations. **HABITAT:** Primarily royal palm savannas, also other open areas with scattered trees.

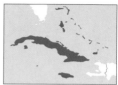

CEDAR WAXWING *Bombycilla cedrorum* 18–18.5cm (7–7.25in). Crest; yellow-tipped tail. Forms flocks. **VOICE:** Clear, short, high-pitched trill. Also unmusical *che-che-check*. **STATUS AND RANGE:** Rare non-breeding resident; numbers vary greatly year to year. Most frequent in Cuba: sometimes fairly common October through April. Rare in Jamaica and Cayman Islands primarily December through April; very rare in Bahamas. Vagrant elsewhere in West Indies. **HABITAT:** Mountain rain forests to lowland cultivated edges and urban gardens.

CUBAN GNATCATCHER *Polioptila lembeyei* 10.5cm (4in). Small and slender. Gray above, grayish-white below. Long black tail (often cocked upward) has white outer feathers. White eye-ring; black crescent from eye to behind ear. (Blue-gray Gnatcatcher lacks black facial crescent.) **FEMALE:** Paler. **VOICE:** Loud and melodious. Song begins with 4 whistles, followed by trill and thin varied whisper, *pss-psss-psss-psss-tttiizzzt-zzzz-ttizzz-tzi-tzi-tzi*. **STATUS AND RANGE:** Endemic to Cuba: common in east, absent in west and patchily distributed in between. **HABITAT:** Fairly dense coastal thorn-scrub, sometimes inland in similar vegetation.

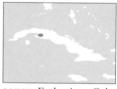

BLUE-GRAY GNATCATCHER *Polioptila caerulea* 11cm (4.25in). Small and active. Grayish above, white below; white eye-ring. Long black tail (often cocked upward) has white outer feathers. **MALE:** Bluish tint to upperparts and fine black eyebrow stripe during breeding. **FEMALE:** Paler; lacks eyebrow stripe. **VOICE:** Mew-like call, similar to Gray Catbird, usually 2 syllables, *zpee-zpee*. Also soft whisper-like song. **STATUS AND RANGE:** Common resident on larger islands of Bahamas, augmented by migrants September through November. Common non-breeding resident in Cuba September through April. Uncommon on Cayman Islands. **HABITAT:** Scrubland. In Cayman Islands, also mangroves. In Cuba, all lowland and mid-elevation habitats from forests to gardens.

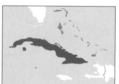

ZAPATA WREN *Ferminia cerverai* 16cm (6.25in). Sparrow-sized. Brown striped black except for grayish underparts. Tail, bill, and legs long. Wings short and round. Highly secretive. (House Wren smaller, less heavily barred, does not occur in sawgrass marshes.) **VOICE:** High, strong, and very musical. Starts with low guttural note transforming to canary-like warble. Usually repeats song 3 times. Also harsh notes and sharp *chip*s of various tones. **STATUS AND RANGE:** Endemic to Cuba: limited to Zapata Swamp. Threatened. **HABITAT:** Sawgrass marshes.

BROWN-HEADED NUTHATCH *Sitta pusilla* 9.5–11cm (3.75–4.25in). Bluish-gray upperparts; brown crown; dark brown line through eye; white hindneck patch. Climbs up and down pine trunks and limbs, often upside down. **VOICE:** Weak, fast, squeaky high-pitched chatter. **STATUS AND RANGE:** Very rare and local resident on Grand Bahama in Bahamas. Endangered. **HABITAT:** Limited to pine barrens.

HOUSE WREN *Troglodytes aedon* 11.5–13cm (4.5–5in). Small, active, brown bird with relatively large head. **ADULT:** Reddish-gray above; pale eyebrow stripe; variably dark brown to whitish below. Bill all dark or with lower mandible yellow; wings and tail heavily barred black. **VOICE:** Bursting, gurgling warble. Also sharp chatter. **STATUS AND RANGE:** Common resident in Dominica; locally so in lowlands of Grenada; uncommon in St Vincent; rare and local in St Lucia where confined to northeastern dry coastal scrub. St Lucia and St Vincent races are threatened. Very rare migrant in northern Bahamas. **HABITAT:** Moist upland forests to arid coastal areas and human settlements.

PALMCHAT

CEDAR
WAXWING

imm

adult

CUBAN
GNATCATCHER

♂

ZAPATA
WREN

BLUE-GRAY
GNATCATCHER

♀

br ♂

adult

BROWN-HEADED
NUTHATCH

St Lucia race

HOUSE
WREN

Grenada race

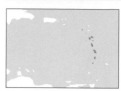

BROWN TREMBLER *Cinclocerthia ruficauda* 23–26cm (9–10in). Dark reddish-olive upperparts; buffish-brown underparts; long bill, slightly down-curved near tip; yellow eye. Often droops wings and trembles; cocks tail over back. (Gray Trembler grayer above, whiter below.) **VOICE:** Semi-melodic phrases; harsh alarm notes. **STATUS AND RANGE:** Fairly common resident in Saba, Guadeloupe, and Dominica; uncommon in St Christopher, Nevis, Montserrat, St Lucia, and St Vincent; rare in Martinique and Grenada. These islands comprise entire range. **HABITAT:** Wet forests, also secondary forests and drier woodlands. In St Lucia, only dry forests and scrub.

GRAY TREMBLER *Cinclocerthia gutturalis* 23–26cm (9–10in). Upperparts dark olive-gray, underparts grayish-white (Martinique) or bright white (St Lucia). Bill very long and slightly down-curved near tip; eye white. Often droops wings and trembles; cocks tail over back. **VOICE:** Wavering, whistled phrases; also harsh alarm notes. **STATUS AND RANGE:** Fairly common resident in Martinique and St Lucia which account for entire range. **HABITAT:** Mature moist forests, usually at higher elevations. Less often in second growth, dry scrub, and open woodlands at lower elevations.

GRAY CATBIRD *Dumetella carolinensis* 23cm (9in). Entirely gray with black cap, reddish-brown undertail coverts, and long tail often cocked slightly upwards. **VOICE:** Distinctive soft cat-like *mew*. Also *pert-pert-pert*. Song disconnected phrases including mews, imitations, and pauses. **STATUS AND RANGE:** Common migrant and non-breeding resident in Bahamas, Cayman Islands, and Providencia; uncommon in Cuba, Jamaica, and San Andrés; rare in Hispaniola. Occurs primarily October through April. **HABITAT:** Thickets and dense undergrowth.

WHITE-BREASTED THRASHER *Ramphocinclus brachyurus* Martinique: 20–21cm (7.75–8.25in); St Lucia: 23–25cm (9–10in). **ADULT:** Dark brown upperparts, clear white underparts; red eye; long, slightly down-curved bill. Often droops wings and may twitch or flick wings when excited or curious. **STATUS AND RANGE:** Local, increasingly rare resident in Martinique and St Lucia. In Martinique, found at Presqu'île de la Caravelle. In St Lucia, restricted to east coast from Petite Anse south to Anse Pouvert and Frigate Island Reserve. These islands comprise entire range. Critically endangered. **HABITAT:** Dense thickets of semi-arid wooded stream valleys and ravines.

BAHAMA MOCKINGBIRD *Mimus gundlachii* 28cm (11in). Large; upperparts brownish-gray with fine streaks; underparts whitish with dark streaks on sides. Long, broad tail, almost fan-shaped in flight, tipped with white; 2 white wing bars not conspicuous in flight. (Pearly-Eyed Thrasher has darker upperparts, pale bill, and white eye.) **VOICE:** Series of phrases, each repeated several times. **STATUS AND RANGE:** Generally common resident in Bahamas, cays of northern Cuba, and Hellshire Hills of southern Jamaica. These islands comprise entire range. **HABITAT:** Semi-arid scrub, woodlands, and human habitation.

Guadeloupe race

Dominica race

BROWN TREMBLER

GRAY TREMBLER

Martinique race

GRAY CATBIRD

WHITE-BREASTED THRASHER

BAHAMA MOCKINGBIRD

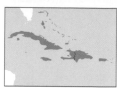

NORTHERN MOCKINGBIRD *Mimus polyglottos* 23–28cm (9–11in). Gray above, grayish-white below. Wings and tail conspicuously marked with white; long tail often cocked upward. (Bahama Mockingbird larger; lacks white in wings.) **VOICE:** Clear, melodious phrases, each repeated several times. Also loud *tchack*. **STATUS AND RANGE:** Common resident throughout Bahamas, Greater Antilles, Virgin and Cayman Islands. Introduced to New Providence. **HABITAT:** Open country with scattered bushes or trees, including semi-arid scrub, open mangrove forests, gardens, parks, and settled areas. Primarily lowlands.

TROPICAL MOCKINGBIRD *Mimus gilvus* 23–24cm (9–9.5in). Gray upperparts and head; broad, blackish eye-line; white eyebrow stripe; wings darker than back; 2 wing bars. Tail long, conspicuously tipped white. **VOICE:** Repeated couplets of musical whistles and phrases lasting several seconds. Also harsh *chuck*. **STATUS AND RANGE:** Fairly common resident on Guiana Island off Antigua, Guadeloupe, Dominica, Martinique, St Lucia, St Vincent, Grenadines, Grenada, and San Andrés. In Guadeloupe, very local at extreme eastern end. Expanding range northward. **HABITAT:** Open areas around human dwellings, dry lowland scrub, and agricultural areas.

BROWN THRASHER *Toxostoma rufum* 29cm (11.5in). Upperparts reddish-brown; long tail; pale white wing bars; buffish-white underparts boldly streaked dark brown; dark brown mustache streak; yellow-orange eye; long dark bill. **STATUS AND RANGE:** Vagrant. Wanderers irregularly reach Bahamas and Cuba October and November. **HABITAT:** Dense undergrowth.

SCALY-BREASTED THRASHER *Allenia fusca* 23cm (9in). White underparts heavily scaled with grayish-brown from throat to belly; 1 whitish wing bar; black bill; yellow-brown eye; tail tipped white. (Pearly-eyed Thrasher larger, with large yellowish bill; no wing bars.) **VOICE:** Repeats phrases similar to Tropical Mockingbird, but with less vigor. **STATUS AND RANGE:** Generally fairly common resident from Saba and St Bartholomew south to St Vincent. Rare and local in Grenada and possibly extirpated on St Eustatius, Barbuda, and Barbados. These islands comprise entire range. **HABITAT:** Moist and semi-arid forests and woodlands.

PEARLY-EYED THRASHER *Margarops fuscatus* 28–30cm (11–12in). Upperparts brown; underparts white, streaked with brown. White eye; large yellowish bill; large white patches on tail tip. (Scaly-breasted Thrasher smaller; bill black; 1 whitish wing bar.) **VOICE:** Series of 1- to 3-syllable phrases with lengthy pauses between. Also many raucous call notes. **STATUS AND RANGE:** Common resident in southern and central Bahamas; spreading northward. Common in Puerto Rico, Virgin Islands, and Lesser Antilles south to St Lucia, except Martinique where uncommon. On Hispaniola, only on Beata Island and northeast corner of Dominican Republic. Outside West Indies occurs on Bonaire. **HABITAT:** Thickets, woodlands, and forests at all elevations from mangroves and coastal palm groves to mountain tops. Also urban areas.

NORTHERN
MOCKINGBIRD

adult

imm

adult

Southern Lesser
Antilles race

adult

TROPICAL
MOCKINGBIRD

San Andrés race

BROWN
THRASHER

SCALY-BREASTED
THRASHER

PEARLY-EYED
THRASHER

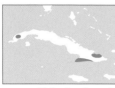

● **CUBAN SOLITAIRE** *Myadestes elisabeth* 19cm (7.5in). Plain-colored; flycatcher-like. White eye-ring; dark mustache stripe; white outertail feathers; small bill. **VOICE:** Very high-pitched flute-like song. Melodious and varied. Similar to rubbing wet finger against fine glass. **STATUS AND RANGE:** Endemic to Cuba: common, but quite local. In western Cuba, only in Sierra de los Organos, Sierra del Rosario and Sierra de la Güira. In east, more widely distributed. Threatened. **HABITAT:** Dense, humid forests of hills and mountains.

● **RUFOUS-THROATED SOLITAIRE** *Myadestes genibarbis* 19cm (7.5in). Reddish-brown throat, foreneck and undertail coverts; light gray breast; white outer feathers visible in flight. St Vincent: black above with olive uppertail-coverts. **VOICE:** Haunt-ingly beautiful minor-key whistle, most often at dawn. **STATUS AND RANGE:** Fairly common resident in Jamaica, Hispaniola, Dominica, Martinique, St Lucia, and St Vincent. These islands comprise entire range. **HABITAT:** Dense, moist mountain forests.

● **SWAINSON'S THRUSH** *Catharus ustulatus* 17.5cm (7in). Grayish-brown above; whitish below, with brownish spots on breast. Buff-colored eye-ring and lores give spectacled appear-ance. **STATUS AND RANGE:** Rare migrant in Cuba, Jamaica, and Cayman Islands; very rare in northern Bahamas. Occurs Septem-ber through November and March through May. Abundance fluctuates year to year. **HABITAT:** Open woods and tree clumps with much leaf-litter and little undergrowth. Also gardens.

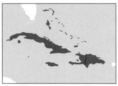

● **VEERY** *Catharus fuscescens* 16–18cm (6.25–7in). Upperparts reddish-brown, rarely olive-brown. Underparts whitish with faint spots on buffish breast. Inconspicuous grayish eye-ring. More reddish-brown above and more lightly spotted below than other migrant thrushes. **STATUS AND RANGE:** Rare migrant in northern Bahamas, Cuba, Jamaica, and Hispaniola; very rare in southern Bahamas and Cayman Islands. Vagrant elsewhere in West Indies. Occurs September through October and April through May. **HABITAT:** Open forests, wood-lands with substantial undergrowth, scrub and gardens.

● **HERMIT THRUSH** *Catharus guttatus* 19cm (7.5in). Olive-brown upperparts, reddish-brown tail, and whitish underparts with buffish wash. Large spots on breast form streaks from sides of throat to flanks. Narrow buffish-white eye-ring. (Swainson's, Bicknell's, and Gray-cheeked Thrushes, and Veery, similar but lack contrasting dark back and reddish-brown tail.) **STATUS AND RANGE:** Very rare non-breeding resident in northern Bahamas October through April. **HABITAT:** Forest thickets.

CUBAN
SOLITAIRE

imm

St Vincent race

Jamaica race

RUFOUS-THROATED SOLITAIRE

SWAINSON'S THRUSH

VEERY

HERMIT THRUSH

● **EASTERN BLUEBIRD** *Sialia sialis* 15–16.5cm (5.75–6.5in). **ADULT MALE:** Bright blue upperparts including tail and wings; reddish throat, breast, sides, flanks, and upper belly; white lower belly and undertail coverts. **ADULT FEMALE:** Duller with whitish eye-ring. **IMMATURE:** Grayish-blue above flecked white; breast and upper belly whitish with conspicuous gray ringlets. **VOICE:** Clear whistle *chur-lee*. **STATUS AND RANGE:** Vagrant in Bahamas, western Cuba and Virgin Islands. **HABITAT:** Field edges and open country with hedgerows.

● **GRAY-CHEEKED THRUSH** *Catharus minimus* 16–20cm (6.25–8in). Grayish-brown above, whitish below; spots on breast and throat. Gray cheeks; no conspicuous eye-ring; no reddish-brown coloration. Extremely similar to Bicknell's Thrush. (Swainson's Thrush has distinct buff-colored eye-ring.) **STATUS AND RANGE:** Rare migrant in western Cuba. Status unclear in Bahamas, eastern Cuba, Hispaniola, Puerto Rico, and Virgin Islands. Probably rare migrant in Jamaica and Cayman Islands. **HABITAT:** Forests and woodlands.

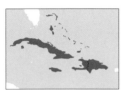

● **BICKNELL'S THRUSH** *Catharus bicknelli* 16–19cm (6.25–7.5in). Buffish-brown upperparts; white underparts and sides of throat; breast cream-buff, boldly spotted black. Grayish cheeks and lores; dark reddish-brown tail. (Gray-cheeked Thrush slightly larger, grayer above with darker lores, whiter breast, and pinkish rather than yellow on lower mandible, but characters overlap. Too similar to separate accurately.) **VOICE:** Generally silent in West Indies. **STATUS AND RANGE:** Uncommon migrant and non-breeding resident in Hispaniola late September through early May. Likely rare migrant in Bahamas, particularly southernmost islands, eastern Cuba, and Jamaica September through November and March through May. **HABITAT:** Broadleaf forests, generally at higher elevations. Also woods or gardens with large trees.

● **WOOD THRUSH** *Hylocichla mustelina* 20cm (8in). Cinnamon-colored crown, conspicuous white eye-ring and white underparts with heavy dark spots. (Ovenbird smaller, with cinnamon-colored crown bordered by black stripes.) **VOICE:** Emits short *pit-pit-pit* notes. **STATUS AND RANGE:** Rare migrant in Cuba and very rare in northern Bahamas. Vagrant elsewhere. Occurs primarily mid-September through November and March through April. A few may remain in Cuba December through February. **HABITAT:** Tree plantations and large gardens.

● **AMERICAN ROBIN** *Turdus migratorius* 23–28cm (9–11in). Primarily dull red underparts. **MALE:** Blackish head and tail. **FEMALE:** Paler. **STATUS AND RANGE:** Rare non-breeding resident October through April in northern Bahamas and Cuba. Numbers vary year to year. **HABITAT:** Open woodlands, gardens, parks, and open scrub.

● **WHITE-EYED THRUSH** *Turdus jamaicensis* 23cm (9in). **ADULT:** Dark gray above, paler below. Reddish-brown head, conspicuous whitish eye, white breast bar. **VOICE:** Repeated phrases like Northern Mockingbird, but louder and less variable. Whistled *hee-haw* often included. Also other high-pitched, harsh call notes. **STATUS AND RANGE:** Endemic to Jamaica: fairly common in mountains. **HABITAT:** Wet forests from hills to mountain summits. Also shade coffee plantations and other wooded areas at moderate elevations.

● **LA SELLE THRUSH** *Turdus swalesi* 26cm (10in). Grayish-black head and upperparts; a few white streaks on throat. Red lower breast and sides; broad, white streak on belly. **VOICE:** Series of deliberate *tu-re-oo* and *cho-ho-cho* calls continued indefinitely. Also loud *wheury-wheury-wheury* and gurgling notes. **STATUS AND RANGE:** Endemic to Hispaniola: locally common in Haiti in Massif de la Selle; rare and local in Dominican Republic in Sierra de Baoruco, Sierra de Neiba, and Cordillera Central. Endangered. **HABITAT:** Low, dense vegetation and wet forests, including pines in high mountains.

adult ♀

GRAY-CHEEKED/
BICKNELL'S THRUSH

adult ♂

EASTERN BLUEBIRD

WOOD THRUSH

AMERICAN ROBIN

WHITE-EYED THRUSH

LA SELLE
THRUSH

FOREST THRUSH *Cichlherminia lherminieri* 25–27cm (10–10.5in). Upperparts grayish-brown; underparts brown with white spots on breast, flanks, and upper belly giving scaled effect. Legs, bill and skin around eye yellow. Scaled underparts distinguish it from Bare-eyed Robin. **VOICE:** Soft, musical clear notes. **STATUS AND RANGE:** Uncommon resident in Montserrat, Guadeloupe, and Dominica; rare in St Lucia. These islands comprise entire range. **HABITAT:** Moist mountain forests.

COCOA THRUSH *Turdus fumigatus* 23cm (9in). **ADULT:** Upperparts entirely rich brown; underparts paler. Whitish throat patch with brown streaks; dark bill. **VOICE:** Series of loud, musical phrases, each short and differing from one another, with brief pause between each. Sometimes plaintive, 4-note call, first 2 notes higher, last 2 lower. Also *weeo, weeo, weeo*. **STATUS AND RANGE:** Fairly common resident in St Vincent and Grenada. **HABITAT:** Forests, cacao plantations, and croplands with scattered trees. More frequent at higher elevations.

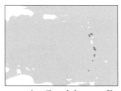

BARE-EYED ROBIN *Turdus nudigenis* 23cm (9in). **ADULT:** Plain olive-gray upperparts, paler underparts; white throat with brown streaks. Broad, pale yellow eye-ring; yellowish bill and feet. (Forest Thrush has scaled underparts.) **VOICE:** Loud, liquid, variable *cheerily cheer-up cheerio*, especially at dawn. Also squeaky *miter-ee*. **STATUS AND RANGE:** Fairly common resident in Martinique, St Lucia, St Vincent, Grenadines, and Grenada. Uncommon in Guadeloupe. Expanding range northward through Lesser Antilles. **HABITAT:** Primarily lowlands in drier and moderately moist open woodlands, plantations, second growth, and forest borders.

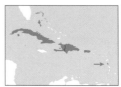

RED-LEGGED THRUSH *Turdus plumbeus* 25–28cm (10–11in). Gray upperparts; reddish legs and bill; red eye-ring; large white tail tips. Underparts very variable. **VOICE:** *low wéecha*; a rapid, high-pitched *chu-wéek, chu-wéek, chu-wéek*; and a loud *wheet-wheet*. Song melodious, but monotonous 1- to 3-syllabled phrases similar to Pearly-eyed Thrasher. **STATUS AND RANGE:** Common and widespread resident in northern Bahamas, Cuba, Hispaniola, Puerto Rico, and Dominica. Fairly common in Cayman Islands (Cayman Brac). These islands comprise entire range. **HABITAT:** Woodlands and forests at all elevations, scrub, thick undergrowth, gardens, and shade coffee plantations.

WHITE-CHINNED THRUSH *Turdus aurantius* 24cm (9.5in). Highly terrestrial. **ADULT:** Dark gray above, paler below; conspicuous white diagonal bar on wing; white chin; orange bill and legs; and cocks tail upward. **VOICE:** Variable. Musical song, a shrill whistle *p'lice, p'lice*, and repeated chicken-like clucking. **STATUS AND RANGE:** Endemic to Jamaica: common and widespread. **HABITAT:** Primarily forests, woodlands, road edges, cultivated areas, and gardens, in mountains at middle and high elevations. Less frequent in lowlands.

FOREST THRUSH

Dominica race

Montserrat race

BARE-EYED
ROBIN

COCOA THRUSH

adult

Hispaniola &
Puerto Rico race

Cuba race

RED-LEGGED THRUSH

WHITE-CHINNED
THRUSH

adult

● **ST ANDREW VIREO** *Vireo caribaeus* 12.5cm (5in). Pale yellow stripe above bill to eye; grayish-brown eye; whitish to pale yellow underparts; 2 white wing bars. **VOICE:** Chatter on single syllable; 2-syllable *se-wi*, repeated. **STATUS AND RANGE:** Endemic to San Andrés: fairly common in southern third of island. **HABITAT:** Mangroves, bushes, scrubby pastures.

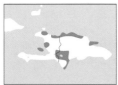

● **THICK-BILLED VIREO** *Vireo crassirostris* 13.5cm (5.25in). Variable. Blackish lores; dark eye; 2 white wing bars; bright yellow spectacles sometimes broken around eye. Underparts in southern Bahamas yellow; in northern Bahamas and Cayman Islands grayish with yellow tint. **IMMATURE:** Lacks blackish lores. **VOICE:** Bubbly, variable *chik-didle-wer-chip*, like White-eyed Vireo, but slower and less emphatic. **STATUS AND RANGE:** Common resident in Bahamas, Hispaniola (Île Tortue), Cayman Islands, and Providencia. Uncommon migrant to coastal north-central Cuba in October. **HABITAT:** Undergrowth, woodland edges, and bushes.

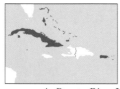

● **FLAT-BILLED VIREO** *Vireo nanus* 12–13cm (4.75–5in). Light gray below, washed pale yellow. Outertail feathers have white tips; 2 white wing bars; white eye. **VOICE:** Chattering, high-pitched *weet-weet-weet-* etc., often repeated. **STATUS AND RANGE:** Endemic to Hispaniola: uncommon and local. **HABITAT:** Primarily lowlands in semi-arid scrub and undergrowth. Also moist hills.

● **YELLOW-THROATED VIREO** *Vireo flavifrons* 12.5cm (5.5in). Yellow spectacles; 2 white wing bars; dark eye. Chin, throat, and breast yellow. **VOICE:** Wheezy *chee-wee, chee-woo, u-wee, chee-wee....* Also scolding *chi-chi-chur-chur-chur-chur-chur.* **STATUS AND RANGE:** Locally common in Cuba; uncommon in Bahamas, Virgin Islands (St John and St Thomas), and Cayman Islands September through April. Rare in southern Bahamas and Barbados; very rare in Puerto Rico. Vagrant elsewhere in West Indies. **HABITAT:** Widespread in many forest types and scrub.

● **WHITE-EYED VIREO** *Vireo griseus* 12.5cm (5in). Whitish below; yellow sides and spectacles; 2 white wing bars. **ADULT:** White eye. **IMMATURE:** Duller; dark eye. **VOICE:** Loud, slurred, 3–7 syllables. Also churring note. **STATUS AND RANGE:** Generally uncommon non-breeding resident in Bahamas, Cuba, and Cayman Islands; rare in Jamaica and Puerto Rico; very rare in Hispaniola and Virgin Islands (St John). Occurs primarily October through March. **HABITAT:** Undergrowth, scrub, coastal thickets, and brushy woodlands.

● **CUBAN VIREO** *Vireo gundlachii* 13cm (5in). Chunkier than warbler, with larger bill. Bulging eyes bordered by smudgy yellowish eye-ring. Yellowish underparts; faint wing bars. **VOICE:** High, oft-repeated *wi-chiví, wi-chiví, wi-chiví....* **STATUS AND RANGE:** Endemic to Cuba, where common and widespread. **HABITAT:** Brushland, forest edges, and dense scrub and thickets primarily in lowlands, but also in hills and mountains.

● **MANGROVE VIREO** *Vireo pallens* 11.5cm (4.5in). Dull yellow eyebrow stripe and underparts; 2 white wing bars. (Thick-billed Vireo has grayish-green crown and hindneck that contrasts with brownish-green upperparts.) **STATUS AND RANGE:** Reports of Thick-billed Vireo from Providencia likely pertain to Mangrove Vireo. **HABITAT:** Mangroves.

● **JAMAICAN VIREO** *Vireo modestus* 12.5cm (5in). 2 whitish wing bars; pinkish lower mandible; whitish eye. Flicks tail up. **IMMATURE:** Dark eye; yellow of underparts confined to central stripe. **VOICE:** Repeats phrase several minutes, then changes. Phrases rapid and high-pitched, often *sewi-sewi.* **STATUS AND RANGE:** Endemic to Jamaica: widespread and common. **HABITAT:** Most forests, forest edges, thickets, particularly arid lowlands.

● **BLUE-HEADED VIREO** *Vireo solitarius* 12.5–15cm (5–5.75in). Blue-gray head with white spectacles; 2 white wing bars. **VOICE:** Short, garbled 2- to 3-syllable phrases. **STATUS AND RANGE:** Very rare non-breeding resident in northern Bahamas and Cuba September through April. **HABITAT:** Low, dense shrubs.

ST ANDREW
VIREO

THICK-BILLED VIREO

Bahamas
race

Île Tortue race

FLAT-BILLED
VIREO

YELLOW-
THROATED
VIREO

WHITE-EYED
VIREO

CUBAN VIREO

MANGROVE
VIREO

JAMAICAN
VIREO

BLUE-HEADED
VIREO

PUERTO RICAN VIREO *Vireo latimeri* 12.5cm (5in). Two-toned underparts—throat and breast pale gray, belly and abdomen pale yellow. Incomplete white eye-ring and brown eye. VOICE: Melodious whistle, usually 3–4 syllables repeated for several minutes, then changed. STATUS AND RANGE: Endemic to western Puerto Rico: common. Does not occur east of Loíza Aldea, Caguas, and Patillas. Most common in haystack hills of north coast and forested valleys of south coast. HABITAT: Forests of all types and all elevations including mangroves, dry coastal scrub, moist limestone hills, and wet mountain forests.

WARBLING VIREO *Vireo gilvus* 12.5–15cm (5–5.75in). Pale gray upperparts; slightly lighter crown and hindneck; whitish eyebrow stripe. Throat to belly whitish, often with wash of pale or greenish-yellow. (Orange-crowned Warbler lacks gray crown and has faint greenish-yellow eyebrow stripe.) STATUS AND RANGE: Vagrant in western Cuba and Jamaica September and October. HABITAT: Forests and gardens.

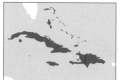

RED-EYED VIREO *Vireo olivaceus* 15cm (5.75in). Gray cap; white eyebrow stripe bordered by black eye-line; crown stripe. Lacks black 'whisker.' (Black-whiskered Vireo has black whisker stripe, buffer underparts, duller green on back and paler gray on crown.) ADULT: Red eye. VOICE: Calls primarily in April. Nasal, high *chway*. Also, abrupt phrases, oft-repeated. (Black-whiskered Vireo has longer phrases.) STATUS AND RANGE: Uncommon and somewhat irregular migrant in Bahamas, Cuba, Jamaica, and Cayman Islands (Grand Cayman) September through November and in April. Rare in Hispaniola. Vagrant elsewhere in West Indies. HABITAT: Dry and wet forests, open woodlands, scrub, and gardens, from coast to mountains.

BLUE MOUNTAIN VIREO *Vireo osburni* 13cm (5in). Robust gray vireo; large, with dark bill. Lacks facial markings and wing bars. VOICE: Trilling or bubbling whistle, descending slightly in tone. Also harsh *burr*, descending at end. STATUS AND RANGE: Endemic to Jamaica: uncommon. HABITAT: Mainly humid and moist mountain forests, also upland woods and shade coffee.

BLACK-WHISKERED VIREO *Vireo altiloquus* 15–16.5cm (5.75–6.5in). Whitish eyebrow stripe; dark eye-line; black mustache stripe; no wing bars. ADULT: Red iris. VOICE: Monotonous, throughout day. Short, melodious 2- to 3-syllable phrases, each different, separated by pauses. STATUS AND RANGE: Common breeding resident nearly throughout West Indies. Resident in Hispaniola and Lesser Antilles year-round, but in Bahamas, Cuba, Jamaica, Puerto Rico, and Cayman Islands (absent from Grand Cayman), absent September to January. HABITAT: All forest types at all elevations.

YUCATAN VIREO *Vireo magister* 15cm (5.75in). Olive-gray crown and back; whitish or buff eyebrow stripe; dark gray eye-line; white underparts with yellowish abdomen; brown eye; no wing bars. VOICE: 2-note whistle *whoi whu* and 3-syllable *sweet, brid-get*, very similar to Black-whiskered Vireo. STATUS AND RANGE: Fairly common resident on Grand Cayman (Cayman Islands). HABITAT: Low-elevation woodlands and mangroves.

PHILADELPHIA VIREO *Vireo philadelphicus* 12.5cm (5in). Gray crown; gray-olive upperparts; variable yellow below. Dark lores; whitish eyebrow stripe; brown eye; no wing bars. (Warbling Vireo has whiter breast and lacks dark lores. Tennessee Warbler has more slender bill; in non-breeding plumage, has yellowish eyebrow stripe and greenish crown. In breeding plumage, much whiter below.) STATUS AND RANGE: Rare migrant in Bahamas, Cuba, and Jamaica primarily October, though as late as February. Vagrant elsewhere in West Indies. HABITAT: Forests, woodlands, and gardens.

PUERTO
RICAN VIREO

imm

adult

WARBLING VIREO

RED-EYED VIREO

BLUE MOUNTAIN
VIREO

BLACK-WHISKERED
VIREO

YUCATAN VIREO

PHILADELPHIA VIREO

ELFIN-WOODS WARBLER *Dendroica angelae* 12.5cm (5in). ADULT: Thin white eyebrow stripe; white patches on ear-coverts and neck; incomplete eye-ring; black crown. IMMATURE: Black replaced by greenish. VOICE: Short, rapid, unmusical notes on one pitch, swelling and terminating with s'.ort double syllables slightly lower. STATUS AND RANGE: Endemic to Puerto Rico: uncommon and local. Threatened. HABITAT: Dense vines of canopy in humid mountain forests; sometimes at lower elevations.

BLACKPOLL WARBLER *Dendroica striata* 12.5–14cm (5–5.5in). BREEDING MALE: Black cap, white cheek. BREEDING FEMALE: Grayish above, whitish below; lightly streaked sides; white wing bars and undertail coverts. NON-BREEDING ADULT AND IMMATURE: *See* Plate 76. VOICE: Thin, high-pitched *zeet-zeet-zeet-zeet*.... STATUS AND RANGE: Fairly common migrant in Bahamas, Cuba, Hispaniola, and Puerto Rico; uncommon to rare on most other islands. Occurs primarily October through November and in May. HABITAT: Mangroves, brush, scrub forests, open areas with trees, and mixed woodlands.

ARROWHEAD WARBLER *Dendroica pharetra* 13cm (5in). Flicks tail down. ADULT MALE: Streaked black and white; 2 white wing bars. ADULT FEMALE: Dark gray streaks. IMMATURE: Yellowish-olive above, pale yellowish below with fine grayish streaks; wing bars; yellowish eye-ring; some white in tail. (Jamaican Vireo similar to immature, but lacks eye-ring, dark eye-line, and white in tail. Flicks tail up.) VOICE: Soft, generally 2 series of rising *tswee* notes followed by jumble of notes. Also, watery *chip*. STATUS AND RANGE: Endemic to Jamaica where locally common. HABITAT: Moist and humid forests at all elevations. Infrequently, wet lowland forests.

BLACK-AND-WHITE WARBLER *Mniotilta varia* 12.5–14cm (5–5.5in). Black-and-white striped crown. Climbs tree trunks. MALE: Black cheek patch. FEMALE: Whiter, particularly on cheek, throat, and sides. VOICE: Thin *tee-zee, tee-zee, tee-zee, tee-zee,* varying in length. STATUS AND RANGE: Non-breeding resident in West Indies primarily August through April. Common in Bahamas, Greater Antilles, Cayman and Virgin Islands, Providencia, and San Andrés; varies in Lesser Antilles from common to very rare. HABITAT: Forests and wooded areas at all elevations.

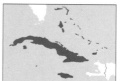

CERULEAN WARBLER *Dendroica cerulea* 10–13cm (4–5in). 2 white wing bars. ADULT MALE: Light blue head and upperparts; dark band across breast. ADULT FEMALE AND IMMATURE MALE: Upperparts grayish-blue, underparts dull white with yellowish tinge on throat and upper breast and faint streaks on sides. IMMATURE FEMALE: *See* Plate 77. STATUS AND RANGE: Very rare migrant in Bahamas, western Cuba, Jamaica, and Cayman Islands (Grand Cayman) primarily September and October, less frequent in April. HABITAT: Forest canopy, also low bushes and small trees.

NORTHERN WATERTHRUSH *Seiurus noveboracensis* 12.5–15cm (5–5.75in). Pale buff below with dark brown streaks. Prominent buff eyebrow stripe which narrows behind eye, and fine blackish-brown streaks on throat. Terrestrial. Bobs and teeters. Similar to Louisiana Waterthrush. VOICE: Sharp, emphatic *tchip*. STATUS AND RANGE: Generally fairly common non-breeding resident throughout West Indies primarily September through April. HABITAT: Borders of standing water, primarily saline and brackish, in or near mangroves and coastal scrub forests.

LOUISIANA WATERTHRUSH *Seiurus motacilla* 14.5–16cm (5.5–6.25in). White below with dark brown streaks. White eyebrow stripe, broader behind eye; lacks streaks on throat. Terrestrial. Bobs and teeters. (Northern Waterthrush has fine streaks on throat, and buffer eyebrow stripe does not broaden behind eye.) VOICE: Sharp *chink*, higher and more ringing than Northern Waterthrush. STATUS AND RANGE: Non-breeding resident in West Indies August through March. Common in Greater Antilles; uncommon in Bahamas; rare in Virgin and Cayman Islands; generally vagrant in Lesser Antilles south to St Vincent. HABITAT: Edges of flowing fresh water, often at higher elevations. Also sinkhole lakes and standing pools.

OVENBIRD *Seiurus aurocapillus* 14–16.5cm (5.5–6.5in). Orange crown bordered with blackish stripes; bold white eye-ring; white underparts heavily marked with large dark streaks. Terrestrial. FEMALE: Slightly duller. STATUS AND RANGE: Fairly common non-breeding resident in Bahamas, Greater Antilles and San Andrés August through May; uncommon in Virgin and Cayman Islands, and Providencia; generally rare in Lesser Antilles south to St Vincent. HABITAT: Principally woodlands and primary forest floors, often near streams or pools.

adult

ELFIN-WOODS
WARBLER

imm

br ♂

BLACKPOLL
WARBLER

br ♀

BLACK-AND-
WHITE WARBLER

adult ♂

ARROWHEAD
WARBLER

imm

♂

♀

adult ♂

CERULEAN
WARBLER

adult ♀ & imm ♂

LOUISIANA
WATERTHRUSH

NORTHERN
TERTHRUSH

OVENBIRD

● **PRAIRIE WARBLER** *Dendroica discolor* 12cm (4.75in). Yellow underparts; black side streaks. Bobs tail. **IMMATURE FEMALE:** *See* Plate 76. **STATUS AND RANGE:** Non-breeding resident in West Indies primarily late August through April. Common in Bahamas, Greater Antilles, and Cayman Islands; fairly common in Virgin Islands; rare in Lesser Antilles. **HABITAT:** Dry coastal forests, thickets, pastures with scattered trees, mangroves, and gardens, at all elevations.

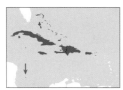

● **PALM WARBLER** *Dendroica palmarum* 12.5–14cm (5–5.5in). Bobs tail. **BREEDING:** Dark reddish-brown crown. **NON-BREEDING:** *See* Plate 76. **STATUS AND RANGE:** Non-breeding resident in West Indies primarily October through April. Common in Bahamas; somewhat less so in Cuba, Jamaica, Hispaniola, and Cayman Islands; uncommon in Puerto Rico and San Andrés; generally rare in Virgin Islands; vagrant in Lesser Antilles. **HABITAT:** Generally brush and bushes near coast including mangroves. Also open areas with sparse brush, plantation edges, and gardens.

● **YELLOW-THROATED WARBLER** *Dendroica dominica* 13cm (5in). Yellow throat, white eyebrow stripe and white neck patch. Bahamas race—yellow extends to abdomen; less white facial markings. Bahamas race often climbs pine trunks. Does not bob tail like Kirtland's Warbler. **VOICE:** Soft, high-pitched, slightly metallic *tsip.* **STATUS AND RANGE:** Common resident in northern Bahamas (Grand Bahama and Abaco). Generally common migrant in Bahamas, Cuba, and Cayman Islands; uncommon in Jamaica, Hispaniola, and Puerto Rico; vagrant in Virgin Islands and Lesser Antilles. Occurs primarily August through March. **HABITAT:** Pine forests, gardens, developed areas, Australian pine (Casuarina), lowland forests, and coconut palms.

● **YELLOW-RUMPED WARBLER** *Dendroica coronata* 14cm (5.5in). Yellow rump and patch on side of breast; white throat. **IMMATURE:** *See* Plate 76. **VOICE:** Hard, characteristic *check.* **STATUS AND RANGE:** Generally fairly common non-breeding resident in Bahamas, Cuba, Jamaica, and San Andrés; uncommon in Hispaniola, Puerto Rico, Virgin and Cayman Islands, Providencia. Rare in Lesser Antilles. Occurs primarily November through March. **HABITAT:** Gardens, woodlands, thickets, areas with scattered vegetation. Also mangroves and swamp edges.

● **OLIVE-CAPPED WARBLER** *Dendroica pityophila* 12.5cm (5in). Greenish-yellow crown; yellow throat and breast bordered by black spots; 2 whitish wing bars. (Yellow-throated Warbler has white eyebrow stripe and white patch on side of neck.) **VOICE:** High, melodious whistle-like song, generally 8 quick notes, *wisi-wisi-wisi* ... dropping, then rising on last note. Also characteristic *tsip.* **STATUS AND RANGE:** Endemic to Cuba and Bahamas: common, but extremely local. Cuba: confined to Pinar del Río and eastern region of Oriente. Bahamas: only on Grand Bahama and Abaco. **HABITAT:** Pine forests, sometimes nearby mixed pine-hardwood forests.

● **CANADA WARBLER** *Wilsonia canadensis* 12.5–15.5cm (5–5.75in). **ADULT MALE:** Bluish-gray upperparts; bold yellow spectacles; yellow underparts with black stripes forming a necklace. (Oriente Warbler has yellow cheeks and lacks stripes on breast.) **ADULT FEMALE:** *See* Plate 76. **IMMATURE:** Olive-brown wash on upperparts; virtually no necklace. **STATUS AND RANGE:** Very rare migrant and less frequent non-breeding resident in northern Bahamas and Cuba. Vagrant elsewhere in West Indies. Occurs primarily September and October. **HABITAT:** Primarily lowlands in moderately open vegetation among scattered trees, usually near swamps or other standing water.

PRAIRIE
WARBLER

adult

br

PALM WARBLER

imm & non-br ♂

Bahamas race

br adult

YELLOW-THROATED
WARBLER

br ♂

YELLOW-RUMPED
WARBLER

adult ♀ & non-br ♂

OLIVE-CAPPED
WARBLER

CANADA
WARBLER

adult ♂

MAGNOLIA WARBLER *Dendroica magnolia* 11.5–12.5cm (4.5–5in). White tail markings; white eyebrow stripe and wing bars; yellow throat and rump. (Yellow-rumped Warbler has some white in tail and has white, not yellow, throat.) **NON-BREEDING ADULT AND IMMATURE:** *See* Plate 76. **VOICE:** Hard, sonorous *tseek*. **STATUS AND RANGE:** Generally fairly common migrant in Bahamas, Cuba, and San Andrés; uncommon in Jamaica, Hispaniola, Puerto Rico, Cayman Islands, and Providencia; rare in Virgin Islands, Antigua, and Barbados; very rare elsewhere in Lesser Antilles. Occurs September to May. **HABITAT:** Open woodlands in lowlands, swamp edges, and bushes. Sometimes gardens.

CAPE MAY WARBLER *Dendroica tigrina* 12.5–14cm (5–5.5in). Heavy striping on breast; yellowish rump. Usually a yellow neck patch. (Magnolia Warbler lacks yellow neck patch.) **IMMATURE:** *See* Plate 76. **STATUS AND RANGE:** Non-breeding resident throughout West Indies primarily October through April. Common in Bahamas, Greater Antilles, Cayman Islands, and San Andrés; uncommon in Virgin Islands; generally rare to very rare in Lesser Antilles. **HABITAT:** Mountain forests to coastal thickets, mangroves, and gardens. Almost anywhere plants are flowering.

BLACK-THROATED GREEN WARBLER *Dendroica virens* 12.5cm (5in). Yellowish-gray cheeks surrounded by characteristic yellow band. **ADULT MALE:** Black chin, throat, upper breast, and side streaks. **ADULT FEMALE AND IMMATURE MALE:** Duller; chin yellowish. **IMMATURE FEMALE:** *See* Plate 77. **STATUS AND RANGE:** Non-breeding resident in West Indies September through May. Common in western Cuba; uncommon in Bahamas, eastern Cuba, Jamaica, and Hispaniola; rare in Cayman Islands and San Andrés; very rare in Puerto Rico, Virgin Islands, and some Lesser Antilles. **HABITAT:** Primarily low- and mid-elevation forests. Sometimes woodlands and gardens.

PINE WARBLER *Dendroica pinus* 12.5–14.5cm (5–5.75in). **ADULT MALE:** Greenish-olive upperparts; unstreaked back; 2 white wing bars; faint yellow eyebrow stripe; variable yellow on chin and throat; faint gray to blackish streaking on breast and upper flanks. (Bay-breasted Warbler has streaked back.) **ADULT FEMALE:** Duller. **IMMATURE:** *See* Plate 77. **VOICE:** Musical trill usually on one pitch. Also strong *tzip*. **STATUS AND RANGE:** Common resident in northern Bahamas and Dominican Republic. Theatened in Haiti. Very rare wanderer to western Cuba and Cayman Islands October and November. Vagrant elsewhere in West Indies. **HABITAT:** Mature pine forests or barrens.

KIRTLAND'S WARBLER *Dendroica kirtlandii* 15cm (5.75in). Bobs tail. **BREEDING MALE:** Bluish-gray above; black streaks on back; 2 inconspicuous whitish wing bars; broken white eye-ring; bright yellow throat and belly; black streaks on sides. Forehead and lores black; more contrast. **IMMATURE FEMALE:** Brownish-gray above with eye-ring and flank streaks fainter. **ADULT FEMALE AND NON-BREEDING MALE:** *See* Plate 77. Similar Yellow-Throated Warbler does not bob tail. **STATUS AND RANGE:** Rare non-breeding resident in Bahamas primarily October through April. Endangered. **HABITAT:** Low broadleaved scrub, thickets, and understory. Infrequently, pine forests.

BLACKBURNIAN WARBLER *Dendroica fusca* 13cm (5in). **ADULT FEMALE, NON-BREEDING MALE, AND IMMATURE MALE:** Bright orange-yellow throat, breast, eyebrow stripe, and sides of neck. White back stripes and wing bars; dark side stripes. **BREEDING MALE:** Orange throat and facial markings. **IMMATURE FEMALE:** *See* Plate 77. **VOICE:** Fine, weak *tsseek, tsseek*. **STATUS AND RANGE:** Uncommon migrant in Cuba; rare in Bahamas, Jamaica, Hispaniola, and Cayman Islands; very rare in Puerto Rico and Virgin Islands (St John); and vagrant in Lesser Antilles. Occurs primarily September through October and April through May. **HABITAT:** Conifers, tall trees, and botanical gardens.

TOWNSEND'S WARBLER *Dendroica townsendi* 13cm (5in). Dark cheek ringed with yellow. **ADULT MALE:** Black cheek, chin, throat, and side streaks; yellow lower breast and belly; white outertail feathers. **ADULT FEMALE:** Slightly duller; yellow chin and throat; white belly. **IMMATURE:** Paler. Cheeks olive-green; underparts may lack black or have only fine streaks. (Black-throated Green Warbler has paler, yellower cheeks; less yellow on breast. Backburnian Warbler has striped back.) **STATUS AND RANGE:** Vagrant in Bahamas. **HABITAT:** Forests, primarily conifers.

MAGNOLIA
WARBLER

br ♂

br ♀

CAPE MAY
WARBLER

adult ♂

adult ♀

BLACK-THROATED
GREEN WARBLER

adult ♂

adult ♂

adult ♀

PINE
WARBLER

KIRTLAND'S
WARBLER

adult ♂

br ♂

adult ♀, non-br ♂
& imm ♂

TOWNSEND'S
WARBLER

adult ♂

BLACKBURNIAN
WARBLER

●**NASHVILLE WARBLER** *Vermivora ruficapilla* 11.5–12.5cm (4.5–5in). Conspicuous white eye-ring in all plumages; grayish head contrasts with yellowish-green upperparts. **ADULT:** Pale bluish-gray head, yellow underparts except for white belly. **IMMATURE:** *See* Plate 78. **STATUS AND RANGE:** Rare non-breeding resident in northern Bahamas and Cayman Islands mid-September through mid-April. **HABITAT:** Woodlands.

●**ORIENTE WARBLER** *Teretistris fornsi* 13cm (5in). Gray upperparts; yellow underparts. No wing bars nor white in plumage. Yellow eye-ring; long, slightly down-curved bill. (Female Prothonotary Warbler has less distinctive separation between yellowish-olive crown and yellow of face; also has white in tail.) **VOICE:** Shrill *tsi-tsi-tsi…,* repeated several times, practically indistinguishable from Yellow-headed Warbler. **STATUS AND RANGE:** Endemic to Cuba: locally common in eastern part of island. Particularly common in southern provinces of Granma, Santiago de Cuba, and Guantánamo. **HABITAT:** Forests, scrub, and borders of swamps from coast to highest mountains.

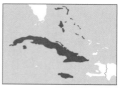

●**WILSON'S WARBLER** *Wilsonia pusilla* 11–12.5cm (4.25–5in). **ADULT MALE:** Distinct black cap; bright yellow forehead and eyebrow stripe. **ADULT FEMALE AND IMMATURE MALE:** Duller; hint of black cap. **IMMATURE FEMALE:** *See* Plate 78. **STATUS AND RANGE:** Very rare migrant and even rarer non-breeding resident in northern Bahamas, western and central Cuba, and Jamaica September through April. Vagrant elsewhere in West Indies. **HABITAT:** Dense vegetation at all altitudes, but primarily in lowlands.

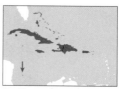

●**KENTUCKY WARBLER** *Oporornis formosus* 12.5–14.5cm (5–5.75in). **ADULT MALE:** Yellow spectacles; black facial mark and crown; yellow underparts. **ADULT FEMALE AND IMMATURE MALE:** Less black on face and crown. **IMMATURE FEMALE:** *See* Plate 79. **STATUS AND RANGE:** Rare migrant and very rare non-breeding resident in Bahamas, Cuba, Jamaica, Hispaniola, Puerto Rico, Virgin and Cayman Islands, and Providencia late August through April. **HABITAT:** Dense undergrowth and thickets in moist forest understory.

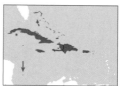

●**HOODED WARBLER** *Wilsonia citrina* 12.5–14.5cm (5–5.75in). Flicks and fans tail showing white outertail feathers. **MALE:** Distinctive black hood. **ADULT FEMALE:** Variable hood, from almost complete to only black markings on crown. *See also* Plate 79. **IMMATURE FEMALE:** Lacks hood; yellow face sharply demarcated. (Adult female and immature Wilson's Warblers smaller, with yellow eyebrow stripe and no white in tail.) **STATUS AND RANGE:** Uncommon to rare non-breeding resident in Bahamas, Cuba, and Jamaica September through April. Rare in Hispaniola, Puerto Rico, Virgin and Cayman Islands. Common on San Andrés. Vagrant elsewhere in West Indies. **HABITAT:** Moist forest undergrowth and mangroves.

NASHVILLE
WARBLER

adult

ORIENTE
WARBLER

WILSON'S
WARBLER

adult ♂

adult ♂

KENTUCKY
WARBLER

♂

HOODED
WARBLER

♀

● **BACHMAN'S WARBLER** *Vermivora bachmanii* 11–11.5cm (4.25–4.5in). Yellow eye-ring. **ADULT MALE:** Large black patch on throat and breast; black patch on crown; yellow fore-head, chin, and belly. **ADULT FEMALE:** Duller; black on breast reduced to fine streaks or absent; crown and hindneck gray. **STATUS AND RANGE:** Critically endangered if not extinct, formerly uncommon and local non-breeding resident in Cuba September through April. Last widely accepted record 1964. 1980 report dubious. **HABITAT:** Undergrowth in moist woods, canebrakes, and forest edges bordering swamps.

● **BAHAMA YELLOWTHROAT** *Geothlypis rostrata* 15cm (5.75in). Relatively large, slow-moving, with relatively heavy bill. **MALE:** Black mask; gray cap; yellow throat, breast, and upper belly. Mask edging varies from whitish to yellow. **FEMALE:** Lacks mask. Yellow throat, breast, and belly; gray crown; whitish eye-ring and eyebrow stripe. Similar to Common Yellowthroat. *See also* Plate 79. **VOICE:** Loud, clear *witchity-whitchity-witchit*, very similar to Common Yellowthroat. Also deep, sharp *tchit*, less gravelly than Common Yellowthroat. **STATUS AND RANGE:** Endemic to northern Bahamas: common on Grand Bahama, Abaco, Eleuthera, Cat Island; uncommon on Andros; rare on New Providence. **HABITAT:** Scrub, coppice edges, and pine woods with thatch palm understory.

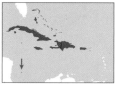

● **COMMON YELLOWTHROAT** *Geothlypis trichas* 11.5–14cm (4.5–5.5in). **ADULT MALE:** Conspicuous black facial mask, edged above by whitish; yellow throat and breast. **ADULT FEMALE:** Lacks facial mask; bright yellow throat and breast contrast with whitish belly; narrow, whitish eye-ring; usually pale, buffish eyebrow stripe. *See also* Plate 79. **IMMATURE:** Duller and browner than adult female. (Bahama Yellowthroat larger; less active; heavier bill; yellow of underparts extends to belly; crown gray.) **VOICE:** Gravelly. **STATUS AND RANGE:** Common non-breeding resident in Bahamas, Greater Antilles, Cayman Islands, and San Andrés; uncommon to rare in Virgin Islands and Providencia; vagrant in Lesser Antilles. Occurs primarily October through early May. **HABITAT:** Wet grass and brush, usually at freshwater edges.

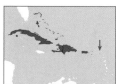

● **CONNECTICUT WARBLER** *Oporornis agilis* 13.5–15cm (5.25–5.75in). Large, stocky, with distinctive hood and white eye-ring. Dull yellow from belly to undertail coverts which extend nearly to end of tail. (Mourning Warbler sometimes has eye-ring, but this is thin and broken in front; undertail coverts shorter.) Primarily terrestrial. **ADULT MALE:** Hood bluish-gray. **ADULT FEMALE AND IMMATURE:** Hood pale gray-brown; whitish throat. *See also* Plate 79. **STATUS AND RANGE:** Very rare migrant in Bahamas, Cuba, Hispaniola, Puerto Rico, Virgin Islands (St Croix), St Bartholomew, and St Martin. Primarily occurs September and October. **HABITAT:** Moist woodland understory, usually near water.

● **MOURNING WARBLER** *Oporornis philadelphia* 13–14.5cm (5–5.75in). Primarily ter-restrial. **ADULT MALE:** Bluish-gray hood; black breast patch; no eye-ring. **ADULT FEMALE:** Hood pale gray or brownish; incomplete eye-ring; whitish throat; lacks black on breast. **IMMATURE:** *See* Plate 79. (Connecticut Warbler has bold white, complete eye-ring and longer undertail coverts.) **STATUS AND RANGE:** Vagrant in Bahamas, Cuba, Jamaica, Hispaniola (Dominican Republic), Puerto Rico, and Virgin Islands primarily September and October. **HABITAT:** Wet thickets, second growth, and swamp edges.

BACHMAN'S
WARBLER

adult ♀

adult ♂

Andros and New
Providence race

♂

♀

BAHAMA
YELLOWTHROAT

COMMON
YELLOWTHROAT

adult ♂

adult ♀

adult ♂

adult ♀ & imm

CONNECTICUT
WARBLER

MOURNING
WARBLER

adult ♀

adult ♂

● **VITELLINE WARBLER** *Dendroica vitellina* 13cm (5in). Bobs tail. **ADULT MALE:** Olive-green above, entirely yellow below with faint side stripes and distinct facial pattern. **ADULT FEMALE:** *See* Plate 77. **IMMATURE:** Crown and throat pale gray; facial markings buffish. (Prairie Warbler has more conspicuous side stripes, whitish undertail coverts, more contrast in facial markings.) **VOICE:** Slightly harsh 4- to 5-syllable *szwee-szwee-szwee-zee*. Also shorter, deeper call. **STATUS AND RANGE:** Endemic to Cayman and Swan Islands: common. **HABITAT:** Dry scrub and woodlands, particularly inland. Also disturbed urban areas and gardens.

● **YELLOW WARBLER** *Dendroica petechia* 11.5–13.5cm (4.5–5.25in). **ADULT MALE:** Yellow overall including outertail feathers; reddish streaks on breast and sides. Head varies from yellow (Bahamas and Cuba) to entirely reddish-brown (Martinique). **ADULT FEMALE AND IMMATURE:** *See* Plates 76 and 78. **VOICE:** Variable; typically loud, clear and rapid *sweet-sweet-sweet-ti-ti-ti-weet*. Also, thin *zeet* and hard *chip*. **STATUS AND RANGE:** Common resident widely in West Indies. Uncommon in northern Bahamas; non-breeding in Grenada, St Vincent, and some Grenadines. Rare on Providencia, vagrant on Saba. Barbados race endangered. **HABITAT:** Primarily mangroves, coastal scrub on some islands. In Martinique, ranges to mountain forests.

● **NORTHERN PARULA** *Parula americana* 10.5–12cm (4–4.75in). Grayish-blue above with greenish-yellow back; yellow throat and breast; white wing bars; incomplete white eye-ring. **NON-BREEDING ADULT AND IMMATURE:** May have faint black and reddish band across breast. **BREEDING MALE:** Breast band conspicuous. **VOICE:** Ascending insect-like buzz with sharp end note; heard March through May. **STATUS AND RANGE:** Widespread in West Indies. Common non-breeding resident August through May in Bahamas, Greater Antilles, Virgin and Cayman Islands, and San Andrés. Generally uncommon in northern Lesser Antilles and rarer further south. **HABITAT:** Primarily dry forests and scrub of lowlands; also moist mountain forests.

● **BLUE-WINGED WARBLER** *Vermivora pinus* 12cm (4.75in). Overall bright yellow with bluish wings, white wing bars, and black eye-line. (Prothonotary Warbler lacks white wing bars and black eye-line.) **STATUS AND RANGE:** Rare non-breeding resident in Bahamas, Cuba, Jamaica, Hispaniola, larger Virgin Islands, and Cayman Islands primarily October through March. Vagrant elsewhere in West Indies. **HABITAT:** Moist forests, trees in vicinity of Australian Pine (Casuarina), and sometimes bushes.

● **PROTHONOTARY WARBLER** *Protonotaria citrea* 13.5cm (5.25in). **MALE:** Golden-yellow overall except blue-gray wings and tail. **FEMALE:** *See* Plate 79. **STATUS AND RANGE:** Generally uncommon migrant in Bahamas, Cuba, Jamaica, and Hispaniola primarily August through October and March through early April. Rare in Cayman Islands, Providencia, and San Andrés. Uncommon in Puerto Rico; rare in Virgin Islands and Lesser Antilles. **HABITAT:** In or near mangrove swamps. In Cuba, also gardens and tree clumps.

YELLOW
WARBLER

adult ♂

Martinique race

adult ♂,
Bahamas &
Cuba race

adult ♂

adult ♂

Anegada & most
Lesser Antilles race

adult ♂

VITELLINE
WARBLER

imm

br ♂

NORTHERN
PARULA

non-br adult & imm

BLUE-WINGED
WARBLER

♂

PROTHONOTARY
WARBLER

● **YELLOW-HEADED WARBLER** *Teretistris fernandinae* 13cm (5in). Gray overall, paler below; yellowish head and neck; long, slightly down-curved bill; no wing bars. (Prothonotary Warbler primarily yellow below.) **VOICE:** Peculiar, shrill *tsi-tsi-tsi...*, repeated several times. Nearly identical to call of Oriente Warbler. **STATUS AND RANGE:** Endemic to Cuba: common in western and central parts of island. **HABITAT:** Sea level to mid-elevations. Primarily shrub with much tangled vegetation, bushes, and vines. Also open forests.

● **ORANGE-CROWNED WARBLER** *Vermivora celata* 11.5–14cm (4.5–5.5in). Unmarked, dull olive-green upperparts; faint greenish-yellow eyebrow stripe; thin, broken yellow eye-ring; greenish-yellow underparts faintly streaked pale gray; yellow undertail coverts. *See also* Plate 77. (Tennessee Warbler unstreaked below and has white undertail coverts. Philadelphia and Warbling Vireos have white eyebrow stripe and gray cap.) **STATUS AND RANGE:** Rare non-breeding resident in northern Bahamas primarily October to January. **HABITAT:** Scrubby areas.

● **ST LUCIA WARBLER** *Dendroica delicata* 12.5cm (5in). Bluish-gray upperparts; yellow throat and breast; yellow eyebrow stripe and crescent below eye edged black. **FEMALE:** Similar, but black edging to crown stripe less pronounced; less white in tail. **VOICE:** Loud trill variable in pitch and speed. Also medium-strength *chick*. **STATUS AND RANGE:** Endemic to St Lucia: common. **HABITAT:** Principally mid- and high-elevation forests.

● **ADELAIDE'S WARBLER** *Dendroica adelaidae* 12.5cm (5in). Bluish-gray upperparts; yellow throat and breast; yellow and white eyebrow stripe and crescent below eye. **FEMALE:** Similar, but duller facial markings; less white in tail. **VOICE:** Loud trill variable in pitch and speed. Also medium-strength *chick*. **STATUS AND RANGE:** Endemic to Puerto Rico: common in western portion. **HABITAT:** Dry coastal scrubland and thickets and moist limestone forests of haystack hills.

● **BARBUDA WARBLER** *Dendroica subita* 12.5cm (5in). Bluish-gray upperparts; yellow throat and breast. Conspicuous eyebrow stripe and crescent below eye. **FEMALE:** Similar, but duller facial markings; less white in tail. **VOICE:** Loud trill variable in pitch and speed. Also medium-strength *chick*. **STATUS AND RANGE:** Endemic to Barbuda: common. **HABITAT:** Thickets near wetlands and inland canals.

● **YELLOW-BREASTED CHAT** *Icteria virens* 19cm (7.5in). Upperparts, wings, and long tail olive-green. Black, thick bill; white lores and eye-ring. Throat, breast, and upper belly yellow; lower belly and undertail coverts white. **STATUS AND RANGE:** Very rare migrant and less frequent non-breeding resident in northern Bahamas, Cuba, and Cayman Islands (Grand Cayman) late August through early May. **HABITAT:** Low, dense vegetation.

YELLOW-HEADED WARBLER

ORANGE-CROWNED
WARBLER

ST LUCIA
WARBLER

ADELAIDE'S
WARBLER

BARBUDA
WARBLER

YELLOW-BREASTED
CHAT

● **AMERICAN REDSTART** *Setophaga ruticilla* 11–13.5cm (4.25–5.25in). **ADULT MALE:** Black upperparts, throat, and breast; large orange patches in wings and tail. **ADULT FEMALE:** Head gray; upperparts greenish-gray; large yellow patches in wings and tail. **IMMATURE:** Head greenish-gray; yellow patches reduced. **STATUS AND RANGE:** Common non-breeding resident in Bahamas, Greater Antilles, Cayman and Virgin Islands, northern Lesser Antilles, San Andrés; generally uncommon in southern Lesser Antilles. Occurs primarily late August through early May. **HABITAT:** Usually forests and woodlands from coast to mountains. Also gardens and shrubby areas.

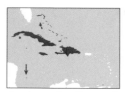

● **GOLDEN-WINGED WARBLER** *Vermivora chrysoptera* 12.5cm (5in). Yellow wing patch; gray or black throat; cheek patch. Forehead yellow; underparts whitish. **ADULT MALE:** Throat and cheek patch black. **FEMALE AND IMMATURE:** Paler and more subdued. Throat and cheek patch gray. **VOICE:** A rather strong *chip*. **STATUS AND RANGE:** Rare migrant in Puerto Rico and Virgin and Cayman Islands; very rare in Bahamas, Cuba, Jamaica, and Hispaniola primarily September, October and April. **HABITAT:** Cuba: gardens and woodlands; Puerto Rico: high mountain forests. Prefers tree canopies.

● **TENNESSEE WARBLER** *Vermivora peregrina* 11.5–12.5cm (4.5–5in). **NON-BREEDING ADULT:** Olive-green above, yellowish below; yellowish eyebrow stripe, noticeable eye-line. **BREEDING MALE:** Bright olive-green above, white below; gray crown; white eyebrow stripe, pale gray line through eye. **BREEDING FEMALE:** Crown duller and greenish; breast with yellowish wash. **IMMATURE:** *See* Plate 78. (Orange-crowned Warbler has faint breast streaks and yellow undertail coverts.) **VOICE:** Short, fine *tseet-tseet-tseet*... repeated frequently. **STATUS AND RANGE:** Uncommon non-breeding resident through Bahamas, Cuba, Cayman Islands, and San Andrés September through May; rare in Jamaica, Hispaniola, and Providencia. **HABITAT:** Woodlands, gardens, and scrub.

● **RUBY-CROWNED KINGLET** *Regulus calendula* 11.5cm (4.5in). Tiny, with olive-colored upperparts, bold white eye-ring, and 2 whitish wing bars. **MALE:** Usually concealed red crest. **FEMALE:** *See* Plate 78. **STATUS AND RANGE:** Very rare non-breeding resident in northern Bahamas October through March. Vagrant elsewhere in West Indies. **HABITAT:** Generally low, scrubby vegetation.

● **BLACK-THROATED BLUE WARBLER** *Dendroica caerulescens* 12–14cm (4.75–5.5in). **MALE:** Blue above; black face and band along sides; white wing spot. **FEMALE:** *See* Plate 79. **STATUS AND RANGE:** Common non-breeding resident in Bahamas and Greater Antilles September to May; fairly common in Cayman Islands; uncommon on San Andrés; rare in Virgin Islands, decidedly so in Lesser Antilles. **HABITAT:** Forests, forest edges, and woodlands, primarily in mountains. Also moist to wet lowlands. Infrequently dry forests.

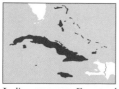

● **BAY-BREASTED WARBLER** *Dendroica castanea* 12.5–15cm (5–5.75in). **BREEDING MALE:** Reddish-brown cap and band on chin, throat, and sides; buffish neck patch. **BREEDING FEMALE:** Duller. **NON-BREEDING ADULT AND IMMATURE:** *See* Plate 76. **VOICE:** Weak *tsee-tsee-tsee*. **STATUS AND RANGE:** Rare migrant in Bahamas, Cuba, Jamaica, Cayman Islands, and San Andrés primarily October through November and April through May. Vagrant elsewhere in West Indies. **HABITAT:** Forest edges, woodlands, gardens, and open areas with scattered trees.

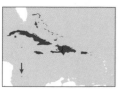

● **CHESTNUT-SIDED WARBLER** *Dendroica pensylvanica* 11.5–13.5cm (4.5–5.25in). **BREEDING MALE:** Yellow cap; reddish band along sides; white underparts. **BREEDING FEMALE:** Duller. **NON-BREEDING ADULT AND IMMATURE:** *See* Plate 78. **STATUS AND RANGE:** Uncommon non-breeding resident in Cuba; rare in Bahamas, Jamaica, Hispaniola, Puerto Rico, Virgin and Cayman Islands September through May. Vagrant in Lesser Antilles. Uncommon on San Andrés. **HABITAT:** Open woodlands, gardens with trees.

adult ♂

AMERICAN
REDSTART

adult ♀

GOLDEN-WINGED
WARBLER

adult ♂

TENNESSEE
WARBLER

br ♂

♂

RUBY-CROWNED
KINGLET

BLACK-THROATED
BLUE WARBLER

♂

br ♂

BAY-BREASTED
WARBLER

br ♀

CHESTNUT-SIDED
WARBLER

br ♂

SWAINSON'S WARBLER *Limnothlypis swainsonii* 14cm (5.5in). Head brownish-gray with brown crown, whitish eyebrow stripe, and blackish line through eye. Back, wings, and tail unmarked olive grayish-brown. Underparts whitish, grayer on sides. Primarily terrestrial. **VOICE:** Sharp, metallic *chip*. **STATUS AND RANGE:** Uncommon non-breeding resident in Cuba and Jamaica; rare in Bahamas, Puerto Rico, Hispaniola, and Cayman Islands. Occurs September through April. **HABITAT:** Heavy leaf-litter in canebrakes, thickets, dense woodland understory, and wet limestone forests.

WORM-EATING WARBLER *Helmitheros vermivorus* 14cm (5.5in). Plain greenish-gray upperparts, wings, and tail; buffish head with black stripes on crown and through eye; underparts whitish-buff, whiter on throat and belly. **STATUS AND RANGE:** Fairly common non-breeding resident in Bahamas, Cuba, Cayman Islands, and San Andrés September through April; uncommon in Jamaica, Hispaniola, Puerto Rico, and Providencia; rare in Virgin Islands. Vagrant elsewhere in West Indies. **HABITAT:** Dense forests at all elevations.

WHISTLING WARBLER *Catharopeza bishopi* 14.5cm (5.75in). **ADULT:** Blackish hood, upperparts, and broad breast band; broad white eye-ring, chin, and mark by bill. **IMMATURE:** Brownish-gray hood, upperparts, and breast band; white eye-ring and mark by bill. **VOICE:** Rising notes, increasingly loud, ending with 2–3 emphatic ones. **STATUS AND RANGE:** Endemic to St Vincent: rare and threatened. Occurs primarily at Colonaire and Perserence Valleys and Richmond Peak. **HABITAT:** Primary or secondary mountain forest undergrowth and underside of forest canopy.

PLUMBEOUS WARBLER *Dendroica plumbea* 12cm (4.75in). Flicks tail. **ADULT:** Plain gray upperparts; white eyebrow stripe, especially in front of eye; 2 white wing bars; underparts mostly pale gray with some white through center of breast. **IMMATURE:** *See* Plate 78. **VOICE:** Musical 3-syllable *pa-pi-a*. Also loud rattle. **STATUS AND RANGE:** Common resident in Guadeloupe and Dominica. These islands encompass entire range. **HABITAT:** Moist mountain forests, sometimes drier scrub forests and mangroves.

WHITE-WINGED WARBLER *Xenoligea montana* 13.5–14cm (5.25–5.5in). Bold white wing patch; white outertail feathers; white line above eye to forehead. **VOICE:** Low chattering *suit...suit...suit...chir...suit...suit...suit...suit...chir...chi....* Also thin *tseep*. **STATUS AND RANGE:** Endemic to Hispaniola: common very locally in Dominican Republic in Cordillera Central, Sierra de Baoruco, and Sierra de Neiba; in Haiti, very rare in Massif de la Hotte and Massif de la Selle. Endangered. **HABITAT:** Primarily mature broadleaf forest undergrowth, low trees, and thickets and wet shrubs in higher mountains.

GREEN-TAILED WARBLER *Microligea palustris* 12–14cm (4.75–5.5in). Slender, with long tail. **ADULT:** Incomplete white eye-ring; red eye; greenish lower back, rump, wings, and tail. **IMMATURE:** Greener above and tinted olive below; brown iris. **VOICE:** *Sip-sip-sip*; also rasping notes. **STATUS AND RANGE:** Endemic to Hispaniola: common, but declining. Haiti: high elevations in Massif de la Selle and near sea level in far northwest. Dominican Republic: local from sea level to high mountains. **HABITAT:** Dense thickets or disturbed patches of wet broadleaf forests, primarily in mountains. Also moist forest, scrub, and semi-arid areas.

SEMPER'S WARBLER *Leucopeza semperi* 14.5cm (5.75in). Long, pale legs; pale feet. **ADULT:** Nearly uniform dark gray upperparts and whitish underparts. **IMMATURE:** Upperparts including rump gray washed with olive-brown; brownish-buff below. **VOICE:** Soft *tuck-tick-tick-tuck*. **STATUS AND RANGE:** Endemic to St Lucia; critically endangered and very possibly extinct. Last certain report 1961. Most reports from ridge between Piton Flore and Piton Canaries. **HABITAT:** Primary or secondary moist forests at mid-elevations with thick undergrowth, mountain thickets, and dwarf forests. Believed to forage on or close to ground.

SWAINSON'S WARBLER

WORM-EATING WARBLER

WHISTLING WARBLER
adult
imm

PLUMBEOUS WARBLER
adult

WHITE-WINGED WARBLER

SEMPER'S WARBLER
adult
imm

GREEN-TAILED WARBLER
adult
imm

CANADA WARBLER *Wilsonia canadensis* 12.5–15.5cm (5–5.75in). **ADULT FEMALE:** Gray streaks on breast; yellow spectacles. **ADULT MALE:** *See* Plate 68.

PALM WARBLER *Dendroica palmarum* 12.5–14cm (5–5.5in). Bobs tail. **NON-BREEDING:** Yellowish undertail coverts; olive-colored rump; faint eyebrow stripe; brownish back. **BREEDING:** *See* Plate 68.

YELLOW WARBLER *Dendroica petechia* 11.5–13.5cm (4.5–5.25in). **ADULT FEMALE:** Yellow overall. Faintly streaked or unstreaked below; no reddish-brown on head. *See also* Plate 78. **IMMATURE:** Upperparts olive-gray; underparts grayish-white; yellow in wings. **ADULT MALE:** *See* Plate 72.

CAPE MAY WARBLER *Dendroica tigrina* 12.5–14cm (5–5.5in). **IMMATURE:** Striped breast; yellowish rump; buffish patch behind cheek. **ADULT:** *See* Plate 69.

MAGNOLIA WARBLER *Dendroica magnolia* 11.5–12.5cm (4.5–5in). **NON-BREEDING ADULT AND IMMATURE:** Pale eyebrow stripe; white eye-ring; gray head. Yellow underparts, buff band nearly across breast. **BREEDING ADULT:** *See* Plate 69.

PRAIRIE WARBLER *Dendroica discolor* 12cm (4.75in). Bobs tail. **IMMATURE FEMALE:** Yellow underparts; blackish streaks on sides; whitish facial markings. **ADULT MALE:** *See* Plate 68.

BLACKPOLL WARBLER *Dendroica striata* 12.5–14cm (5–5.5in). **NON-BREEDING ADULT AND IMMATURE:** Difficult to identify. White wing bars and undertail coverts; faint side streaks; pale legs. (Non-breeding adult and immature Bay-breasted Warbler unstreaked below; buffish undertail coverts; black legs.) **BREEDING ADULT:** *See* Plate 67.

YELLOW-RUMPED WARBLER *Dendroica coronata* 14cm (5.5in). Yellow rump and patch on side of breast; white throat. **IMMATURE:** Duller. **ADULT AND NON-BREEDING MALE:** *See* Plate 68.

BAY-BREASTED WARBLER *Dendroica castanea* 12.5–15cm (5–5.75in). **NON-BREEDING ADULT AND IMMATURE:** Back greenish-gray; unstreaked buffish below, including undertail coverts; creamy-buff on flanks; white wing bars; usually blackish legs. (Non-breeding adult and immature Blackpoll Warbler finely streaked below, pale legs, white undertail coverts. Pine Warbler has unstreaked back.) **BREEDING ADULT:** *See* Plate 74.

CANADA
WARBLER

adult ♀

PALM
WARBLER

non-br

adult ♀

YELLOW
WARBLER

imm

CAPE MAY
WARBLER

imm

MAGNOLIA
WARBLER

non-br adult & imm

imm ♀

PRAIRIE
WARBLER

imm

non-br adult & imm

YELLOW-RUMPED
WARBLER

BLACKPOLL
WARBLER

BAY-BREASTED
WARBLER

non-br adult & imm

CERULEAN WARBLER *Dendroica cerulea* 10–13cm (4–5in). **IMMATURE FEMALE:** Olive-green above, yellower below; 2 white wing bars. **ADULT AND IMMATURE MALE:** *See* Plate 67.

VITELLINE WARBLER *Dendroica vitellina* 13cm (5in). Cayman and Swan Islands. Bobs tail. **ADULT FEMALE:** Upperparts olive-green, underparts entirely yellow; faint facial pattern; may lack side stripes. **ADULT MALE AND IMMATURE:** *See* Plate 72.

BLACK-THROATED GREEN WARBLER *Dendroica virens* 12.5cm. (5in). **IMMATURE FEMALE:** Yellowish-gray cheek; faint side streaks. **ADULT AND IMMATURE MALE:** *See* Plate 69.

ORANGE-CROWNED WARBLER *Vermivora celata* 11.5–14cm (4.5–5.5in). Upperparts unmarked olive-green; underparts greenish-yellow, streaked pale gray; yellow undertail coverts; greenish-yellow eyebrow stripe; thin broken yellow eye-ring. *See also* Plate 73.

BLACKBURNIAN WARBLER *Dendroica fusca* 13cm (5in). **IMMATURE FEMALE:** Yellowish throat, breast, eyebrow stripe and sides of neck; white back stripes and wing bars. **OTHER PLUMAGES:** *See* Plate 69.

PINE WARBLER *Dendroica pinus* 12.5–14.5cm (5–5.75in). **IMMATURE:** Grayish-brown above; buffish-white below; 2 white wing bars; whitish eyebrow stripe. **ADULT:** *See* Plate 69.

KIRTLAND'S WARBLER *Dendroica kirtlandii* 15cm (5.75in). **ADULT FEMALE AND NON-BREEDING MALE:** Upperparts bluish-gray; black streaks on back; throat and belly yellow; black side streaks; broken eye-ring; forehead and lores dark gray. Bobs tail. **BREEDING MALE:** *See* Plate 69.

imm ♀

CERULEAN
WARBLER

adult ♀

VITELLINE
WARBLER

BLACK-THROATED
GREEN WARBLER

imm ♀

ORANGE-CROWNED
WARBLER

imm ♀

BLACKBURNIAN
WARBLER

imm

PINE WARBLER

adult ♀ & non-br ♂

KIRTLAND'S
WARBLER

CHESTNUT-SIDED WARBLER *Dendroica pensylvanica* 11.5–13.5cm (4.5–5.25in). **NON-BREEDING ADULT AND IMMATURE:** Yellowish-green above; white eye-ring; pale gray underparts; 2 yellowish wing bars. **BREEDING MALE:** *See* Plate 74.

WILSON'S WARBLER *Wilsonia pusilla* 11–12.5cm (4.25–5in). **IMMATURE FEMALE:** Lacks black on cap. Yellow forehead, eyebrow stripe, lores, and underparts. **ADULT:** *See* Plate 70.

YELLOW WARBLER *Dendroica petechia* 11.5–13.5cm (4.5–5.25in). **ADULT FEMALE:** Yellow overall. Faintly streaked or unstreaked below; no reddish-brown on head. *See also* Plate 76. **NON-BREEDING FEMALE:** Underparts with some buffish-white. **IMMATURE:** *See* Plate 76. **ADULT MALE:** *See* Plate 72.

RUBY-CROWNED KINGLET *Regulus calendula* 11.5cm (4.5in). Tiny, with olive-colored upperparts, bold white eye-ring, and 2 whitish wing bars. **FEMALE:** Lacks red crest. **MALE:** *See* Plate 74.

TENNESSEE WARBLER *Vermivora peregrina* 11.5–12.5cm (4.5–5in). **IMMATURE:** Olive-green above; yellowish-green below except for white undertail coverts. **BREEDING MALE:** *See* Plate 74.

PLUMBEOUS WARBLER *Dendroica plumbea* 12cm (4.75in). Flicks tail. **IMMATURE:** Greenish-gray upperparts; eyebrow stripe either white or buffish; underparts buffish. **ADULT:** *See* Plate 75.

NASHVILLE WARBLER *Vermivora ruficapilla* 11.5–12.5cm (4.5–5in). **IMMATURE:** White eye-ring; brownish-gray head contrasts with yellowish-green upperparts; underparts paler yellow with whitish throat and tan sides. **ADULT:** *See* Plate 70.

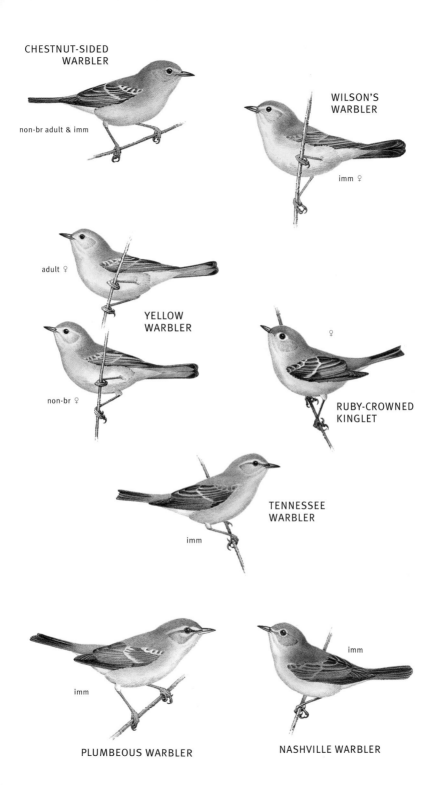

CHESTNUT-SIDED
WARBLER

non-br adult & imm

WILSON'S
WARBLER

imm ♀

adult ♀

YELLOW
WARBLER

non-br ♀

♀

RUBY-CROWNED
KINGLET

TENNESSEE
WARBLER

imm

imm

PLUMBEOUS WARBLER

imm

NASHVILLE WARBLER

● **COMMON YELLOWTHROAT** *Geothlypis trichas* 11.5–14cm (4.5–5.5in). **ADULT FEMALE:** Lacks facial mask; bright yellow throat and breast contrast with whitish belly; narrow, whitish eye-ring; usually pale, buffish eyebrow stripe. *See also* Plate 71. **IMMATURE:** Duller and browner than adult female. **MALE:** *See* Plate 71.

● **HOODED WARBLER** *Wilsonia citrina* 12.5–14.5cm (5–5.75in). Flicks and fans tail showing white outertail feathers. **ADULT FEMALE:** Variable hood, from almost complete to only black markings on crown. **MALE:** *See* Plate 70.

● **BLACK-THROATED BLUE WARBLER** *Dendroica caerulescens* 12–14cm (4.75–5.5in). **FEMALE:** Narrow, whitish eyebrow stripe; white wing spot, sometimes absent in young females. **MALE:** *See* Plate 74.

● **PROTHONOTARY WARBLER** *Protonotaria citrea* 13.5cm (5.25in). **FEMALE:** Golden yellow face, throat, and breast; blue-gray wings and tail. **MALE:** *See* Plate 72.

● **KENTUCKY WARBLER** *Oporornis formosus* 12.5–14.5cm (5–5.75in). **IMMATURE FEMALE:** Black on face absent, replaced by gray on lores. **ADULT:** *See* Plate 70.

● **MOURNING WARBLER** *Oporornis philadelphia* 13–14.5cm (5–5.75in). Primarily terrestrial. **IMMATURE:** Hood pale gray or brownish; incomplete whitish eye-ring; throat yellowish. **ADULT:** *See* Plate 71.

● **BAHAMA YELLOWTHROAT** *Geothlypis rostrata* 15cm (5.75in). Relatively large, slow-moving, with relatively heavy bill. **FEMALE:** Lacks mask. Yellow throat, breast, and belly; gray crown; whitish eye-ring and eyebrow stripe. **MALE:** *See* Plate 71.

● **CONNECTICUT WARBLER** *Oporornis agilis* 13.5–15cm (5.25–5.75in). Primarily terrestrial. Large, stocky. **ADULT FEMALE AND IMMATURE:** Pale gray-brown hood; whitish throat; white eye-ring; undertail coverts extend nearly to end of tail. **ADULT MALE:** *See* Plate 71.

COMMON
YELLOWTHROAT

adult ♀

HOODED
WARBLER

adult ♀

♀

BLACK-THROATED
BLUE WARBLER

♀

PROTHONOTARY
WARBLER

imm ♀

KENTUCKY
WARBLER

MOURNING
WARBLER

imm

♀

BAHAMA
YELLOWTHROAT

CONNECTICUT
WARBLER

adult ♀ & imm

ANTILLEAN EUPHONIA *Euphonia musica* 12cm (4.75in). Small and compact, with sky-blue crown and hindneck. **MALE:** Variable, from greenish like female (Lesser Antilles) to primarily dark above and rich yellow below, on rump and forehead (Puerto Rico). **FEMALE:** Duller. Greenish above, yellowish-green below; yellowish rump and forehead. **VOICE:** Rapid, subdued, almost tinkling *ti-tit*; hard, metallic *chi-chink*; plaintive *whee*; jumbled, tinkling song mixed with explosive notes. **STATUS AND RANGE:** Locally common in Hispaniola and Puerto Rico. Threatened in Haiti. Uncommon in Lesser Antilles, including Barbuda, Antigua, Guadeloupe, Dominica, Martinique, St Lucia, St Vincent, and Grenada. **HABITAT:** Dense forests from dry lowlands to wet mountain tops, particularly those with mistletoe.

JAMAICAN EUPHONIA *Euphonia jamaica* 11.5cm (4.5in). Small, compact, and drab, with stubby, dark bill. Arboreal. **ADULT MALE:** Grayish-blue overall; yellow belly. **FEMALE AND IMMATURE:** Two-toned: head and underparts bluish-gray; back, wings, and flanks olive-green. **VOICE:** Staccato churring, like motor starting. Also pleasant, squeaky whistle. **STATUS AND RANGE:** Endemic to Jamaica: common and widespread. **HABITAT:** Primarily open secondary forests of lowland hills, but at all elevations in open areas with trees, woodlands, forest edges, shrubbery, and gardens.

RED-LEGGED HONEYCREEPER *Cyanerpes cyaneus* 13cm (5in). Small, with long, slender, down-curved bill. **BREEDING MALE:** Purplish-blue; light blue crown; red legs. Underwing mostly yellow. **ADULT FEMALE:** Dull olive-green, paler below with faint whitish streaks. **NON-BREEDING ADULT MALE:** Similar to female, wings and tail black. **IMMATURE:** Similar to adult female, more lightly streaked. **VOICE:** Short, harsh *chrik-chrik*. **STATUS AND RANGE:** Rather rare and local resident in Cuba. **HABITAT:** Forests and forest edges.

ORANGEQUIT *Euneornis campestris* 14cm (5.5in). Small, with slightly down-curved black bill. **ADULT MALE:** Gray-blue overall with orangish-red throat. **FEMALE AND IMMATURE:** Crown and hindneck olive-gray; grayish-white below with faint streaks. **VOICE:** Thin, high-pitched *tseet* or *swee*. **STATUS AND RANGE:** Endemic to Jamaica: locally common, especially at Newcastle, Hardwar Gap, Mandeville, and Anchovy. **HABITAT:** Humid forests and woodlands at all altitudes, most frequently mid-elevations.

BANANAQUIT *Coereba flaveola* 10–12.5cm (4–5in). Highly variable. **ADULT:** In most, curved bill; white eyebrow stripe and wing spot; yellow breast, belly, and rump. Black color phase in Grenada and St Vincent has slight greenish-yellow wash on breast and lacks white eyebrow stripe and wing spot. **IMMATURE:** Duller. **VOICE:** Variable. Generally thin, high-pitched ticks, clicks and insect-like buzzes. Call note unmusical *tsip*. **STATUS AND RANGE:** Very common resident throughout West Indies except Cuba where vagrant. **HABITAT:** All habitats, except highest peaks and driest lowlands.

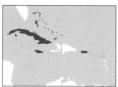

SCARLET TANAGER *Piranga olivacea* 18cm (7in). **FEMALE:** Overall yellowish-green plumage; distinctive bill shape; white wing linings in flight. **NON-BREEDING MALE:** Similar to female, but wings black. (Female Baltimore Oriole more yellowish, with more pointed bill and whitish wing bars.) **BREEDING MALE:** Red with black wings and tail. **STATUS AND RANGE:** Rare migrant primarily September and October, less frequent March through May in Bahamas, Cuba, Jamaica, and Cayman Islands. Very rare on Puerto Rico, Virgin Islands, and northern Lesser Antilles south to Antigua. Generally vagrant in southern Lesser Antilles. **HABITAT:** Open woods, forest edges, and gardens with trees.

SUMMER TANAGER *Piranga rubra* 18–19.5cm (7–7.5in). Large-billed tanager. **ADULT MALE:** Entirely red, brighter below; wings slightly darker. **FEMALE:** Yellowish olive-green above; yellowish-orange below. **IMMATURE MALE:** Similar to female, but with reddish tinge. (Female Scarlet Tanager yellow-green below; lacks orange tinge; has whitish rather than yellow wing linings.) **STATUS AND RANGE:** Uncommon migrant and rare non-breeding resident in Bahamas, Cuba, Jamaica, and Cayman Islands September through May. Vagrant elsewhere in West Indies. **HABITAT:** Woodlands, forest edges, and gardens, primarily at mid-elevations.

ANTILLEAN
EUPHONIA

♀

♂ Hispaniola race

♂ Puerto
Rico race

JAMAICAN
EUPHONIA

adult ♂

♀ & imm

adult ♀

♂

RED-LEGGED
HONEYCREEPER

br ♂

ORANGEQUIT

adult ♂

♀ & imm

BANANAQUIT

adult
Bahamas
race

imm

adult
Puerto
Rico race

adult St
Vincent
race

non-br ♂   SCARLET TANAGER

♀

br ♂

♀

adult ♂

SUMMER TANAGER

PUERTO RICAN STRIPE-HEADED TANAGER *Spindalis portoricensis* 16.5cm (6.5in). **MALE:** Black head striped white. Underparts primarily yellow; reddish-orange wash on breast and hindneck. **FEMALE:** Underparts dull whitish; gray streaks on sides and flanks; whitish mustache stripe; inconspicuous white eyebrow stripe. **VOICE:** Variable thin, high-pitched whistle *zeé-tit-zeé-tittit-zeé*. Also soft *teweep*. **STATUS AND RANGE:** Endemic to Puerto Rico: common and widespread. **HABITAT:** Woodlands and forests at all elevations.

HISPANIOLAN STRIPE-HEADED TANAGER *Spindalis dominicensis* 16.5cm (6.5in). **MALE:** Black head striped white. Underparts yellow; reddish-brown wash on breast. **FEMALE:** Underparts whitish with fine stripes; whitish mustache stripe. **VOICE:** Weak, high-pitched *thseep*. Also thin, high-pitched whistle. **STATUS AND RANGE:** Endemic to Hispaniola: common in mountains, less so on coast. **HABITAT:** Forests.

WESTERN STRIPE-HEADED TANAGER *Spindalis zena* 15cm (5.75in). **MALE:** Black head striped white. **FEMALE:** 2 whitish facial stripes. **VOICE:** Variable, generally very high-pitched, thin, ventriloquial whistle. **STATUS AND RANGE:** Common resident throughout Cuba and Bahamas. Fairly common resident on Grand Cayman (Cayman Islands). **HABITAT:** Bahamas: native and Australian pines, coppice. Cayman Islands: open woods, brush. Cuba: all elevations in open woods, brush, and mangroves.

JAMAICAN STRIPE-HEADED TANAGER *Spindalis nigricephala* 18cm (7in). Primarily orangish-yellow underparts. **MALE:** Black head striped white; considerable white on wings. **FEMALE:** Gray throat and upper breast. **VOICE:** Soft *seep* and high, fast notes. **STATUS AND RANGE:** Endemic to Jamaica: common and widespread, particularly hills and mountains. **HABITAT:** Forests, woodlands, and brushy areas.

PUERTO RICAN STRIPE-
HEADED TANAGER

♀

♂

HISPANIOLAN STRIPE-
HEADED TANAGER

♂

♀

Cuba race

WESTERN STRIPE-
HEADED TANAGER

Bahamas race

JAMAICAN STRIPE-
HEADED TANAGER

♀

♂

LESSER ANTILLEAN TANAGER *Tangara cucullata* 15cm (5.75in). **MALE:** Iridescent orangish-yellow above, sometimes with greenish cast; dark reddish-brown cap; bluish-green wings and tail. **FEMALE:** Duller, with greenish upperparts. **VOICE:** Weak, high-pitched series of single notes followed by twitter. **STATUS AND RANGE:** Uncommon resident known only from St Vincent and Grenada. **HABITAT:** Forests, gardens, and second growth at all elevations.

BLACK-CROWNED PALM-TANAGER *Phaenicophilus palmarum* 18cm (7in). **ADULT:** Black crown; white throat blends to gray breast. **VOICE:** Nasal *pi-au*, pleasant dawn song, and low *chep*. **STATUS AND RANGE:** Endemic to Hispaniola: common in lowlands, less frequently high elevations. In Haiti, generally common, but rare west of Port-au-Prince. **HABITAT:** Primarily semi-arid and humid thickets, but wherever there are trees, from towns to dense forests.

GRAY-CROWNED PALM-TANAGER *Phaenicophilus poliocephalus* 18cm (7in). **ADULT:** Black mask; gray crown; sharp contrast between white throat and gray breast. **VOICE:** *Peee-u*. **STATUS AND RANGE:** Endemic to Hispaniola: common, but local on southern peninsula of Haiti and islands of Île-à-Vache, Grande Cayemite, and Gonâve. In Dominican Republic, rare in Sierra de Baoruco and southern part of Loma de Toro and Hoyo de Pelempito. Endangered. **HABITAT:** Forests at all elevations. Also open areas and gardens.

PUERTO RICAN TANAGER *Nesospingus speculiferus* 18–20cm (7–8in). **ADULT:** Olive-brown above, white below; pale brownish stripes on breast; white wing spot. **IMMATURE:** Lacks wing spot. **VOICE:** Noisy. Harsh *chuck* or *chewp* frequently runs into chatter. **STATUS AND RANGE:** Endemic to Puerto Rico: common in higher mountains, but regular locally at moderate altitudes. **HABITAT:** Undisturbed mountain forests, also second growth.

WESTERN CHAT-TANAGER *Calyptophilus tertius* 20cm (8in). Mockingbird-shaped, with long, rounded tail. Dark brown above; white throat and breast; yellow lores; fringe on bend of wing. Lacks eye-ring. Primarily terrestrial. **VOICE:** Emphatic, clear whistling *chip-chip-swerp-swerp-swerp*, a buzzy *wee-chee-chee-chee-chee* or *chirri-chirri-chirri-chip-chip-chip*, repeated. Also sharp *chick*. **STATUS AND RANGE:** Endemic to Hispaniola. Haiti: locally common in higher mountains. Dominican Republic: fairly common, but local in Sierra de Baoruco. Endangered. **HABITAT:** Wet broadleaf forests.

EASTERN CHAT-TANAGER *Calyptophilus frugivorus* 17cm (6.75in). Similar to Western Chat-tanager, but smaller, with yellow eye-ring. Primarily terrestrial. **VOICE:** Similar to Western Chat-tanager. **STATUS AND RANGE:** Endemic to Hispaniola. Dominican Republic: uncommon and local in Cordillera Central and Sierra de Neiba. Unrecorded for decades from Samaná Peninsula and Gonave Island. Endangered. **HABITAT:** Primarily dense undergrowth along streams in deciduous forests.

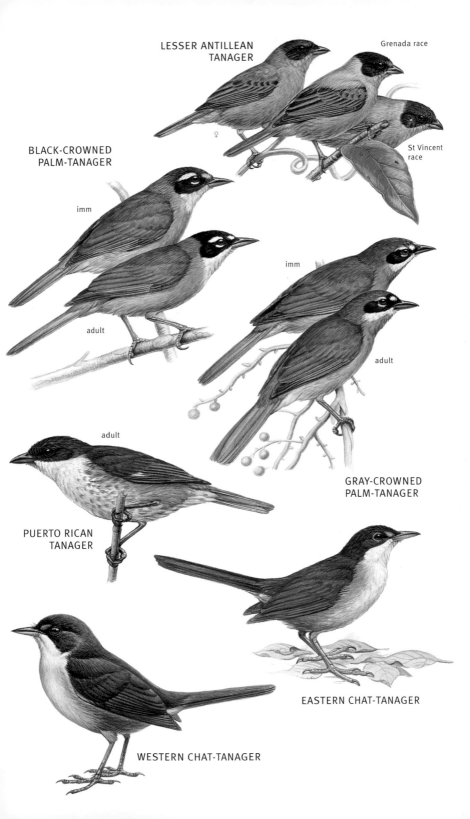

LESSER ANTILLEAN
TANAGER

Grenada race

St Vincent
race

♀

BLACK-CROWNED
PALM-TANAGER

imm

adult

imm

adult

GRAY-CROWNED
PALM-TANAGER

adult

PUERTO RICAN
TANAGER

EASTERN CHAT-TANAGER

WESTERN CHAT-TANAGER

ORCHARD ORIOLE *Icterus spurius* 16.5–18cm (6.5–7in). **ADULT MALE:** Reddish-brown breast, belly, lower back, and bend of wing. **FEMALE:** Grayish olive-green above; brighter on head and rump; dull yellow below; 2 white wing bars; bright olive-green tail. **IMMATURE MALE:** Similar to female, but with black chin and throat. **STATUS AND RANGE:** Very rare migrant in Cuba in October, April, and May. **HABITAT:** Woodlands and gardens.

BALTIMORE ORIOLE *Icterus galbula* 18–20cm (7–8in). **ADULT MALE:** Orange and black plumage; white wing bar; orange tail patches. **ADULT FEMALE AND IMMATURE:** Brownish above, orange-yellow below with 2 whitish wing bars. **STATUS AND RANGE:** Uncommon migrant and rare non-breeding resident in Bahamas, Cuba, and Jamaica September through May. Rarer in Hispaniola, Puerto Rico, larger Virgin Islands, and Cayman Islands. **HABITAT:** All elevations in gardens with trees, semi-arid scrubland, open woodlands, swamps, and forest edges.

HOODED ORIOLE *Icterus cucullatus* 7.5cm (7in). **ADULT MALE:** Orange-yellow with black throat, breast, wings, back, and tail; 2 white wing bars. **FEMALE AND IMMATURE:** Olive-yellow overall; 2 white wing bars, lower less conspicuous. Longer, more slender, down-curved bill and longer tail than Orchard Oriole. **STATUS AND RANGE:** Vagrant in Cuba. **HABITAT:** Palms, woodlands, and thickets.

JAMAICAN ORIOLE *Icterus leucopteryx* 21cm (8in). Bright yellow to dull greenish-yellow with black mask and large white wing patch. **IMMATURE:** 2 wing bars. **VOICE:** Whistled *you cheat* or *cheat-you*. **STATUS AND RANGE:** Common resident in Jamaica and San Andrés. These islands comprise entire range. **HABITAT:** Jamaica: nearly all forests, woodlands, and areas with trees except mangroves. Also gardens.

TROUPIAL *Icterus icterus* 25cm (9.75in). Large size, orange-yellow and black, extensive white wing patches. **VOICE:** Clear whistles *troup, troup…* or *troup-ial, troup-ial….* **STATUS AND RANGE:** Probably introduced. Puerto Rico: common in southwest. Virgin Islands: south and east coasts of St Thomas, on Water Island and St John. Lesser Antilles: recent reports from Antigua, Dominica, and Grenada. **HABITAT:** Principally arid scrublands.

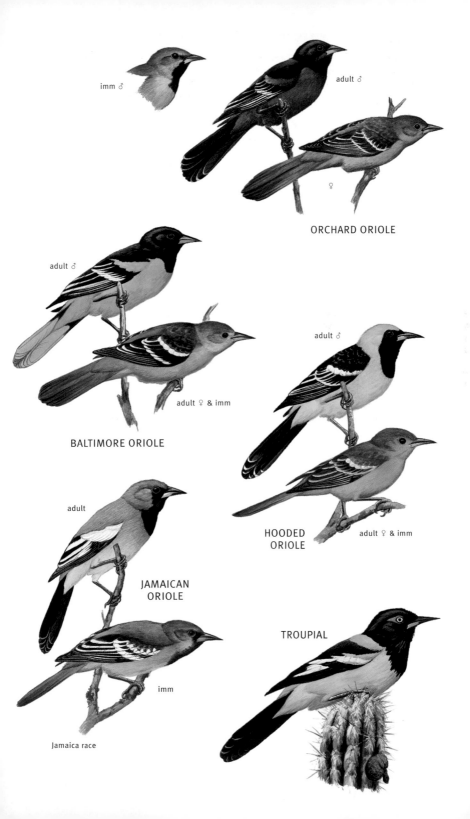

imm ♂

adult ♂

♀

ORCHARD ORIOLE

adult ♂

adult ♀ & imm

BALTIMORE ORIOLE

adult ♂

adult ♀ & imm

HOODED ORIOLE

adult

JAMAICAN ORIOLE

TROUPIAL

imm

Jamaica race

MARTINIQUE ORIOLE *Icterus bonana* 18–21cm (7–8in). **ADULT:** Reddish-brown hood and reddish-orange shoulder, rump, lower belly, and abdomen. **VOICE:** Clear whistles and harsh, scolding call. **STATUS AND RANGE:** Endemic to Martinique: uncommon. Most frequent in south and north center. Endangered. **HABITAT:** Nearly all forests from dry coast to humid mountains. Also plantations and gardens with trees.

MONTSERRAT ORIOLE *Icterus oberi* 20–22cm (8–8.5in). **ADULT MALE:** Yellowish lower back, rump, shoulder, lower breast, belly, and abdomen. **ADULT FEMALE:** Mainly yellowish-green above; underparts bright yellow. **IMMATURE:** Duller. **VOICE:** Loud whistles; also harsh, scolding *chuur.* **STATUS AND RANGE:** Endemic to Montserrat: rare. Found only in Soufrière Hills and Centre Hills. Endangered. **HABITAT:** Mid-elevation forests.

ST LUCIA ORIOLE *Icterus laudabilis* 20–22cm (8–8.5in). **ADULT MALE:** Primarily black; lower back, rump, shoulder, and lower belly orange or orange-yellow. **ADULT FEMALE:** Duller. **IMMATURE:** Mostly greenish, with blackish throat. **VOICE:** Drawn-out melodic whistles. **STATUS AND RANGE:** Endemic to St Lucia: uncommon and becoming scarcer. Threatened. **HABITAT:** Woodlands, including moderately dry and moist forests from near sea level to about 700m (2300ft); often associated with palms.

GREATER ANTILLEAN ORIOLE *Icterus dominicensis* 20–22cm (8–8.5in). **ADULT:** Yellow shoulders, rump, and undertail coverts extending to lower breast in Bahamas birds. **IMMATURE:** Upperparts mainly olive, underparts dull yellow; wings black; throat black or reddish-brown. **VOICE:** Hard, sharp *keek* or *check.* **STATUS AND RANGE:** Fairly common resident in Cuba, Hispaniola, and Puerto Rico. In Bahamas, only Andros, where common, and Abaco, where near extirpation. Bahamas race threatened. These islands comprise entire range. **HABITAT:** Forests, forest edges, woodlands, and gardens from coast to mid-elevations, particularly near palms.

MARTINIQUE
ORIOLE

adult

adult ♂

adult ♀

MONTSERRAT
ORIOLE

adult ♂

ST LUCIA
ORIOLE

imm

Puerto Rico
race

adult

Bahamas
race

adult

GREATER
ANTILLEAN
ORIOLE

imm

adult

Hispaniola race

CUBAN BLACKBIRD *Dives atroviolacea* 25–28cm (10–11in). Grackle-sized black bird with glossy purplish iridescence, dark eye, and square tail. Forms flocks. (Female Red-shouldered Blackbird smaller. Male Shiny Cowbird smaller, with more conspicuous sheen.) **VOICE:** Vast variety of calls; most typical is loud, repetitive *tí-o*, with metallic tone. **STATUS AND RANGE:** Endemic to Cuba: common and widespread. **HABITAT:** Primarily gardens in urban and rural areas, also woodlands from lowlands to mid-elevations.

SHINY COWBIRD *Molothrus bonariensis* 18–20cm (7–8in). Medium-sized dark bird with conical bill. Often in flocks. **ADULT MALE:** Glossy black with purplish sheen. (Female Red-shouldered Blackbird has finer bill and lacks purplish sheen.) **ADULT FEMALE:** Drab grayish-brown upperparts; lighter brown underparts; faint eyebrow stripe. **IMMATURE:** Resembles adult female, but underparts finely streaked. **VOICE:** Whistles followed by melodious trill. Variety of short call notes. **STATUS AND RANGE:** Common resident through much of West Indies. Range expanding. **HABITAT:** Primarily open country and edges in lowlands. Favors dairies.

BROWN-HEADED COWBIRD *Molothrus ater* 16.5cm (6.5in). **MALE:** Black with metallic greenish sheen; head brown. **FEMALE:** Brownish-gray. Grayer than Shiny Cowbird, with whitish throat and no eyebrow stripe. **VOICE:** Distinctive harsh rattle and creaky whistles. **STATUS AND RANGE:** Rare non-breeding resident in Bahamas primarily October through February. Records from Cuba. Expanding range. **HABITAT:** Farms, gardens, and rural areas.

GREATER ANTILLEAN GRACKLE *Quiscalus niger* 25–30cm (10–12in). Fairly large, with dark plumage, long tail, and conical, pointed bill. Forms flocks. **ADULT MALE:** Glossy metallic-blue to violet-black plumage; yellow eye; deep, V-shaped tail. **ADULT FEMALE:** Duller; tail with smaller 'V'. **IMMATURE:** Dull brownish black; tail flat; eye pale brown. (All other black birds within range lack V-shaped tail.) **VOICE:** Highly variable, including high *cling, cling, cling.* **STATUS AND RANGE:** Common resident in Cuba, Jamaica, Hispaniola, Puerto Rico, and Cayman Islands. These islands comprise entire range. **HABITAT:** Primarily open areas in lowlands.

JAMAICAN BLACKBIRD *Nesopsar nigerrimus* 18cm (7in). Medium-sized, entirely black, with slender, pointed bill and short tail. Arboreal. (Shiny Cowbird has more conical bill; not strictly arboreal. Male Jamaican Becard stockier, with stubbier bill.) **VOICE:** Loud, wheezy *zwheezoo-whezoo whe.* Also *check.* **STATUS AND RANGE:** Endemic to Jamaica: uncommon. Widely distributed, mostly higher elevations. Threatened. **HABITAT:** Wet mountain forests with bromeliads and mosses. Occasionally lower elevations.

CARIB GRACKLE *Quiscalus lugubris* 24–28cm (9.5–11in). Forms flocks. **ADULT MALE:** Black with violet, green or steel-blue sheen; yellowish-white eye; tail long and V-shaped. **ADULT FEMALE:** Smaller; varies from relatively dark to quite pale; tail shorter, less V-shaped. **IMMATURE:** Brownish-black. **VOICE:** 3–7 syllables with rising inflection. Also whistles and chucks. **STATUS AND RANGE:** Common year-round resident on most Lesser Antilles from Anguilla to Grenada. Possibly introduced to Lesser Antilles north of Montserrat. **HABITAT:** Primarily open areas in lowlands.

CUBAN BLACKBIRD

SHINY
COWBIRD

adult ♀

adult ♂

GREATER ANTILLEAN
GRACKLE

adult ♂

BROWN-HEADED
COWBIRD

♀

♂

JAMAICAN
BLACKBIRD

adult ♀

adult ♂

CARIB GRACKLE

TAWNY-SHOULDERED BLACKBIRD *Agelaius humeralis* 19–22cm (7.5–8.5in).
Medium-sized, black, with tawny shoulder patch, most conspicuous in flight. Forms flocks.
IMMATURE: Shoulder patch much smaller. Shoulder patch sometimes not visible, giving
appearance of female Red-shouldered Blackbird. **VOICE:** Strong, short *chic-chic* resembles
chip of Northern Yellowthroat. Sometimes harsh call similar to Red-shouldered Blackbird,
but softer, shorter, and less shrill. **STATUS AND RANGE:** Known only from Cuba, where common, and Haiti, where uncommon and local. Threatened on Haiti. **HABITAT:** Woodlands,
gardens, farms, swamp edges, pastures, rice fields, only in lowlands.

YELLOW-SHOULDERED BLACKBIRD *Agelaius xanthomus* 20–23cm (8–9in).
ADULT: Entirely glossy black with yellow shoulder patches. (Greater Antillean Oriole more
extensively yellow.) **IMMATURE:** Duller; abdomen brown. **VOICE:** Raspy *tnaaa*; whistle *tsuu*,
descending scale; melodious *eh-up*, second syllable lower and accented; *chuck*. **STATUS AND
RANGE:** Endemic to Puerto Rico: local along southwestern coast and on Mona Island.
Decidedly uncommon elsewhere. Critically endangered. **HABITAT:** Primarily mangroves and
arid scrublands.

EASTERN MEADOWLARK *Sturnella magna* 23cm (9in). Medium-sized, with yellow
underparts and conspicuous black 'V' on breast. Outertail feathers white; crown and upperparts striped. **VOICE:** Distinctive, high call on 3 tones. Also peculiar harsh, loud alarm note.
STATUS AND RANGE: Common resident in Cuba. **HABITAT:** Open grasslands, savannas,
marshes, and pastures with only scattered trees or bushes primarily in lowlands. Often
perches on fence posts or wires.

BOBOLINK *Dolichonyx oryzivorus* 18.5cm (7.25in). Large; forms flocks. **NON-BREEDING
ADULT:** Central buff crown stripe; unmarked buffish throat; streaked sides and abdomen;
pointed tail. **BREEDING MALE:** Black below, buff hindneck, white patches on wings and lower
back. **BREEDING FEMALE:** Similar, but with whitish throat. **VOICE:** Distinctive *pink*. **STATUS
AND RANGE:** Primarily migrant August through December, less frequent February through
May. Generally common in Bahamas, Cuba, Jamaica, and Cayman Islands; uncommon and
local in Puerto Rico, Virgin Islands, and Barbados; rare on Hispaniola, St Bartholomew,
Antigua, and Dominica; very rare among other Lesser Antilles. **HABITAT:** Rice fields, pastures, and grassy areas.

RED-WINGED BLACKBIRD *Agelaius phoeniceus* 19–23cm (7.5–9in). Medium-sized,
black. Sometimes in large flocks. **ADULT MALE:** Scarlet shoulder patch edged yellowish. Identical to male Red-shouldered. **FEMALE:** Brown above; buffish below, heavily streaked dark
brown; light buffish eyebrow stripe. **IMMATURE MALE:** Dark mottled brown; faint pale eyebrow stripe; small reddish-brown shoulder patch. **VOICE:** Bubbling, shrill *ok-a-lee*, repeated
often. Also sharp *chek*. **STATUS AND RANGE:** Common resident very locally in northern
Bahamas south to Andros and Eleuthera. **HABITAT:** Swamps and marshes.

RED-SHOULDERED BLACKBIRD *Agelaius assimilis*
19–23cm (7.5–9in). Medium-sized, black. Sometimes in large
flocks. **ADULT MALE:** Scarlet shoulder patch edged yellowish.
FEMALE: Entirely black. **IMMATURE MALE:** Shoulder patch reddish-
brown. (Male Shiny Cowbird has purplish sheen and heavier bill.
Cuban Blackbird larger; no shoulder patch. Red-winged Blackbird does not overlap in range.) **VOICE:** Harsh creaking and rather
shrill, non-melodious *o-wi-hiiii*, repeated often. Also, short *cheap*, *chek-chek-chek* or single
chek. **STATUS AND RANGE:** Endemic to Cuba: confined to western part of island where locally common. **HABITAT:** Swamps and marshes.

YELLOW-HEADED BLACKBIRD *Xanthocephalus xanthocephalus* 21–28cm (8–11in).
ADULT MALE: Black overall with orange-yellow hood and white wing patch. **ADULT FEMALE:**
Grayish-brown above; yellowish-orange eyebrow stripe, throat, breast and line below cheek.
STATUS AND RANGE: Vagrant in Bahamas, Cuba, and Cayman Islands. **HABITAT:** Swamps and
marshes.

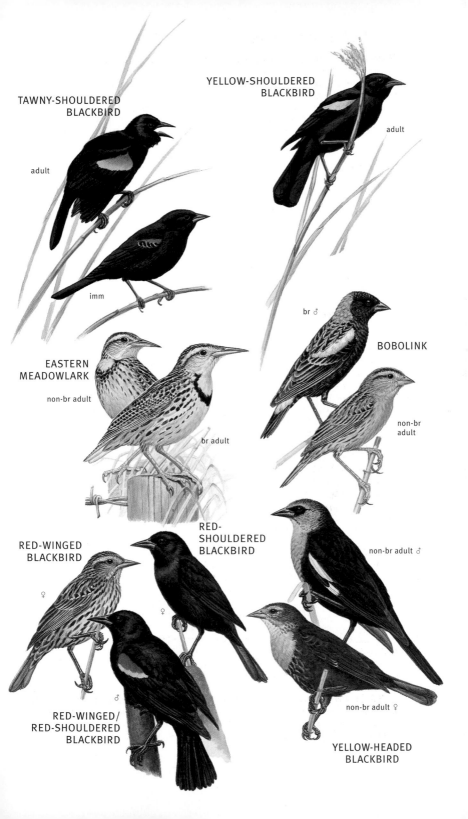

TAWNY-SHOULDERED
BLACKBIRD

adult

imm

YELLOW-SHOULDERED
BLACKBIRD

adult

EASTERN
MEADOWLARK

non-br adult

br adult

br ♂

BOBOLINK

non-br
adult

RED-WINGED
BLACKBIRD

♀

RED-
SHOULDERED
BLACKBIRD

♀

non-br adult ♂

RED-WINGED/
RED-SHOULDERED
BLACKBIRD

♂

non-br adult ♀

YELLOW-HEADED
BLACKBIRD

● **CUBAN GRASSQUIT** *Tiaris canora* 11.5cm (4.5in). Small, with olive upperparts. Conspicuous yellow crescent divides face and breast. Forms flocks. **MALE:** Black face and breast. **FEMALE:** Yellow less marked; face dark reddish-brown. **VOICE:** Shrill, raspy *chiri-wichi-wichi, chibiri-wichi-wichi* resembling Bee Hummingbird. Also *chip*. **STATUS AND RANGE:** Endemic to Cuba: common. Introduced to New Providence (Bahamas), where fairly common throughout island. **HABITAT:** Primarily semi-arid country; also pine undergrowth, edges of woods, bushy areas, shade coffee and citrus plantations, farms with much shrubbery, from coast to mid-elevations.

● **YELLOW-SHOULDERED GRASSQUIT** *Loxipasser anoxanthus* 10cm (4in). **ADULT MALE:** Two-toned: black head and underparts, yellowish wings and back; undertail coverts reddish-brown. **ADULT FEMALE:** Gray below, yellowish-green above; yellow patch on bend of wing. Undertail coverts pale reddish-brown. Yellowish in wing and rusty undertail coverts distinguish it from Black-faced Grassquit. **VOICE:** 5 notes, descending with echo-like quality. **STATUS AND RANGE:** Endemic to Jamaica: fairly common and widespread. **HABITAT:** Forest edges from wet to dry and all elevations. Also woodlands and gardens near wooded areas.

● **YELLOW-FACED GRASSQUIT** *Tiaris olivacea* 11.5cm (4.5in). **MALE:** Yellow throat and eyebrow stripe; black breast. **FEMALE AND IMMATURE:** Yellowish-olive coloration and usually faint yellowish eyebrow stripe, eye-ring, and chin. (Female and immature Black-faced Grassquit less olive, and lack facial markings.) **VOICE:** Soft *tek*; also thin trill, sometimes sequentially at different pitches. **STATUS AND RANGE:** Common resident in Cuba, Jamaica, Hispaniola, Puerto Rico, and Cayman Islands. **HABITAT:** Primarily open grassy areas from lowlands to moderate elevations, sometimes high mountains.

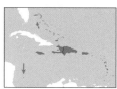

● **BLACK-FACED GRASSQUIT** *Tiaris bicolor* 11.5cm (4.5in). **MALE:** Black head and underparts. **FEMALE AND IMMATURE:** Drab brownish-olive overall. Female and immature drabber than Yellow-faced Grassquit and lack faint facial markings. (Male Yellow-shouldered Grassquit has yellowish back and wings; female a yellow wing patch.) **VOICE:** Emphatic buzz often followed by second louder effort. Also soft musical *tsip*. **STATUS AND RANGE:** Generally common resident throughout West Indies, though rare and very local in Cuba. Absent from Cayman Islands. **HABITAT:** Open areas with grasses and shrubs, forest clearings, road edges, sugarcane plantations, and gardens.

● **YELLOW-BELLIED SEEDEATER** *Sporophila nigricollis* 10.5cm (4.5in). **ADULT MALE:** Black hood; pale blue-gray bill; yellowish-white underparts. **FEMALE AND IMMATURE:** Olive-brown above, yellowish-buff below; dark bill. **VOICE:** Brief melodious warbling song frequently followed by buzzy notes. **STATUS AND RANGE:** Uncommon and local breeding resident on Grenada and Carriaçou in Grenadines March through November. Migrates outside breeding season. **HABITAT:** Shrubby fields and thickets, field edges, and roadsides.

● **RED SISKIN** *Carduelis cucullata* 10cm (4in). Small; forms flocks. **MALE:** Primarily orange-red with black hood. **FEMALE:** Orange rump, wing markings, and wash on breast. **VOICE:** High-pitched twitter and *chi-tit* similar to Warbling Silverbill. **STATUS AND RANGE:** Introduced to Puerto Rico: rare and local in dry foothills. Declining. **HABITAT:** Thick scrub, often in dry ravines.

● **ANTILLEAN SISKIN** *Carduelis dominicensis* 11cm (4.25in). Small, chunky bird with light yellow bill. Forms flocks. **MALE:** Black head and yellowish body; tail black with 2 yellow patches. **FEMALE:** Olive-green above, yellowish-white below, with faint pale gray streaks; 2 yellow wing bars; pale yellowish rump. **VOICE:** Soft *chut-chut* and higher-pitched *swee-ee*. Also low, bubbling trill. **STATUS AND RANGE:** Endemic to Hispaniola: common and widespread in western Dominican Republic. In Haiti, uncommon, but increasing, in Massif de la Hotte. **HABITAT:** Pine forests and associated grassy clearings and forest edges in mountains; wanders to lower altitudes.

CUBAN
GRASSQUIT

♂

♀

YELLOW-SHOULDERED
GRASSQUIT

adult ♂

adult ♀

YELLOW-FACED
GRASSQUIT

♂

Puerto Rico
race

♀ & imm

BLACK-FACED
GRASSQUIT

♂

♀ & imm

YELLOW-BELLIED
SEEDEATER

adult ♂

♀ & imm

♀

♂

ANTILLEAN
SISKIN

♀

RED SISKIN

♂

● **AMERICAN GOLDFINCH** *Carduelis tristis* 11–12cm (4.25–4.75in). **NON-BREEDING ADULT AND IMMATURE:** Brownish or grayish above; black wings with white wing bars; light gray to whitish below; whitish rump; often some yellowish on face. **BREEDING MALE:** Bright yellow overall with black cap, wings, and tail. **BREEDING FEMALE:** Olive above, yellowish below; black wings with white wing bars and white rump. **STATUS AND RANGE:** Vagrant in Bahamas (Grand Bahama, Abaco, and Eleuthera) and Cuba. Occurs mid-October through December and also April. **HABITAT:** Weedy fields, roadsides, thickets, and second growth.

● **GRASSLAND YELLOW-FINCH** *Sicalis luteola* 12cm (4.75in). **ADULT MALE:** Upperparts pale yellow, heavily streaked with blackish; underparts and rump yellow. **ADULT FEMALE:** Similar, but duller. **IMMATURE:** Like female, but with blackish streaks on breast. **VOICE:** Distinctive buzzy trill. **STATUS AND RANGE:** Probably introduced. Uncommon and local resident in Antigua, Guadeloupe, Martinique, St Lucia, Barbados, St Vincent, and Grenada. **HABITAT:** Open grassy fields and runway edges.

● **SAFFRON FINCH** *Sicalis flaveola* 14cm (5.5in). **ADULT:** Medium-sized; entirely yellow with an orange crown. **MALE:** Crown bright orange. **FEMALE:** Crown yellowish-orange. **IMMATURE:** Generally gray, paler below, with yellow undertail coverts and, with age, a yellow breast band. (Yellow and Prothonotary Warblers smaller; finer bill; not in grassy habitats.) **VOICE:** Soft or loud, sharp *pink*; a whistle *wheat* on one pitch; a fairly loud, melodious, but slightly harsh *chit, chit, chit, chi-chit,* of differing length. **STATUS AND RANGE:** Introduced. Jamaica: widespread and common; Puerto Rico: fairly common, but local in and around San Juan. **HABITAT:** Puerto Rico: cultivated lawns; Jamaica: also roadsides and farmlands with seeding grasses.

● **HOUSE SPARROW** *Passer domesticus* 15cm (5.75in). Forms flocks. **MALE:** Black bib, gray crown, and pale cheek. **FEMALE AND IMMATURE:** Buff-colored eyebrow stripe and underparts; brown upperparts streaked with black. **VOICE:** Distinctive *chirp.* **STATUS AND RANGE:** Introduced. Cuba: very common and widespread. Bahamas (Northern Bahamas and Great Inagua), Dominican Republic, Puerto Rico, Virgin Islands (St Thomas and St John), St Martin, and Guadeloupe: locally common. Range expanding. **HABITAT:** Urban areas.

● **VILLAGE WEAVER** *Ploceus cucullatus* 17cm (6.75in). Chunky with heavy bill. Often in flocks. **MALE:** Distinctive orange-yellow overall, with black hood and red eye. (Adult male Baltimore Oriole also black and orange-yellow, but slimmer with longer bill and tail.) **FEMALE:** Yellowish-green on face and breast with yellow wing bars. (Female Antillean Siskin smaller, with paler and less massive bill, and no eyebrow stripe.) **VOICE:** Steady high-pitched chatter with musical whistling calls. **STATUS AND RANGE:** Introduced. Hispaniola: common and widespread. Martinique: common very locally on northern end of island. **HABITAT:** Mostly lowlands in rice fields, vegetation near water, and open woodlands and scrub. Also gardens.

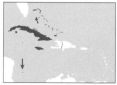

● **DICKCISSEL** *Spiza americana* 15–18cm (5.75–7in). Yellowish wash on breast; dull yellow eyebrow stripe; thick bill; reddish-brown bend of wing. **NON-BREEDING MALE:** Pale but noticeable black throat patch. **FEMALE:** Black on throat confined to few streaks. **BREEDING MALE:** Dark black throat patch; yellow below more extensive. **STATUS AND RANGE:** Rare migrant September through November and March through April in Bahamas, San Andrés, and Providencia; very rare in Cuba and Jamaica; vagrant elsewhere in West Indies. **HABITAT:** Open grasslands with scattered trees.

AMERICAN
GOLDFINCH

br ♂

non-br ♀

non-br ♂

GRASSLAND
YELLOW-FINCH

adult ♂

imm

SAFFRON
FINCH

♂

imm

HOUSE
SPARROW

adult ♂

♀ & imm

♀ & non-br ♂

VILLAGE
WEAVER

♀

♂

DICKCISSEL

br ♂

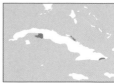

ZAPATA SPARROW *Torreornis inexpectata* 16.5cm (6.5in). Plump; yellow underparts; white throat; dark mustache stripe; dark reddish-brown crown; olive-gray upperparts. **VOICE:** 4 distinct calls. Most typical is short, somewhat metallic trill, repeated at intervals. It is high-pitched and penetrating, *tziii-tzziii-tzzi-ii....* **STATUS AND RANGE:** Endemic to Cuba: very local. Common on Cayo Coco; uncommon in Zapata Swamp north of Santo Tomás; rarer in coastal areas east of Guantánamo Bay. Threatened. **HABITAT:** Sawgrass country with scattered bushes; dry vegetation, semi-deciduous woods, and swampy areas.

ROSE-BREASTED GROSBEAK *Pheucticus ludovicianus* 19–20cm (7.5–8in). **MALE:** Pinkish-red breast; black head and back; white wing bars; pink wing linings in flight. **FEMALE:** Large, with heavy bill, white crown stripes, and white wing bars. Streaked underparts; yellow wing linings in flight. **STATUS AND RANGE:** Non-breeding resident in West Indies October through April, most frequent during migration. Generally uncommon in Bahamas, Cuba, and Cayman Islands; rare in Jamaica, Hispaniola, Puerto Rico, and Virgin Islands; vagrant among larger Lesser Antilles. Common migrant on Providencia and San Andrés. **HABITAT:** Scrub, woodlands, forest edges. Also gardens.

LESSER ANTILLEAN SALTATOR *Saltator albicollis* 22cm (8.5in). Upperparts dull green. **ADULT:** Whitish eyebrow stripe; black bill with orange-white tip; underparts streaked with olive-green; black mustache stripe. **IMMATURE:** Duller facial markings and breast streaks. **VOICE:** Series of harsh, loud notes that rise and fall. **STATUS AND RANGE:** Common resident in Guadeloupe, Dominica, Martinique, and St Lucia. These islands comprise entire range. **HABITAT:** Thickets, second growth, dry scrub, and forest edge undergrowth.

WHITE-WINGED CROSSBILL *Loxia leucoptera* 15cm (5.75in). Crossed bill tips; 2 broad, white wing bars on black wings. Forms flocks. **ADULT MALE:** Pale red overall. **ADULT FEMALE:** Yellowish rump and finely streaked breast. **IMMATURE:** Browner and more heavily streaked. **VOICE:** High-pitched, emphatic, repeated *chu-chu-chu-chu.* **STATUS AND RANGE:** Resident in Hispaniola: uncommon and local in highest mountains. Declining. Endangered. **HABITAT:** Pine forests.

PUERTO RICAN BULLFINCH *Loxigilla portoricensis* 16.5–19cm (6.5–7.5in). **ADULT:** Black, with reddish-brown throat, undertail coverts, and crown band. (Greater Antillean Bullfinch has less reddish-brown in crown. Lesser Antillean Bullfinch nearly lacks this color in crown.) **IMMATURE:** Dark olive-green; only undertail coverts reddish-brown. **VOICE:** Distinctive 2–10 rising whistles followed by buzz. Also, whistled *coochi, coochi, coochi,* and medium-strength *check.* **STATUS AND RANGE:** Endemic to Puerto Rico: common. Absent from extreme eastern tip of island. **HABITAT:** Forests and dense thickets of all types and at all elevations.

CUBAN BULLFINCH *Melopyrrha nigra* 14–15cm (5.5–5.75in). Small, dark, with thick, curved bill, and white band on edge of wing. **MALE:** Primarily black. **FEMALE:** Cuba—grayish-black; Grand Cayman—paler olive-gray. **IMMATURE:** White absent from wing, bill pale. **VOICE:** Buzzing *chip,* ventriloquial quality. Also thin, long, melodious trill, descending, then ascending, *ti, ti, ti, ti-si-sssiiittt-sssiii.* **STATUS AND RANGE:** Known only from Cuba and Grand Cayman in Cayman Islands. Cuba: common and widespread. Grand Cayman: most abundant at North Side, North Sound Estates, and South Sound Swamp. **HABITAT:** Forests including mangroves, woodlands, brushy areas, and undergrowth in pine country. Found at all elevations.

ST LUCIA BLACK FINCH *Melanospiza richardsoni* 13–14cm (5–5.5in). Heavy bill, pink legs. Bobs tail. Primarily terrestrial. **ADULT MALE:** Entirely black. **FEMALE:** Gray crown contrasts with brown back; buffish below. (Lesser Antillean Bullfinch has smaller bill; lacks pink legs; does not bob tail; female has grayish underparts and lacks gray crown.) **VOICE:** Burry *tick-zwee-swisiwis-you* with accents on 2nd and last notes; similar to Bananaquit. **STATUS AND RANGE:** Endemic to St Lucia: uncommon and local. **HABITAT:** Moist and semi-arid forests to 700m (2300ft).

ZAPATA
SPARROW

ROSE-BREASTED
GROSBEAK

♀

♂

WHITE-WINGED
CROSSBILL

adult ♀

adult ♂

LESSER ANTILLEAN
SALTATOR

adult

imm

adult

PUERTO RICAN BULLFINCH

Grand
Cayman
race

Cuba
race

♀

♂

CUBAN BULLFINCH

♀ & imm

adult ♂

ST LUCIA BLACK FINCH

● **GREATER ANTILLEAN BULLFINCH** *Loxigilla violacea* 15–18cm (5.75–7in). Chunky, with thick bill, reddish-brown eyebrow stripe, throat, and undertail coverts. **ADULT MALE:** Black overall. **ADULT FEMALE:** Duller black. **IMMATURE:** Olive-brown. (Puerto Rican Bullfinch has reddish-brown crown band.) **VOICE:** Shrill, insect-like *t'zeet, t'seet, t'seet, tseet, seet, seet, seet, seet, seet.* Also thin *spit.* **STATUS AND RANGE:** Common resident on most larger islands of Bahamas, Hispaniola, and Jamaica. These islands comprise entire range. **HABITAT:** Dense thickets and undergrowth at all elevations from dry coastal scrub to wet mountain forests, including gardens.

● **LESSER ANTILLEAN BULLFINCH** *Loxigilla noctis* 14–15.5cm (5.5–6in). **MALE (EXCEPT BARBADOS):** All black with reddish-brown chin, throat, and in front of eye. Some have red undertail coverts. **FEMALE, BARBADOS MALE, AND IMMATURE:** Brownish-olive above, gray below; orangish undertail coverts. (St Lucia Black Finch has pink legs and larger bill; bobs tail; female has gray crown.) **VOICE:** Short, crisp trill; harsh *chuk*; thin, wiry *tseep, tseep*; and a lengthy twitter. **STATUS AND RANGE:** Common resident through Lesser Antilles, but absent from Grenadines. Locally common in Virgin Islands (St John, St Croix). These islands comprise entire range. **HABITAT:** Shrubbery, gardens, thickets, and forest understory at all elevations.

● **BLUE-BLACK GRASSQUIT** *Volatinia jacarina* 11cm (4.25in). **ADULT MALE:** Entirely glossy blue-black; wingpits sometimes white. Frequently hops off perch into air, typically while singing. **ADULT FEMALE:** Olive-brown above and yellowish-buff below, heavily streaked with gray on breast and sides. **IMMATURE:** Similar, but grayer above and more darkly streaked below. **VOICE:** Emphatic *eee-slick.* **STATUS AND RANGE:** Common breeding resident in Grenada June through September. Most abundant in dry southwest. Migrates outside breeding season. **HABITAT:** Shrubby fields, roadsides, low scrubby second growth, farms, primarily at low elevations.

● **INDIGO BUNTING** *Passerina cyanea* 14cm (5.5in). **NON-BREEDING MALE:** Brown overall; traces of blue in wings and tail. **FEMALE:** Dull brown; very pale breast stripes and wing bars; no conspicuous markings. Female's faint breast stripes and wing bars distinguish it from immature mannikins. **BREEDING MALE:** Entirely blue. **VOICE:** Emphatic *twit.* Sometimes thin song of paired phrases. **STATUS AND RANGE:** Non-breeding resident in West Indies October to early May. Common in Bahamas, Cuba, larger Virgin Islands, and San Andrés; uncommon in Jamaica, Hispaniola, and Cayman Islands; rare in Puerto Rico and Providencia. **HABITAT:** Rice fields, grassy areas bounded by heavy thickets, rows of trees or woodlands, pasture edges and scrub.

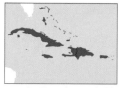

● **BLUE GROSBEAK** *Passerina caerulea* 16.5–19cm (6.5–7.5in). Flicks tail. **MALE:** Entirely blue with reddish-brown wing bars. **FEMALE:** Brown overall; large with heavy bill; reddish-brown wing bars. Hints of blue sometimes on wings and rump. **STATUS AND RANGE:** Non-breeding resident September through April, most common during migrations. Uncommon in Bahamas and Cayman Islands; rare in Cuba, Hispaniola, and Puerto Rico; very rare in Jamaica and Virgin Islands. **HABITAT:** Forest edges, Australian pine (Casuarina) groves, rice fields, seeding grass near thickets or woodlands. Also gardens with trees.

● **PAINTED BUNTING** *Passerina ciris* 13cm (5in). **ADULT MALE:** Blue head, red underparts, and green back. **FEMALE AND YOUNG MALE:** Green above, yellowish-green below. Brighter green than vireos and bill is much heavier. **IMMATURE:** Much duller, but hints of green. **VOICE:** Loud *chip.* **STATUS AND RANGE:** Non-breeding resident in Bahamas and Cuba primarily October to April. Bahamas: fairly common November and March as migrant, uncommon as resident. Cuba: uncommon migrant and rare remaining months. Vagrant elsewhere in West Indies. **HABITAT:** Thickets, brush, and grassy areas, particularly semi-arid areas, often near water.

GREATER
ANTILLEAN
BULLFINCH

imm

adult ♂

St Lucia race

LESSER
ANTILLEAN
BULLFINCH

♂

♀, Barbados
& imm

BLUE-BLACK
GRASSQUIT

adult ♂

adult ♀

Guadeloupe–
Dominica race

INDIGO
BUNTING

♀

br ♂

BLUE
GROSBEAK

♀

adult ♀ & young ♂

♂

♂

PAINTED BUNTING

● **PIN-TAILED WHYDAH** *Vidua macroura* Breeding male: 30–33cm (12–13in); female and non-breeding male: 11.5cm (4.5in). Often flocks. **BREEDING MALE:** Black and white with long tail plumes and red bill. **FEMALE AND NON-BREEDING MALE:** Mottled reddish-brown above; red bill; black-and-white facial stripes. **IMMATURE:** More grayish-brown; buff-colored eyebrow stripe. Bill blackish, pinkish-red at base. **VOICE:** Twittering sometimes with loud chattering and whistles. Also emphatic *sweet*. **STATUS AND RANGE:** Introduced. Puerto Rico: uncommon and local on coast, less frequent in mountains. **HABITAT:** Lawns and fields with short grass.

● **YELLOW-CROWNED BISHOP** *Euplectes afer* 11.5–12.5cm (4.5–5in). Forms flocks. **BREEDING MALE:** Yellow rump and crown; entirely black underparts. **FEMALE AND NON-BREEDING MALE:** Mottled brown above and buff-colored below. Yellowish eyebrow stripe contrasts sharply with dark brown eye-line. Breast and crown finely striped. (Female and non-breeding male Orange Bishops have paler cheek patch; pale, rather than dark brown, eye-line; no yellow in eyebrow stripe. Grasshopper Sparrow has whitish central crown stripe.) **VOICE:** Series of *sweet* and *chuck* notes similar to Orange Bishop. **STATUS AND RANGE:** Introduced. Puerto Rico and Jamaica: uncommon and very local. **HABITAT:** High grass and reeds near fresh water.

● **ORANGE BISHOP** *Euplectes franciscanus* 12.5cm (5in). Forms flocks. **BREEDING MALE:** Orange-red plumage with black belly and crown. **FEMALE AND NON-BREEDING MALE:** Mottled brown above and buff-colored below with buff-colored eyebrow stripe. Breast and crown finely striped. *See also* Plate 93. **IMMATURE:** Like female, but more buffish. (Grasshopper Sparrow has golden spot near bill and single, central whitish crown stripe.) **VOICE:** Breeding males sing sputtering song. **STATUS AND RANGE:** Introduced. Puerto Rico: uncommon locally from San Juan to Arecibo. Rare elsewhere in lowlands. Martinique and Guadeloupe: uncommon and local. **HABITAT:** Primarily sugarcane fields bordered by grassy edges.

● **JAVA SPARROW** *Padda oryzivora* 15–16.5cm (5.75–6.5in). Forms flocks. **ADULT:** Primarily gray above and below; broad, pinkish-red bill; white cheek patch; black crown. **IMMATURE:** Similar but duller bill, buff-colored cheeks, and brownish body. **VOICE:** Hard, metallic *chink*. **STATUS AND RANGE:** Introduced. Puerto Rico: fairly common in San Juan area. Jamaica: recent reports. **HABITAT:** Primarily urban areas with short grass, such as athletic fields and large lawns.

PIN-TAILED
WHYDAH

♀ & non-br ♂

br ♂

♀ & non-br ♂

YELLOW-CROWNED
BISHOP

br ♂

ORANGE BISHOP

br ♂

♀ & non-br ♂

JAVA SPARROW

imm

adult

RED AVADAVAT *Amandava amandava* 10cm (4in). Forms flocks. **BREEDING MALE:** Primarily deep red with white spots on wings, flanks, and sides. **ADULT FEMALE AND NON-BREEDING MALE:** Brown above, paler below. Red uppertail-coverts and bill; white spots on wing; dark eye-line. **IMMATURE:** Similar, but lacks red; wing spots buff-colored. **VOICE:** Musical *sweet* and *sweet-eet*. Also melodious whistles and warbles. **STATUS AND RANGE:** Introduced. Guadeloupe and Martinique: common. Puerto Rico and Dominican Republic: uncommon and local. **HABITAT:** Grassy edges of freshwater swamps and canals, also sugarcane borders.

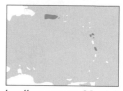

BLACK-RUMPED WAXBILL *Estrilda troglodytes* 10cm (4in). Forms flocks. **ADULT:** Red eye-line; red bill; gray uppertail-coverts. (Orange-cheeked Waxbill has orange cheek patch and reddish uppertail-coverts.) **IMMATURE:** Lacks red eye-line; bill pale pink. **VOICE:** Call notes include *pit, cheww* or *chit-cheww*, like bullet ricocheting off rock. **STATUS AND RANGE:** Introduced. Puerto Rico: uncommon, but widespread on coastal plain. Guadeloupe: locally common. Martinique: uncommon and local. **HABITAT:** High grass by sugarcane fields.

INDIAN SILVERBILL *Lonchura malabarica* 11.5cm (4.5 in). Overall light brown upperparts, white underparts and rump, and dark tail. Heavy bill is bluish. Forms flocks. **VOICE:** Usually quick, 2-syllable *chit-tit*. **STATUS AND RANGE:** Introduced. Puerto Rico: common in metropolitan San Juan and southwestern coast. Recent records from Virgin Islands (St Croix). **HABITAT:** Arid scrub, pastures, and gardens where grass in seed.

NUTMEG MANNIKIN *Lonchura punctulata* 11.5cm (4.5in). Forms flocks. **ADULT:** Cinnamon-colored hood and scalloped underparts are diagnostic. **IMMATURE:** Cinnamon-colored above; paler below. **VOICE:** Soft, plaintive whistle *peet* dropping in pitch and fading at end. **STATUS AND RANGE:** Introduced. Puerto Rico: common on northeastern coast and less frequently throughout island. Dominican Republic and Guadeloupe: locally common. Cuba, Jamaica, and Martinique: decidedly uncommon and local. **HABITAT:** Lowland open areas such as sugarcane borders, road edges, and urban parks.

ORANGE-CHEEKED WAXBILL *Estrilda melpoda* 10cm (4in). Forms flocks. **ADULT:** Orange cheek patch; reddish bill and uppertail-coverts. **IMMATURE:** Lacks orange cheek; bill pale pink. **VOICE:** Clear *pee* singly or in series. Flocks have characteristic twitter. **STATUS AND RANGE:** Introduced. Puerto Rico: common on coastal plain. Guadeloupe and Martinique: recent records. **HABITAT:** Tall seeding grass in agricultural areas, sugarcane borders, and road edges.

BRONZE MANNIKIN *Lonchura cucullata* 10cm (4in). Forms flocks. **ADULT:** Black hood, dark grayish-brown back and white belly with scalloped pattern on sides and flanks. **IMMATURE:** Hood and scalloped markings faint or lacking. **VOICE:** Coarse *crrit*. **STATUS AND RANGE:** Introduced. Puerto Rico: common around coast. **HABITAT:** Fields, lawns, and wherever grass is in seed.

CHESTNUT MANNIKIN *Lonchura atricapilla* 11.5cm (4.5in). Forms flocks. **ADULT:** Black hood; cinnamon-colored back. Underparts pale brown with black belly patch. **IMMATURE:** Cinnamon-brown above and buffish below. **VOICE:** Thin, nasal *honk*. **STATUS AND RANGE:** Introduced. Uncommon and very local in Jamaica and Martinique. **HABITAT:** High grass bordering dense vegetation.

TRICOLORED MANNIKIN *Lonchura malacca* 11.5cm (4.5in). Forms flocks. **ADULT:** Black hood; cinnamon-colored back. Underparts white with black belly patch. **IMMATURE:** Cinnamon-brown above and buffish below. **VOICE:** Thin, nasal *honk*. **STATUS AND RANGE:** Introduced. Locally common in Cuba and Hispaniola; uncommon in Puerto Rico; uncommon and very local in Jamaica and Martinique. **HABITAT:** High grass bordering dense vegetation.

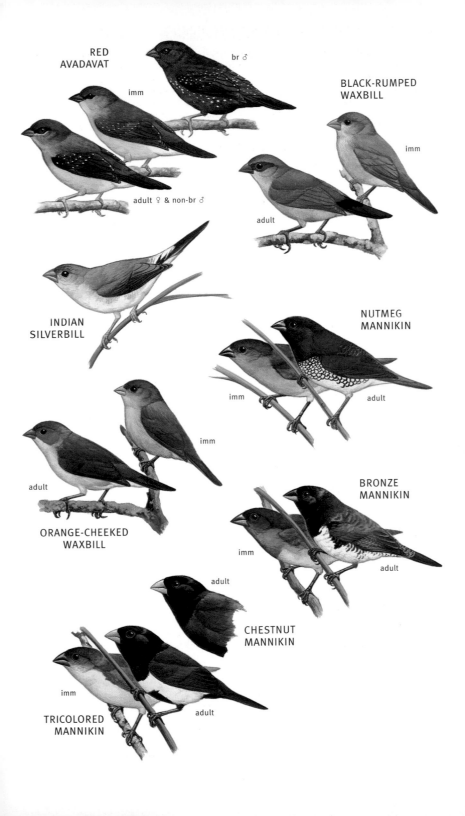

RED
AVADAVAT

br ♂

imm

adult ♀ & non-br ♂

BLACK-RUMPED
WAXBILL

imm

adult

INDIAN
SILVERBILL

NUTMEG
MANNIKIN

imm

adult

ORANGE-CHEEKED
WAXBILL

adult

imm

BRONZE
MANNIKIN

imm

adult

CHESTNUT
MANNIKIN

adult

imm

adult

TRICOLORED
MANNIKIN

● **WHITE-CROWNED SPARROW** *Zonotrichia leucophrys* 18cm (7in). **ADULT:** Conspicuously black-and-white striped crown; gray underparts. **IMMATURE:** Crown stripes brown and buff. **STATUS AND RANGE:** Rare migrant October through November and rarer still December through April in Bahamas and Cuba. **HABITAT:** Open woodlands, gardens with trees, forest edges, and brushy fields.

● **RUFOUS-COLLARED SPARROW** *Zonotrichia capensis* 15–16.5cm (5.75–6.5in). **ADULT:** Black neck band; reddish-brown hindneck; gray crown with black stripes. Often displays slight crest. **IMMATURE:** Duller and spotted below. Lacks black or reddish-brown markings. **VOICE:** Accelerating trill *whis-whis-whis-whis-whiswhisu-whiswhis.* **STATUS AND RANGE:** Locally common resident in Hispaniola. **HABITAT:** Mountains, in forest edges and streamside thickets. Also undergrowth of pine forests.

● **LARK SPARROW** *Chondestes grammacus* 15cm (5.75in). **ADULT:** Bold head and facial pattern; black breast spot; large white patches on outer corners of tail. **IMMATURE:** Head pattern less distinct; breast buffish and heavily streaked. **STATUS AND RANGE:** Vagrant in northern Bahamas, Cuba, and Jamaica August through March. **HABITAT:** Open semi-arid areas with scattered bushes.

● **CLAY-COLORED SPARROW** *Spizella pallida* 12–13.5cm (4.75–5.25in). **ADULT:** Buff-brown above; bold black streaks on back; brownish or buffish rump; white median stripe on crown; wide whitish eyebrow and mustache stripes; brown cheek patch outlined by thin, dark lines; pale lores; gray hindneck contrasting with back. **IMMATURE:** Similar, but fine streaks on breast; head pattern less well defined. **STATUS AND RANGE:** Vagrant in northern Bahamas and Cuba October through February. **HABITAT:** Coastal thickets, borders of salt ponds, and bushy areas.

● **CHIPPING SPARROW** *Spizella passerina* 12.5–14.5cm (5–5.75in). **NON-BREEDING ADULT AND IMMATURE:** Crown brown (immature) or reddish-brown (adult) with black streaks, dark eye-line, and buffish or brown cheeks. Underparts gray in adult and buffish in immature. **BREEDING ADULT:** Reddish-brown crown; gray cheeks; white eyebrow stripe; black line through eye. (Grasshopper Sparrow has golden spot in front of eye.) *See also* Clay-colored Sparrow. **STATUS AND RANGE:** Very rare non-breeding resident in northern Bahamas and Cuba October through April. Vagrant in southern Bahamas. **HABITAT:** Pastures, open areas, grassy fields, bushy thickets, and croplands.

● **ORANGE BISHOP** *Euplectes franciscanus* 12.5cm (5in). **FEMALE AND NON-BREEDING MALE:** Mottled brown; buff eyebrow stripe; underparts, crown and breast finely striped. *See also* Plate 91.

● **GRASSHOPPER SPARROW** *Ammodramus savannarum* 12.5cm (5in). **ADULT:** Golden mark forward of eyebrow stripe; whitish central crown stripe. (Brown-plumaged Yellow-crowned and Orange Bishops lack single central crown stripe.) **IMMATURE:** Paler mark by bill; fine streaks on breast and flanks. **VOICE:** Long, thin, insect-like *buzz,* then hiccup. Very thin, high-pitched twitter. Gritty, insect-like *kr-r-it.* **STATUS AND RANGE:** Common but local resident in Jamaica, Hispaniola, and Puerto Rico. Non-breeding resident October through April in Cuba, where common, and in Bahamas and Cayman Islands, where rare. **HABITAT:** Weedy fields, pastures with tall grass, rice plantations.

WHITE-CROWNED
SPARROW

imm

adult

RUFOUS-COLLARED
SPARROW

imm

adult

CLAY-COLORED
SPARROW

adult

LARK
SPARROW

adult

non-br adult & imm

br adult

CHIPPING SPARROW

♀ & non-br ♂

ORANGE BISHOP

GRASSHOPPER
SPARROW

Hispaniola race

adult

imm

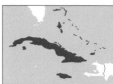

LINCOLN'S SPARROW *Melospiza lincolnii* 13.5–15cm (5.25–5.75in). **ADULT:** Central crown stripe, eyebrow stripe, ear-patch, and sides of neck pale gray. Breast buffish, finely streaked black. **IMMATURE:** Similar, but eyebrow stripe buffish-white. **STATUS AND RANGE:** Rare migrant and perhaps non-breeding resident in Bahamas, Cuba, Jamaica, and Hispaniola. October to April. Vagrant elsewhere in West Indies. **HABITAT:** Moist highland forest thickets, especially around clearings. Also coastal thickets and borders of dense forests.

SWAMP SPARROW *Melospiza georgiana* 15cm (5.75in). **NON-BREEDING ADULT:** Gray central crown stripe, eyebrow stripe, cheek patch, and sides of neck; blackish mustache mark; white throat; breast grayish with a few blackish streaks. **IMMATURE:** Similar, but breast and throat unstreaked gray; buffish cheek patch. **BREEDING ADULT:** Crown reddish-brown. **STATUS AND RANGE:** Vagrant in Bahamas. Primarily occurs November to May. **HABITAT:** Marshes and brushy areas.

AMERICAN PIPIT *Anthus spinoletta* 16.5cm (6.5in). Thin bill; long tail; regularly bobs tail. Conspicuous white outertail feathers in flight. Terrestrial. **NON-BREEDING ADULT:** Buffish eyebrow stripe, 2 faint wing bars; pinkish-buff underparts (October, November) or pale gray underparts (January to March) with blackish stripes concentrated on breast. **STATUS AND RANGE:** Very rare non-breeding resident in Bahamas south to San Salvador October through March. **HABITAT:** Open fields and sandy areas.

DARK-EYED JUNCO *Junco hyemalis* 16cm (6.25in). Blackish-gray overall; white belly and outertail feathers; pink bill. **STATUS AND RANGE:** Vagrant in northern Bahamas, Jamaica, Puerto Rico, and Virgin Islands. **HABITAT:** Cultivated areas, field edges, hedgerows, lawns, and roadsides.

SAVANNAH SPARROW *Passerculus sandwichensis* 15–19cm (5.75–7.5in). Slender; underparts heavily streaked brown; eyebrow stripe usually yellowish, conspicuous, sometimes buff-colored; pale central crown stripe; dark mustache stripe. (Immature Grasshopper Sparrow finer; paler streaks below.) **VOICE:** High-pitched, melodious call of 3 *chip*s, then 2 wispy notes, the last shorter and lower, *chip-chip-chip-tisisiiii-tisi.* **STATUS AND RANGE:** Generally uncommon non-breeding resident in northern Bahamas and Cuba. Rare in Cayman Islands (Grand Cayman). Occurs October through April. **HABITAT:** Open fields, pastures, bushy savannas, and sparse thickets near coast.

NORTHERN WHEATEAR *Oenanthe oenanthe* 15cm (6in). White rump and tail patches. Has habit of flicking and fanning tail. Active, ground-dwelling. **FEMALE AND NON-BREEDING MALE:** Pale reddish-brown below, grayish-brown above; white eyebrow stripe. **BREEDING MALE:** Gray upperparts, black ear-patch. **STATUS AND RANGE:** Vagrant in West Indies where recorded from Bahamas, Cuba, Puerto Rico, and Barbados.

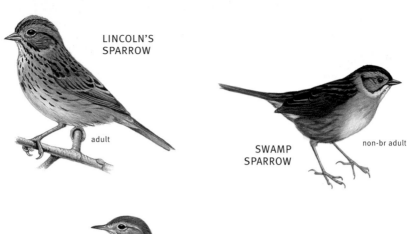

LINCOLN'S
SPARROW

adult

SWAMP
SPARROW

non-br adult

non-br adult

AMERICAN PIPIT

SAVANNAH SPARROW

DARK-EYED JUNCO

br ♂

♀ & non-br ♂

NORTHERN WHEATEAR

SELECTED REFERENCES

ISLAND AVIFAUNAS

Barbour, T. 1923. *The Birds of Cuba*. Memoirs of the Nuttall Ornithological Club No. IV, Cambridge.

— 1943. *Cuban Ornithology*. Memoirs of the Nuttall Ornithological Club No. IX, Cambridge.

Benito-Espinal, E. 1990. *Birds of the West Indies*. Les Editions Latanier, St Barthélemy. [Principally the French-speaking Lesser Antilles.]

Blankenship, J.R. 1990. *The Wildlife of Montserrat—Including an Annotated Bird List for the Island*. Montserrat National Trust, Montserrat.

Bradley, P. 1995. *Birds of the Cayman Islands*. (Revised edition.) Caerulea Press, Italy.

— 2000. *The Birds of the Cayman Islands: An Annotated Checklist*. British Ornithologists' Union, Herts.

Brudenell-Bruce, P.G.C. 1975. *The Birds of the Bahamas*. Taplinger Publishing Company, New York.

Buden, D.W. 1987. *The Birds of the Southern Bahamas*. BOU Check-list No. 8. British Ornithologists' Union, London.

Clark, A.H. 1905. Birds of the Southern Lesser Antilles. *Proceedings of the Boston Society of Natural History*, Vol. 32(7): 203–312.

Devas, Fr. R.P. 1970. *Birds of Grenada, St Vincent and The Grenadines*. (Second edition.) Privately printed, Port-of-Spain, Trinidad.

Dod, A.S. 1978. *Aves de la Republiça Dominicana*. Museo Nacional de Historia Natural, Santo Domingo.

Downer, A. and R. Sutton. 1990. *Birds of Jamaica—A Photographic Field Guide*. Cambridge University Press, Cambridge.

Evans, P.G.H. 1990. *Birds of the Eastern Caribbean*. Macmillan Education Ltd., London.

Garrido, O.H. and A. Kirkconnell. 2000. *Field Guide to the Birds of Cuba*. Cornell University Press, Ithaca.

Hilder, P. 1989. *The Birds of Nevis*. Nevis Historical and Conservation Society. Charlestown, Nevis.

Hutt, M.B., H.F. Hutt, P.A. Buckley, F.G. Buckley, E.B. Massiah, and M.D. Frost (in prep.). *The Birds of Barbados*. BOU Check-list. British Ornithologists' Union, London.

Keith, A.R. 1997. *The Birds of St Lucia, West Indies*. BOU Check-list No. 15. British Ornithologists' Union, London.

Keith, A.R., J.W. Wiley, S.C. Latta, and J.A. Ottenwalder. (in press). *The Birds of Hispaniola—Dominican Republic and Haiti*. BOU Check-list No. 21, British Ornithologists' Union, London.

Lack, D. 1976. *Island Biology—Illustrated by the Land Birds of Jamaica*. Studies in Ecology—Volume 3. University of California Press, Berkeley and Los Angeles.

Latta, S.C. 2002. *Aves Comunes de la Republica Dominicana*/Common Birds of the Dominican Republic. Editora Corripio, Santo Domingo.

Pinchon, Fr. R. 1976. *Faune des Antilles Françaises—Les Oiseaux*. (Second edition.) Privately printed, Fort-de-France, Martinique.

Raffaele, H.A. 1989. *A Guide to the Birds of Puerto Rico and the Virgin Islands*. Princeton University Press, Princeton.

Siegel, A. 1983. *Birds of Montserrat*. Montserrat National Trust, Montserrat.

Voous, K.H. 1983. *Birds of the Netherlands Antilles*. De Walburg Press, Curaçao. (English version.)

Wetmore, A. and B.H. Swales. 1931. *The Birds of Haiti and the Dominican Republic*. Smithsonian Institution, US National Museum, Bulletin 155. Washington, DC.

White, A.W. 1998. *A Birder's Guide to the Bahama Islands* (Including Turks & Caicos). American Birding Association, Inc., U.S.A.

BIRD FAMILY AND REGIONAL IDENTIFICATION GUIDES

Adolfsson, K. and S. Cherrug. 1995. Bird Identification—A Reference Guide. *Anser,* Supplement 37 (379pp.). Lund, Sweden.

Alström, P. and P. Colston. 1991. *A Field Guide to the Rare Birds of Britain and Europe.* HarperCollins, London.

Byers, C., J. Curson, and U. Olsson. 1995. *A Guide to the Sparrows and Buntings of North America and the World.* Houghton Mifflin Company, Boston.

Chantler, P. and G. Driessens. 1995. *Swifts—A Guide to the Swifts and Treeswifts of the World.* Pica Press, Sussex.

Clement, P. 1993. *Finches and Sparrows—An Identification Guide.* A & C Black, London.

Curson, J., D. Quinn, and D. Beadle. 1994. *New World Warblers—An Identification Guide.* A & C Black, London.

Grant, P.J. 1986. *Gulls—A Guide to Identification.* Buteo Books, Vermillion, South Dakota.

Harris, A., L. Tucker, and K. Vinicombe. 1993. *The Macmillan Field Guide to Bird Identification.* Macmillan Press, London.

Hayman, P., J. Marchant, and T. Prater. 1986. *Shorebirds—An Identification Guide to the Waders of the World.* A & C Black, London.

Howell, S.N.G. and S. Webb. 1995. *A Guide to the Birds of Mexico and Northern Central America.* Oxford University Press, Oxford.

Jonsson, L. 1993. *Birds of Europe with North Africa and the Middle East.* A & C Black, London.

Kaufman, K. 1990. *A Field Guide to Advanced Birding.* Houghton Mifflin Company, Boston.

Olsen, K.M. and H. Larsson. 1995. *Terns of Europe and North America.* A & C Black, London.

Rising, J.D. 1996. *A Guide to the Identification and Natural History of the Sparrows of the United States and Canada.* Academic Press, London.

Rosair, D. and D. Cottridge. 1995. *Photographic Guide to the Waders of the World.* Hamlyn, London.

Turner, A. and C. Rose. 1989. *A Handbook to the Swallows and Martins of the World.* A & C Black, London.

Wheeler, B.K. and W.S. Clark. 1995. *A Photographic Guide to North American Raptors.* Academic Press, London.

INDEX OF ENGLISH AND SCIENTIFIC NAMES